IN BED
WITH THE
BLUESHIRTS

SHANE ROSS

IN BED WITH THE BLUESHIRTS

Atlantic Books
London

First published in Great Britain and Ireland in 2020 by Atlantic Books,
an imprint of Atlantic Books Ltd.

A CIP catalogue record for this book is available from
the British Library.

Trade paperback ISBN 978 1 83895 291 4
E-Book ISBN 978 1 83895 292 1

Atlantic Books
An Imprint of Atlantic Books Ltd
Ormond House
26–27 Boswell Street
London WC1N 3JZ
www.atlantic-books.co.uk

Printed in Great Britain

10 9 8 7 6 5 4 3 2 1

Contents

The book is dedicated to all who have tragically died on Irish roads. Especially let us thank the victims' groups who have worked so selflessly to ensure that others do not suffer the unspeakable agonies endured by themselves. There is no nobler action than theirs. Their part in supporting the Drink Driving Bill has undoubtedly saved lives. It is sadly too late for members of victims' groups like the Irish Road Victims' Association (IRVA) and Promoting Awareness, Responsibility and Care (PARC) who have lost loved ones, but many people would not be alive today without their endurance and determination.

Prologue

IT LOOKED LIKE the beginning of the end. Enda Kenny was in full flight at the cabinet table. The Constitution held tightly in his hand, the Taoiseach was waving it in anger at Finian McGrath and at me. He was obviously at the end of his tether. We were only six months into government. Everyone knew we could not go on like this. Nearly every week there was a spat, a fudge and a bad taste in the aftermath.

On Tuesday, 22 November 2016 the issue was neutrality. The cabinet had already seen showdowns on abortion, on the Apple tax judgement and on a Fine Gael nominee to the board of the European Investment Bank. On most Tuesday mornings there was a war of attrition. The media waited expectantly for a good leak about the latest row. They were rarely disappointed.

Sinn Féin had put down a mischievous Dáil motion calling for neutrality to be enshrined in the Constitution. Finian, John Halligan and I had voted enthusiastically for an identical measure a few months earlier, when in opposition. It was due to be debated within forty-eight hours. If we opposed it now, we were hypocrites. If we supported it, the government was split. And probably reduced to the status of a divided rabble with a short life.

It was a heated debate, not defused in any way by the interventions of the excitable Minister for Foreign Affairs, Charlie

Flanagan, sitting opposite me. Every cabinet minister paid lip service to Ireland's military neutrality, although many Blueshirts had never been more than token believers. I looked around at my colleagues, silently thinking that collectively they would make a NATO gathering look like a social democratic think tank.

I glanced down the table at Leo Varadkar and Simon Coveney, destined to be locked in a leadership battle to succeed Kenny in less than six months. Leo, already seen as the likely winner, would surely never relish a head-to-head weekly battle on issues like neutrality? We didn't have to wait long to find out.

As the minority group in government, we in the Independent Alliance had a clear position: there was no commitment to any view on neutrality in the Programme for Government. We expected a free vote. A few months earlier, we had rubbed the Fine Gael noses in it, taking a free vote on abortion in the face of fierce opposition from them, our partners in government. No political earthquake followed. Neutrality, a matter of conscience and principle, was in a similar category.

Kenny was not going to allow a repeat. He was adamant. He lifted the Constitution in the air, a copy of which lay permanently on the table in front of Martin Fraser, the influential cabinet secretary, seated beside him. There was silence around a hushed table.

Enda raised his voice in response to our demand for a free vote: 'Bunreacht na hÉireann,' he declared, brandishing the sacred book, 'trumps the Programme for Government.' He demanded total cabinet solidarity. The Constitution requires the cabinet to speak with *una voce*. So did all true Blueshirts.

It was left to Tánaiste Frances Fitzgerald and elder statesman Michael Noonan to broker a compromise with us. We eventually agreed wording for an amendment, with everyone around the table reaffirming their commitment to military neutrality.

News of the row leaked, as it always did. The media had another field day. Two days later Sinn Féin took lumps out of John Halligan, Finian McGrath and me in the Dáil chamber. Finian and I voted with the Blueshirts. John Halligan was away. Martin Kenny and other Sinn Féin deputies taunted us about our deafening silence.

The great experiment was faltering.

1

A Big Idea Is Born

FINE GAEL NORMALLY eat their young. Only amateur pol
innocents have not learned a basic lesson of history: 1
who bounce into bed with the Blueshirts die a painful c
Independents with blind ambition were long ago warned
this fatal political certainty. Nobody has ever survived as
as a flirtation with Fine Gael. Look at Labour today o1
the Democratic Left. Back in 1951, Clann na Poblachta d
grated after supping with the same devil. Oblivion becl
those who fly too close to Fine Gael.

Two days after Christmas in 2014, I set out on a mi
was in search of an answer to a brewing political q·
Independents were on a roll. So, was there an ope1
independents to form a coherent political force? I spen1
ing winter week touring Ireland to test the temperatu
independent councillors from Dublin, Wexford, Cork
and Sligo. And others on the road back to Dublin. In a
— over the 2014/15 new year — thirty councillors off·
views face to face. Nearly all favoured a new departi
independents would co-operate nationally. And form

Some were rural, others urban. Some pro-choice, (
life. A number came from the Fianna Fáil gene pool,
long-term associations with Fine Gael, or were di

Labour, dejected Greens or even closet Sinn Féin support-
ers. Many had started political life as single-issue candidates.
Independents were (and are) a mixed bag with various agendas.
Detractors rubbished them as a motley crew.

It was the first of many similar journeys I undertook over the
next twelve months. It led to the doors of current household
names like Boxer Moran, Michael Collins, Seán Canney and
Paul Gogarty, all independent councillors at the time.

Parallel to that, at national level, similar tentative moves
were being made by sitting independent TDs in Leinster
House. After the 2011 general election, a 'technical' group of
sixteen independents had been formed to ensure that they
had speaking rights in the Dáil. It included such personalities
as the delightful left-winger Joe Higgins and the sometimes
less delightful right-winger Mattie McGrath. We shared a few
parliamentary facilities, but policy differences made political
unity or consensus impossible.

Many independents shared a corridor in Agriculture House,
attached to Leinster House. Sometimes that merely exacerbated
tensions. Deputies Mattie McGrath's and Catherine Murphy's
offices were opposite each other. The two deputies were barely
on speaking terms. Mattie, a devout pro-life Catholic, posted a
sketch of Pope Francis outside his office. Catherine, a passionate pro-choice agnostic, could not avoid passing it every time
she entered or exited her room. No one believed that Mattie
was unaware of the daily effect the picture of His Holiness
would have on Catherine's blood pressure. Catherine, in turn,
had pinned on her door a picture of the victory celebration for
the referendum on marriage equality in Dublin Castle. Mattie
could not miss it, but it was certain to cause the already excitable Tipperary TD one of his familiar apoplectic fits.

Yet, within that group, Catherine Murphy and a few others
saw opportunities for political reform. Herself a veteran of

several left-wing parties, she found common ground with others, but not with Higgins' far left or with Richard Boyd Barrett's brand of socialism. Nor with Clare Daly, a staunch ally of Higgins before a spat threw her into the arms of another colourful independent TD, the ultra-maverick Mick Wallace. The independents had their own Bonnie and Clyde wing.

Catherine Murphy often spoke to several like-minded TDs, seeking a collective, more cohesive political muscle, based on a common radical zeal. In the middle ground of this disparate group stood more flexible, pragmatic politicians, including her former Workers' Party comrade — then independent TD — John Halligan, newly elected TD Stephen Donnelly (known to some as Harry Potter because of his uncanny physical resemblance to J.K. Rowling's hero), left-wing disabilities champion Finian McGrath, Michael Fitzmaurice from Roscommon, Tom Fleming from Kerry and me. None of us, so it seemed at the time, wanted to stay in opposition for ever.

Talks between Murphy, Donnelly, McGrath, Halligan and me had been progressing sporadically. Attempts at sorting policy differences were slow. Murphy and Donnelly wanted a political party structure with the accompanying rules and discipline; I and others wanted a looser alliance that gave independent members the right to free votes according to their individual consciences.

Free votes on matters of conscience had already propelled another player into the crowded independent/new party space. Lucinda Creighton, a former Fine Gael minister, had been ruthlessly expelled from the party in July 2013 as an objector, on the grounds of conscience, to Enda Kenny's abortion legislation. She had been in exploratory talks with both Donnelly and me, but if the difficulties of whether to form a party or an alliance proved a fundamental obstacle, the problem of three runaway egos uniting behind one leader was thought to have been insuperable. The Ross ego, once described by journalist Mark Paul as 'the size of Croke Park', may have just pipped Donnelly's and Creighton's, but they ran me close.

Fine Gael and Labour, with an unassailable majority in the Dáil, watched contentedly. Opposite them in the chamber slumped a discredited Fianna Fáil. Alongside Fianna Fáil sat a group of sometimes articulate independents already splitting into warring factions. Sinn Féin was not then the force it is today.

Under that coalition, legislation was frequently guillotined. Oireachtas committees were controlled by Labour-Fine Gael majorities. The Dáil and the Seanad were rubber stamps. Unpopular legislation, arguably necessary because of the perilous state of the nation's finances, was rammed through both houses. Fundamental changes, like the introduction of property and water taxes, were rushed through Ireland's parliament with indecent haste. Fertile ground was being prepared for left-wingers and independents to foment discontent. Even the Greens, wiped out by their craven support for the previous Fianna Fáil government, managed to plug into the growing unrest. Huge marches in the streets against water charges spooked the Fine Gael-Labour regime. While the opposition was able to unite against the unpopular austerity measures, it split on a multitude of fronts when it came to agreeing a common platform. It proved impossible.

Opposition was an easy place for independent mavericks. It was not difficult to find reasons to oppose austerity, even if the various independents offered different reasons for doing so. Solutions, suggestions, proposals for common future positions prompted immediate splits.

Nevertheless, in early 2015 the political soil was perfectly prepared for the green shoots of an independents' spring. The record success of independents in the summer 2014 local elections proved that their earlier surge in the 2011 general election had been no flash in the pan. Later in 2014, independent

Michael Fitzmaurice had pulled off a surprise coup when he succeeded Luke 'Ming' Flanagan by winning the Roscommon-Galway by-election. Flushed with victory, Deputy Fitzmaurice took only a few weeks to declare the need for a new political force or party. Presumably with himself at the helm. He told TheJournal.ie that he had spoken to twenty-five to thirty like-minded people. Another mega-ego had entered an already crowded arena.

Suddenly 2015 looked likely to be the year of the political adventurer. It was. No sooner had I arrived back from my countrywide tour of independents than Lucinda Creighton broke cover. On 2 January 2015 the worst-kept secret in Irish politics was revealed. Lucinda announced that she would have something else to announce in due course. She would be launching a new political party. But not until March. She held a press conference with consumer champion Eddie Hobbs and an Offaly councillor, John Leahy. Remarkably, no other TDs were sitting on the platform.

Within less than a week, on 6 January, both Fitzmaurice and I appeared on RTE's *Prime Time* to announce that we were joining forces to form an alliance of independents. According to the programme, others to have expressed their enthusiasm for such an idea (but not for either Fitzmaurice or me) included Deputies Denis Naughten, Noel Grealish, Stephen Donnelly, Tom Fleming, Mattie McGrath, Finian McGrath and John Halligan. *Prime Time* headed the programme with Fitzmaurice speaking of me: 'He seems to be a very reasonable guy in any talking I've done with him and yes, I think we can work something together.'

That was the night the Independent Alliance was born. And it was almost stillborn. Not all the dots had been joined up when *Prime Time* jumped the gun. The independents identified as possible allies had been talking in silos. They had never met in a room together with a common purpose.

While Fitzmaurice had been speaking separately to rural TDs and councillors, Finian McGrath, John Halligan and I had been in exploratory conversations for over a year. I had been in a separate dialogue with Stephen Donnelly for several months. There had been little contact between Donnelly, Fitzmaurice and Halligan. Rivalries erupted within twenty-four hours of the RTÉ programme. Several of *Prime Time*'s supporters of an alliance of independents, in theory, ran for cover when confronted by the reality of the names of their prospective allies.

Within days of the programme, three of the independents — Donnelly, Naughten and Grealish — met in secret in Donnelly's Dáil office and resolved to torpedo the Independent Alliance project at birth. Naughten was always a non-runner for our group because he and Fitzmaurice were deadly rivals in the same Roscommon constituency. In any case, Naughten had hedged his bets on *Prime Time*, carefully approving the idea only 'in principle'. Donnelly was unwilling to accept Fitzmaurice because he believed the Roscommon man would be a political obstacle to his ambition of linking up with left-wingers Catherine Murphy and Róisín Shortall. At the time, Donnelly was fond of proclaiming his social democratic convictions. Many found his protests unconvincing because he hailed from a career in McKinsey & Company management consultants, hardly a bedrock of radical economic thinking.

Grealish and Naughten went to ground. Donnelly bolted. He privately explained to me that Fitzmaurice lacked the quality of the sort of TD he wanted to include in his gang. He felt that Naughten outstripped Fitzmaurice in polish and ability by a country mile. Six months later, in July 2015, after tortuous weeks of talking, he fell happily into the more comfortable, urban and conventional hands of Catherine Murphy and Róisín Shortall when the trio launched the Social Democrats.

Donnelly's defection was a blow, but five TDs held firm. Tom Fleming, Michael Fitzmaurice, John Halligan, Finian McGrath and I decided to embark on a great experiment. We were seeking to be part of an independent group in the next government.

The fault lines were drawn. Five independent TDs wanted an independent group without a whip. Donnelly was a cut above the rest of us, in search of a cerebral, social democratic home. Lucinda Creighton was hell-bent on a right of centre anti-abortion party. Catherine Murphy and Róisín Shortall were debating a new social democratic initiative. Other rural TDs — Denis Naughten, Mattie McGrath, Noel Grealish, Michael Lowry and Michael Healy-Rae — decided to remain aloof in their solo positions, detached from the rapidly forming new groups.

It was time for the talking to stop. A general election was expected in autumn 2015. The new Independent Alliance needed candidates to sign up. The long march to shape an effective army out of a group of independent councillors, unused to political discipline, had begun.

The five deputies and our new recruit, Senator Gerard Craughwell, met in my office every week. We needed money, so contributed €1,000 each to start the operation. Over the following two months, we met dozens of sometimes curious observers, sometimes eager disciples. As an introduction to test the waters, independents from around Ireland were asked to join us in the Bridge House Hotel, Tullamore on Saturday, 27 March. The agenda was broad. The attendance of over eighty people included fifty councillors. As one of our supporters, lawyer Tony Williams, pointed out on that day, we had more councillors there than there were Labour councillors in the entire country. Something was stirring, but that something might be difficult to mobilise.

Finally, Lucinda Creighton had formally launched her party two weeks earlier on 13 March. We were just ahead of the rest of the posse. In June, the Social Democratic Party was formed with no less than three co-leaders: Catherine Murphy, Stephen Donnelly and Róisín Shortall. The field for new groupings was officially crowded.

During that summer, my parliamentary assistant and the only de facto member of staff for the Independent Alliance, Aisling Dunne, completed another tour of Ireland to meet councillors and sign up candidates for the forthcoming general election. She kept the momentum going.

Preparations intensified for a possible autumn election. In September 2015, we hosted our second conference, this time at the Hodson Bay Hotel in Athlone. During the summer we had managed to persuade Senator Feargal Quinn to join us as our chairman. Feargal gave us a huge boost. He was beloved of the media, a widely popular, highly successful entrepreneur. Despite his dazzling business success, he was modest, understated and deeply committed to the independent voice in politics. He had been a fellow university senator with me for nearly twenty years. Nevertheless, I was surprised that he accepted the post so readily because he never engaged in the rough and tumble of domestic politics. The rest of us were street fighters. Feargal had no ambitions for a Dáil seat but, I suspect, might have eyed Áras an Uachtaráin from a dignified distance. Other contributors on the day included Eamon Dunphy, Sinead Ryan, Marian Harkin MEP and Dr Jane Suiter. The Independent Alliance was thriving.

It was a good line-up. Jane Suiter, a lecturer at Dublin City University, was a former economics editor of the *Irish Times*. Marian Harkin, a long-time independent member of the European Parliament, and Sinead Ryan, a leading journalist on consumer affairs, were heavyweights in their own fields. They spoke with authority and expertise, adding gravitas to the Athlone conference. But Eamon was different. He was box office. The councillors in Athlone on that day, many of them general election candidates, had come to hear Eamon. So had the media.

He didn't let them down. He promised to support and vote for the Independent Alliance in the coming election. The celebrity football pundit was mobbed afterwards by enthusiastic candidates, seeking to touch his garment and asking him to launch their campaigns. He agreed and delivered in several cases. Eamon Dunphy wanted to be a player.

A few murmurings arose later that evening when it emerged that Eamon had already been flirting with Sinn Féin. He had even been touted as one of that party's candidates for the coming election. But that is Dunphy, a political chameleon par excellence.

Eamon's invitation to the Athlone gig was solely my responsibility. I knew it would guarantee us media attention, although there was always a danger that he would say something outrageous. He easily could have damaged us just as we were on a roll. As luck had it, he didn't.

Eamon Dunphy was probably my oldest friend on the planet. He accepted the gig, at least partly, out of friendship. We had travelled a long road together. Some of it was political, much of it personal. I had been in many scrapes with him over the previous thirty-five years. In our younger days we were as wild as wolves, bonded by booze, nightclubs, journalism and politics. We had enjoyed many all-night sessions, ending up in either the infamous Manhattan café on Dublin's Kelly's Corner or, worse still, in the early houses on the river Liffey's quays. When I ditched the booze, we went out to dinner regularly, in restaurants all over Dublin.

In 2001, Eamon and I challenged the board of Eircom together, using his highly successful *Last Word* programme on Today FM to mobilise support against the directors. Our campaign culminated in a massive small shareholders' revolt with 4,000 people baying for blood at Eircom's annual general meeting in the RDS.

In 2009, I was honoured when Eamon asked me to be his best man at his second marriage, this time to RTÉ staff member Jane Gogan. A seriously talented head of drama, she has generally been a mellowing influence on the seventy-five-year-old tearaway.

In 2011, Eamon and I had joined with two other journalists, the *Irish Times'* Fintan O'Toole and the economist David McWilliams, to set up a radical political group, 'Democracy Now'. We aimed to fight the 2011 general election with all four of us as candidates. We used to plot our strategy secretly over breakfast in the Kildare Street and University Club, on St Stephen's Green. We took a private room, large enough to fit the four biggest egos ever to gather in a small Dublin location.

The project was doomed from day one. After one of the first breakfasts, I knew we were already in deep trouble when my telephone rang. At the end of the line was Eamon. 'Fintan has to go,' he thundered as the price of his continued support. We tottered on for a few more breakfasts until Eamon arrived one morning and announced coyly that he would not, after all, be a candidate. McWilliams soon followed suit, the media found out and the project collapsed.

Nevertheless, I still loved Eamon. He had a big heart. He had been kind to my grandson, Tom, who was mad about football and Manchester United. He came out and campaigned for me in the 2011 and 2016 Dáil elections. He was a huge hit, especially with the more elderly women in the supermarkets who fawned over him. He kissed many of them warmly on both cheeks. It never mattered that he had once been a 'national handler' for Garret FitzGerald's Fine Gael, an infatuated supporter of Mary Harney, Des O'Malley and the Progressive Democrats, and an ally of various Labour candidates. Indeed, he was even two-timing the Independent Alliance, as he was simultaneously in the early days of courtship with Sinn Féin. After the election he told RTÉ's Claire Byrne that he had voted Fianna Fáil, even though he was supporting me in the adjoining constituency. Eamon lives in Ranelagh, Dublin 6, so he presumably gave his vote to top Fianna Fáil lawyer, Jim O'Callaghan.

That was Eamon, a flawed, contradictory, lovable character. He flaunts his flaws. Eamon has marketed himself as the bold boy, the footballer from Dublin's disadvantaged northside who made mistakes and was always in hot water. It was a wonderful formula. Yet he is not all spoof and top-of-the-head soundbites. While his football expertise is widely recognised, it is surpassed by his writing skills. He remains, to this day, one of the most elegant writers of his generation. He made his reputation, in print, attacking icons like Mary Robinson, Seamus Heaney and Jack Charlton, deliberately courting fierce short-term unpopularity. He is a notice box without equal (I should know). Consequently his name is rarely out of the headlines, whether for personal lapses followed by apologies, or political polemics at events like the one we held in Athlone on that September morning in 2015.

Eamon's political contortions had made him many enemies. I knew on that day in Athlone that his support was a double-edged sword. He probably competes with me for having more 'former friends' than anyone else in the country. I was sure of one thing, though. In 2015, we had been comrades for over three decades. Nothing would sunder that friendship. Or so I thought.

As he raised the morale of the troops, I wondered where he would fit into the Independent Alliance? He should be asked by us to promote this new movement in Irish politics. He seemed eager. He volunteered to travel the country to hold meetings of support. He launched Carol Hunt's campaign in Dún Laoghaire, Marie Casserly's in Sligo and John Halligan's in Waterford. He was fully on board. He would undoubtedly have preferred to debate policy and tactics into the long hours of the night. Such sessions would have been entertaining and passionate, but ultimately wherever Dunphy went, he left chaos behind. He was high risk for the Independent Alliance. There was always the chance that he would be a star striker in the first half who scored a series of own goals in the second.

Over the years, Eamon had always joked that if I ever entered government, he would want the chair of Aer Lingus as a reward for his loyalty. Jane would take the chair of the RTÉ Authority. As the possibility of the Independent Alliance achieving office became a reality, he more and more frequently mentioned the attractions of a Taoiseach's nomination for the Seanad. I never knew whether Eamon was serious about being Senator Dunphy. In subsequent government negotiations, the Independent Alliance was denied any Seanad seats. Enda Kenny's refusal to give us a single nominee provided me with perfect cover. In any case, I could never have pushed for Eamon to be parachuted into the Seanad. A key pillar of the Alliance's platform was to banish cronyism.

Initially our friendship survived the Independent Alliance's transfer from opposition into government. We maintained the frequent telephone calls, the regular dinners and enjoyed a particularly amiable evening with both our wives in late August 2016. Eamon was at his best, telling hilarious stories against himself in Bistro One restaurant in fashionable Foxrock.

Less than a fortnight later, I was listening to *Today with Sean O'Rourke* on RTÉ. The topic was the strike by Dublin bus drivers. Suddenly I heard a familiar voice denouncing me from a height. He referred to me as 'Mr Ross', to my behaviour as 'scandalous' and generally insisted that the drivers should be paid a lot more. It was the first of many exocets fired in my direction, without warning and with remarkable venom, over the following months. Eamon, ever a champion of the underdog, lambasted me for not involving myself, as minister, in a very sensitive transport dispute. The attack was more than mildly surprising. At our dinner just two weeks earlier — when the dispute was already well flagged in the media — he had never mentioned the plight of the bus drivers. His passion for their cause must have faltered at the sight of the first glass of prosecco.

Not to worry. Eamon is Eamon. Not Senator Eamon. His point of view had plenty of public support and merit. He was perfectly entitled to express his opinions on any programme and on any subject he chose. I decided not to respond publicly and awaited one of the regular calls we had enjoyed several times a week over many years. It never came. The calls simply stopped.

Fair enough. A few weeks after his outburst on Sean O'Rourke, my mother died following a long illness. The funeral in Enniskerry was well publicised. My friend of so many years did not appear. I was disappointed, for political differences are one thing, but should never sever personal friendships. Maybe, I thought, my oldest pal would drop me a line of solidarity? Perhaps he was away? Sadly, no message of any sort was ever sent. Eamon was the first casualty of the Independent Alliance in government.

But he certainly gave us a great fillip as we entered the Brave New World in Athlone on that September day.

We headed home from the conference that night with a spring in our step. There had been no hiccups or gaffes. Dunphy had behaved himself. The media was really interested and could not ignore us. A roomful of loose cannons had behaved like responsible politicians. But time was short. Enda Kenny was expected to call a November election and we were far from ready. The Alliance had no staff, no organisation, no money and no manifesto. We needed to get down to the hard graft.

We may have had no money, but we did have human assets — five TDs, two senators, over thirty councillors and great ambitions. Tom Fleming, Michael Fitzmaurice, John Halligan, Finian McGrath and I were backed up by Feargal Quinn and Gerry Craughwell in the Seanad. Our seven members of the Oireachtas outstripped Lucinda's three Renua TDs and two senators, the Social Democrats' trio of Catherine Murphy, Róisín Shortall and Stephen Donnelly, and the Greens' tally of zero. The Rural Alliance did not yet exist and Mick Wallace's left-wing group, 'Independents 4 Change', which included Clare Daly and Joan Collins, was not acting as a unit. We were the front runners among the multiple groups competing in the crowded independents' space.

Tom Fleming and Michael Fitzmaurice carried the torch for rural Ireland at our weekly group meetings. Their contributions reflected similar interests. They also shared one common characteristic: I cannot remember a single occasion when either of them arrived, even vaguely, on time!

Fleming was one of the most unassuming men ever to grace Irish politics. He was universally liked, a trifle innocent for a Kerry TD, but was refreshingly lacking in media savvy or the normal devious ways of politicians. He had been a Fianna Fáil local councillor from 1985 until his surprise election to the Dáil as an independent in 2011. He was originally co-opted to Kerry County Council following the death of his father, then a councillor, and was re-elected at every subsequent election. However, he stood unsuccessfully for the Dáil for Fianna Fáil in 2002 and 2007. Tom resigned from the party after being turned down for a nomination in 2011. It was a good decision, because he sailed into the Dáil, relegating no less a superstar than Michael Healy-Rae into third place. Tom's membership of the Independent Alliance ensured that Michael kept his distance from us. There was no advantage in two competing independents fighting for votes in one constituency to join the same grouping. Michael ploughed his own furrow but the two men, somewhat unusually in this situation, managed to maintain a personal friendship. We all confidently expected Tom to retain his seat. A banker for the Independent Alliance.

If Tom lacked political guile, his soulmate in the Independent Alliance, Michael Fitzmaurice, carried enough of it in his thumbnail for both of them. Fitzmaurice was an operator who would devour most of his opponents for breakfast. With hands that look as if they could easily lift a tractor, he was nicknamed 'Shrek' (after the grumpy ogre of animated movie fame, who lived in a swamp) by the wags in the Dáil Members' Bar, where he hammed up his rural street cred by always insisting that he drink his coffee in a large mug. He was the natural focus of the rural councillors in the Independent Alliance, because he had positioned himself to be the voice of rural Ireland ever since his by-election triumph a few months earlier. He was not trusted by Mattie McGrath's wilder gang of rural councillors who wanted to be voices in the wilderness for ever. So the Independent Alliance offered rural TDs an opening, a vehicle for those of them genuinely interested in going into government. Like his patron, Luke 'Ming' Flanagan, Michael had been elected principally because of his commitment to the cause of the turf-cutters in the west of Ireland. His power base was the bogs, which he had been cutting since he was four years old. He had personally defied an EU ban on turf-cutting and was chair of the Turf Cutters and Contractors Association. Fiercely intelligent, with an irritating macho manner, 'Shrek' was widely expected to outpoll arch-rival Denis Naughten in the general election, whenever it came.

No one could have made less likely partners for Fleming and Fitzmaurice in the Independent Alliance than John Halligan and Finian McGrath. I took an instant liking to John Halligan the moment I met him on our first day in the Dáil — back in 2011. I don't think it was mutual. He had a wild look in his eye, but was personally engaging. His background in the hard-left Workers' Party should have been a flashing amber light for a market-led former stockbroker like me. He had been elected as a Workers' Party councillor in 1999 and 2004, but in 2009 he topped the poll and became independent Mayor of Waterford. I still don't know why John left the Workers' Party, but everybody seemed to leave it sooner or later. From time to time, John, who is notoriously indiscreet, would regale us with hilarious, but sometimes hair-raising, tales about his days with his comrades back in the seventies and eighties.

While he was in opposition during the 2011 to 2016 Dáil, he never deserted his roots, but he had definitely seen the benefits of not staying on the backbenches for ever. His Dáil performances were easily the most passionate of all the Independent Alliance TDs. I thoroughly warmed to him one day early in the Dáil term when he landed in the height of trouble with the Ceann Comhairle, Seán Barrett. An out-of-order discussion had erupted in the chamber about a judgement in the Four Courts. John, a heckler with few equals, roared out that the judge in question was a 'Blueshirt judge'. He had thus broken the nonsensical Dáil taboo that the Four Courts (and above all individual judges) are off limits in the House. He is politically fearless, sometimes reckless and was always unflinchingly loyal. He could be relied upon to bat on the stickiest of wickets for a comrade. He was frequently forced to give his colleagues a dig-out and defend the indefensible in the media. He did it with gusto. We did the same for him. He taught us all that there was, after all, quite a lot to be said for the discipline of a Workers' Party background. Back in those days it would have been impossible to envisage John as a bedfellow for the Blueshirts.

Finian McGrath came from a similar stable. While John's mentor might have been the late former socialist president of the Workers' Party, Seán Garland, Finian's was undoubtedly the late independent inner-city TD Tony Gregory. All four men were ideologically driven and were firmly on the left of the spectrum. John was originally hard left, but Finian's background as a primary school principal probably pulled him somewhat closer to the centre. He came to the Dáil as an Independent Health Alliance candidate through the council route in 2002, after sitting on the Dublin City Council since 1999. He was battle-hardened, having stood unsuccessfully for the Dáil on two previous occasions.

Finian was exceptionally popular with Dáil colleagues from all parties. I met him most days in the Members' Bar for lunch where he held court at the table just inside the door. No TD could enter this Dáil 'holy of holies' at lunchtime without exchanging gossip with Finian. He was invariably cheerful, despite the tragic death of his wife Anne, also a schoolteacher, from cancer in 2009. Maybe more than anyone else in the Alliance, Finian was motivated by his own personal experiences. His expertise and passion for those with disabilities was undoubtedly inspired by having a delightful daughter, Clíodhna, with Down's Syndrome.

Finian had form in government formation. He also had sharp political antennae. Back in 2007, he did a deal with Bertie Ahern and Fianna Fáil to support his fellow northsider's ill-fated coalition with the Greens. After securing much of his own personal programme, he suddenly jumped ship and ended the deal in October 2008. The deluge followed, but Finian was not on the ship when it sank. The statement he issued on his break with the Fianna Fáil-led coalition summed up his political beliefs: 'As someone who comes from the tradition of Tone and Connolly, I have to act in the interests of the elderly, the sick and the disabled and the future of our children. I have also supported the call for more patriotism. However, my patriotism does not include hammering the elderly, the sick, the disabled and young children in large class sizes. There are always other creative ways to fund these matters. I have no option but to withdraw my support for the Government.'

A few years later, the man with the picture of Che Guevara in his office was bouncing into bed with the Blueshirts.

And finally, there was me.

In the background, but not in the firing line for the looming Dáil general election, stood independent Senators Feargal Quinn and Gerard Craughwell.

This was the backbone of our team as we headed into battle.

While all five TDs were strong as individuals and were confidently expected to hold their seats, as a team we were one-dimensional. Unfortunately, we were all male. Worse still, the average age of our seven Oireachtas members was a stunning sixty-three. All bar Michael Fitzmaurice were nearing normal retirement age. At our weekly meeting there was far too much fading testosterone in the room. We had a fine logo, but the brand was dismally lacking in fresh female faces.

We needed candidates to contest the election with us who were female and young enough to be our offspring. We needed a manifesto that would be embraced by all the councillors who had signed up at our gatherings in Tullamore and Athlone. It was a tall order but our national coverage and our meetings in the midlands had fired up enthusiasm for a challenge to the big parties. While we had not managed to attract sitting women deputies or senators to our ranks, countrywide women councillors had come calling.

We spent nearly six months in search of recruits with a different profile. We systematically interviewed councillors or others who saw our project as a vehicle for reform.

In Dublin one of Ireland's most vocal newspaper columnists, Carol Hunt, was an early supporter. Carol ended up as our only woman candidate in the general election who was not a councillor. Her motivations were so noble that I gulped twice over my coffee when I met her in Buswells Hotel during the search for candidates. Carol was refreshing. She had ideas and integrity. She thought that it was time for her to become involved in public life. She felt an obligation. Her opinions in the *Sunday Independent* were the most articulate expression of militant feminism in the media in 2015. She believed it was incumbent on someone who expressed so stridently what was wrong in political life to pick up the gauntlet and practise what she had been preaching in her columns.

Carol was different. Unfortunately, she lived in Dublin's inner city, an almost unassailable political fortress for a new candidate. The mantle of local legend, the late Tony Gregory, had long ago been inherited by one of his closest followers, independent Deputy Maureen O'Sullivan. We had tried to attract Maureen to join us in the Independent Alliance, but she had declined. No other independent had a chance of competing with Maureen for the Gregory legacy, besides which Maureen was a hard worker and one of the most idealistic members of the Dáil. Worse still for Carol, Dublin Central had four incumbents, now fighting for only three seats since the constituency had lost one seat to become a three-seater in 2016. Apart from Maureen, the remaining three seats were held by outgoing cabinet minister Paschal Donohoe, Sinn Féin's Mary Lou McDonald and Labour's Joe Costello. Joe was toast, but if Carol was to capture a seat she needed to topple a political giant, either Paschal or Mary Lou. Instead, she decided to head across the Liffey to Dún Laoghaire, where she had grown up and still had strong family ties.

Elsewhere in Dublin we recruited two utterly different women, both hell-bent on taking seats in their respective areas.

Deirdre O'Donovan had volunteered for my 2011 Dáil election campaign in a resolute effort to remove Fianna Fáil from office. Three years later — in 2014 — she was elected to South Dublin County Council, an area that included Tallaght. She was as keen as mustard to run for us in 2016 on an anti-big party platform with a community emphasis. We embraced her — as someone with such naked ambition — with open arms. Deirdre was hungry.

Just as Carol Hunt had Maureen O'Sullivan blocking her chances, Deirdre had her own high-profile, independent obstacle in the Dublin South-West constituency. Senator Katherine Zappone, who ultimately ended up as an independent minister in Enda Kenny's cabinet, had done good work in Tallaght on the Tallaght West Childhood Development Initiative, adding a local base to her high national profile. Deirdre, unimpressed by the big gun in her bailiwick, powered on, dismissing Zappone's chances of success and convinced that she herself would be swept into a seat for the Independent Alliance.

On the other side of the political spectrum — and on the other side of the Liffey — Lorna Nolan was a radical Fingal County councillor from the Mulhuddart ward. She was as hard-working as councillors come, a senior social care worker dedicated to suicide prevention, drugs rehabilitation programmes and people with disabilities. Lorna is one of those women who is far too good for politics. She was deeply committed to the Alliance because she saw it as a way to promote the minority causes she championed, never as a route to self-advancement. We were devastated when she was forced to withdraw as a candidate at the last minute because her brother became seriously ill.

We had wooed some mighty women from Dublin. Outside Dublin, the numbers of women councillors committed to our cause were fewer than the numbers hovering around the edges, eager but unwilling to take the plunge. They were hampered by our inability to offer them funds for a campaign, because the Independent Alliance qualified for no public money. The entrenched parties have long ago stitched up state funding available for political activities. Independents are forced to fund election campaigns from their own resources or from voluntary donations. Nevertheless, we fielded three serious women contenders, itching to take the big parties apart in Donegal, Louth and Sligo.

We were immensely proud of both our women candidates in the north-west: Councillor Marie Casserly in Sligo-Leitrim and Councillor Niamh Kennedy in Donegal. We knew they both had mountains to climb, fighting Dáil constituencies where traditional loyalty to established civil war parties still dominated.

Unfazed, Marie Casserly decided to enter the fray. An Irish teacher and guidance counsellor at St Mary's College in Ballysadare, Marie was a serious contender. A teacher, a mother of five children, a feminist who helped to found the Grange men's shed, was exactly the kind of community activist we needed to broaden our brand. We had to twist her arm to run because she was motivated by passion for her area, not personal ambition. Nothing moved in Sligo of which Marie was unaware. She was unrelenting in badgering ministers on behalf of her home patch and she was an unrepentant advocate for her 'neglected' region. A health enthusiast, she found time to support all local sports clubs and to promote cycling. She was delighted when Eamon Dunphy launched her entry into national politics.

Farther north, Niamh Kennedy flew the flag in the bearpit that is the constituency of Donegal. Anyone caught in the crossfire between such battle-scarred veterans as Fine Gael's Joe McHugh, Sinn Féin's Pearse Doherty, Fianna Fáil's Pat (the Cope) Gallagher and Charlie McConalogue needs to be made of stern stuff. Niamh is. In 2014, she was the first ever independent councillor elected to Donegal County Council. Based in Killybegs, she originally worked in the fishing industry, in both administration and health and safety. More recently she and her husband have run an electronics business. At one point, Niamh was approached by Fine Gael, but happily she spurned the Blueshirt blandishments.

Yet, despite the rich offerings, not a single woman was elected to any of the nine seats in Donegal and Sligo-Leitrim.

While Marie and Niamh were enlightened political outsiders in two of the most rural parts of Ireland, Louth was a real live runner for an independent seat. Maeve Yore from Dundalk was elected to the Louth County Council in third place in the 2014 local elections with a substantial 1,228 votes. She was well placed in the north of the county, had a proud community record, having worked in the Credit Union for fourteen years, and was a founder member of Special Needs Active Parents (SNAP). She was disarmingly blunt in conversation and regularly discarded her natural charm in pursuit of an objective for people with special needs. It often worked. She was highly respected in Dundalk for her steadfast integrity. Unfortunately, her fame did not stretch beyond Dundalk, where she was guaranteed to reap a good vote. She needed a running mate who would deliver votes from the south of the county, namely Drogheda.

Maeve had a potentially ideal running mate in Drogheda. Councillor Kevin Callan had been a Fine Gael mayor of Drogheda in 2011 but had resigned from the party over the water charges, to become an independent in 2014. Kevin was intent on standing for the Dáil. He and Maeve were a perfect fit. One seat was there for the taking provided they agreed on a vote transfer pact. Kevin and Maeve seemed to be a dream ticket to land one of Louth's five seats. Sadly, they were never able to agree on a sensible division of the county.

While our search for candidates met with multiple successes, one ended in a tragedy. Councillor William Crowley from Newbridge, County Kildare, was an enthusiastic promoter of the Independent Alliance, determined to run for us in the constituency of South Kildare. Willie came to Dublin to meet the Independent Alliance deputies one afternoon and dazzled us with his enthusiasm, his experience in politics and his community involvement. I knew him, but only by reputation, as the man who had met Michael Noonan about the future of the troubled Newbridge Credit Union. As that meeting started, Willie opened up: 'Before we begin, Minister, I would like you to tender your resignation in the Dáil tomorrow.' It was a novel approach from a county councillor seeking a sympathetic audience from a senior minister. Willie was a freelance journalist and a highly successful small businessman, setting out on a career in national politics at the age of sixty-five. We were delighted that he had agreed to run for the Independent Alliance.

It was not to be. On 18 December 2015, Willie was mowed down on the streets of Newbridge by a hit-and-run driver just a hundred yards from his home. I was among several public representatives at his huge funeral in St Conleth's, Newbridge, where there was a clear outpouring of grief from the whole community. His death was a terrible loss to his family, to Newbridge and ultimately to Dáil Eireann.

We met all the candidates before giving them our imprimatur. In return, they agreed to sign up to our principles — a 'Charter for Change' as it would eventually become. We did not accept the approaches of all those looking for the blessing of the Independent Alliance. Sometimes we had to make choices between two independents in one constituency. At other times, the prospective candidate turned down our approaches, feeling that joining a group, albeit a loose alliance, could compromise their freedom. Some opted to run solo without being attached to us. Others joined the Greens or the Social Democrats. Generally, those who were not frightened of being in government signed up, while those who probably felt more comfortable in opposition declined.

One of those gagging to join us was none other than a man with the familiar name of Peter Casey, an investor on RTÉ's *Dragons' Den* business programme. He was supposed to be a heavy hitter with a great career behind him. When he rang looking to meet me, I was chuffed. Here was a TV star on the Dunphy scale seeking our support. Casey had founded an outfit called Claddagh Resources, a global recruitment company that placed executives with many Fortune 500 companies. Claddagh had made him a multi-millionaire. His dazzling business success and television stardom made me think he might be a bit above our pay grade.

The problem was, so did he. I met him on a number of occasions. Never before — or since — in my political life have I encountered a candidate with such delusions. Peter, who lived in the United States, was going to build the biggest house in Donegal and would therefore win a Dáil seat. He ignored my protests that we already had a wonderful candidate in Niamh Kennedy, who had an impeccable record as a county councillor. The idea of defeat in an Irish election never occurred to a man who spent most of his time making his fortune in the US. His ego had reached a level that would have made Dunphy blush. I invited him to our conference in Athlone, hoping that he might be afflicted with a shock dose of realpolitik and be halted in his tracks from aping Donald Trump on speed.

I can only guess that he took my advice and spent some of his vast riches on an opinion poll in Donegal. He dropped the idea of running on our ticket and disappeared. To my great relief, he opted for the Seanad election. There, his balloon was pricked. Casey stood on the Industrial and Commercial Panel, having been foolishly nominated by the Irish Business and Employers Confederation (IBEC). The quota was 113 votes. He received 14.

A lucky escape for the Independent Alliance. Unhappily, Peter Casey resurfaced in 2018. Originally a no-hoper candidate in the presidential election, he unashamedly played the racist card to boost his chances. His last-minute piece of insidious rabble-rousing, plugging into anti-traveller prejudice, raised his poll ratings from 2% to 23% by election day. He was runner-up to Michael D. Higgins.

Peter Casey's performance in the battle for president hardly dented Michael D.'s triumph, but it swelled the challenger's already inflated head. In the wake of the result, he suddenly declared that he wanted to lead Fianna Fáil, but was surprised that the disciples of de Valera had a distinct lack of appetite for a messiah who was not even a party member. Undeterred, he stood as an independent for the European Parliament in 2019, again failing to pass the winning post. Disregarding a succession of rebuffs, he decided to double down in the 2020 general election, spurning the idea of winning merely one single seat. Instead, he wanted two! Voters in both Donegal and Dublin West were honoured to find Casey's name on their ballot papers on the same day. He scraped a small (1,143) vote in Donegal, where he expected to do well. Worse still, in a final piece of grotesque vanity, he challenged Taoiseach Leo Varadkar in his home patch of Dublin West. Casey's vote was a derisory 495 against the Taoiseach's 8,478.

We had certainly attracted enough women and men to counter criticism from those opponents who wagged the finger, insisting that we merely represented one gender and one generation. Several younger males were also on the Independent Alliance ticket. We had high hopes of Paul Gogarty (a former

Green Party TD, then an independent) retaking the seat he lost in Dublin Mid-West in the 2011 election.

Gogarty was one of the most colourful TDs during his nine years in the Dáil from 2002. His highly unorthodox outbursts tended to distract from an appreciation of the good work he did for Irish education during his time in the Dáil. To his credit, he played a leading role in protecting education from cutbacks when he was chairman of the Oireachtas Committee on Education and Science under the Fianna Fáil-Green government. But the public was probably more aware of the time he let fly at Labour's Emmet Stagg during a debate on social welfare in 2010. After being niggled by Stagg's heckling, Paul lost the head. 'With all due respect, in the most unparliamentary language, fuck you, Deputy Stagg, fuck you,' he exclaimed. He immediately apologised, but a complaint from Fine Gael's Lucinda Creighton followed. The incident was referred to the Dáil's Committee on Procedure and Privileges after it was found that the 'F' word was, surprisingly, not on the list of expletives forbidden by the House's rules!

In another controversial incident, Paul again landed in hot water after he brought his eighteen-month-old daughter to a Green Party press conference, claiming that his childminder was not available. He was a wild card with good ideas and was a live prospect for an independent seat.

Elsewhere — in the Midlands — we knew that Kevin 'Boxer' Moran had a sporting chance of a win in Longford-Westmeath and — in the West — Seán Canney was a firm favourite to score a gain for us in Galway East. Both were long-time councillors with a record of hard work which was likely to carry them over the line. Another who might have pulled a surprise if he had been able to agree a vote transfer pact with fellow independent Joe Hannigan was former Fianna Fáil member, businessman and councillor John Foley in Offaly. He couldn't, so his chances were dramatically reduced.

We were not going to allow any no-hopers to stand under our banner. All bar Carol Hunt, Boxer Moran's running mate James Morgan, and Diarmuid O'Flynn of the 'Ballyhea Says No' anti-bailout campaign, were already councillors, so had recently tasted electoral triumphs and established a local base in their larger Dáil constituencies. Tony Murphy (Dublin North), Joe Bonner (Meath East), Ger Carthy (Wexford) and Mick Finn (Cork South-Central) were experienced candidates with strong showings under their belts.

We had a good team of twenty-two, but in October 2015 we were far from ready for Enda Kenny to blow the whistle. Thankfully, he didn't.

Enda bottled the most important political decision of his life. Late in 2015, the Taoiseach had encouraged speculation that he would call an election in November. He was reported to be under heavy pressure from both Finance Minister Michael Noonan and European Commissioner Phil Hogan not to leave the contest until February 2016. Enda's personal standing in the polls was at a high point, Fine Gael was recovering after four years of austerity and unemployment was falling. His TDs, including his Mayo constituency colleague Michael Ring, were upbeat about their chances. Many of the Blueshirts wanted to avoid the seasonal winter political pitfalls of ill health and homelessness.

Enda's Tánaiste, Labour Party leader Joan Burton, had different ideas. Labour faced oblivion at the polls if Enda were to call an election in November. Senior members of the junior partner in government made their view public, urging the Taoiseach not to take the plunge. They succeeded in exposing his intentions as nakedly opportunistic. Kenny, looking to Labour to join him again in the next government, backed down publicly, and, to the surprise of most of cabinet, during an interview on RTÉ's *The Week in Politics* in mid-October. Labour breathed a sigh of relief. So did the Independent Alliance.

The extra time gave us space to prepare our 'Charter for Change'. It was no easy task to unite twenty-two independents from totally different backgrounds. It took several months for us to agree. Finally, barely three weeks before the Dáil was dissolved in early February, on 12 January 2016, we launched the document in Dublin's Royal College of Physicians of Ireland. Senator Feargal Quinn chaired the event, supported by nearly all our candidates. In the audience was Eamon Dunphy, ready to lend a hand wherever it was needed.

Critics greeted the 'Charter for Change' as a statement of dull, diluted but worthy principles. They complained that it was a list of lowest common denominator policies, broad brushes assembled by a disparate group that disagreed hopelessly when challenged on the detail. We saw it as an important part of a great experiment in Irish politics. It contained ten basic principles. As constructive independents, we advocated radical, but responsible, government. We offered the prospect of stability. We had resolved to become part of a unique form of government where the party whip was unnecessary. We pledged to build an administration that respected our principles. We would support a government in votes of confidence and Finance Bills, provided the larger party agreed a Programme for Government. We had no party-political preference, maintaining a strict neutrality, almost indifference, between the Blueshirts and the Soldiers of Destiny. Our members included people from virtually every party-political gene pool, or none.

The demands in our Charter were headed by the need to end cronyism in Irish politics. Ireland has always been cursed by political patronage in state appointments, especially the judiciary. One of the low points of the 2011–16 Fine Gael-Labour coalition had been the John McNulty case, where a failed Fine Gael local election candidate was appointed to the board of the Irish Museum of Modern Art to boost his credentials to stand for the Seanad. It ended in a debacle for the partners in government when McNulty was shamed into resignation. More brazenly, with only weeks to go before the general election, Labour leader Joan Burton had appointed Labour trade union-ist David Begg to the chair of The Pensions Authority. Her selection of Begg provoked a motion of no confidence from the Independent Alliance in the Dáil.

High among our priorities was the neglect of rural Ireland. The fingerprints of Tom Fleming and Michael Fitzmaurice were all over the listed catalogue of woes suffered by towns and villages outside the main urban areas, where the lack of broadband was an open wound.

In keeping with our determination to protect Ireland's more vulnerable individuals and stakeholders, we insisted that small business must not be neglected while multinationals were receiving favourable treatment. Similarly, in an item inserted at the insistence of John Halligan and Finian McGrath, the vulnerable would be protected. Special mention was made of Finian's obsession — the ratification of the UN Convention on the Rights of Persons with Disabilities.

Other commitments demanded in the Charter highlighted far-reaching reform of the Houses of the Oireachtas, including an end to the unsavoury Fine Gael-Labour coalition's use of the Dáil guillotine to suppress discussion on unpopular bills.

The Charter also expressed deep scepticism about whether the bankers had really changed their spots. We opposed privati-sation of the banks, at least until competition was fully restored. Discrimination of all sorts was condemned. We should remain in the European Union but would refuse to rubber-stamp the EU's wishes.

It was a charter for reform, not revolution. Unlike others, we wanted to take real responsibility by putting independents into government.

The Charter was, of course, a compromise between the different approaches of the leading members of the Independent Alliance. There had been arguments galore about it. At one point, the attempted input from councillors had prompted an exasperated Michael Fitzmaurice to say that they should be told they would have to accept the 'full duck or no dinner'.

Some took the full duck. Others got no dinner. The 'full duck' men and women were on parade at the presentation of the Charter on that January morning in the Royal College of Physicians. It worked well until the very first question from the floor: 'Would the Alliance go into government with Sinn Féin?'

I saw the danger. Feargal Quinn, somewhat unhelpfully, handed me the hospital pass. I fumbled it for a moment and then rattled off a well-prepared 'personal' response: the Shinners would have to experience a 'Pauline conversion to democracy to convince us that they were suitable partners'. Decoded, to any political anorak, that meant 'Yes'.

Not to my new colleague, Diarmuid O'Flynn of the 'Ballyhea Says No' campaign, who only a few days earlier had been adopted as our candidate in Cork North-West. Diarmuid instantly waded in, volunteering: 'I wouldn't need much convincing and I assume that is where the divisions would come in.'

I could have shot him on the spot. But suddenly, I recalled rapidly that our whole raison d'être was tolerance of different points of view. I bit my tongue and moved on. The media had their headline.

Otherwise, we were in battle order on that morning, ready for the imminent general election.

The Taoiseach did not formally call the election for another three weeks, on 3 February, but the campaign had really started months earlier. It was an odd election for our candidates. We had a good cluster of outgoing Oireachtas members, a good countrywide geographical spread and a manifesto/ charter of sorts. We had unending enthusiasm. But we had no money, no headquarters and, crucially, no rights to television broadcasts because we were not a formal political party. Not a single member of staff dedicated to the Independent Alliance was available to us. Our immediate competitors for the reformist space, the small parties, had state money to burn. Our unfunded war effort depended on the ability of our sitting Oireachtas members to give a dig-out to the councillors. Feargal and I managed to launch campaigns for Kevin Callan in Louth, Tony Murphy in Dublin Fingal and others, while Michael Fitzmaurice and I were among the TDs helping Seán Canney and Boxer Moran in Galway East and Longford-Westmeath respectively. I travelled to Sligo to spend a morning with the irrepressible Marie Casserly, the woman fighting a rearguard action against the mighty MacSharry dynasty and Fine Gael's Tony McLoughlin.

It was on one of those trips that I had to pursue Michael Fitzmaurice around the rural lanes of Roscommon and East Galway, in what was possibly the most hair-raising experience of my life. It seemed as though the area was a speed-limit-free zone. The local Roscommon TD lost me at least once, probably because I obviously had less experience than him of circumnavigating blind corners in the west of Ireland. A few years later, when I introduced the drink-driving and speeding laws into the Dáil, I could not help recalling that evening when I took my life in my hands and (dare I admit it?) broke the road traffic laws.

As Oireachtas members, as the creators of the Independent Alliance project, we were certainly obliged to campaign for others who had rallied to our battle cry. Although we felt nervousness about abandoning our own constituencies in the middle of an election contest, we had high hopes that all five of us would be returned.

We were in for a shock. On 4 February, a day after the election had been called, Deputy Tom Fleming dropped a bombshell. He rang me in Leinster House to say that he was withdrawing from the field. Kerry had been two three-seat constituencies (North and South) when he was first elected in 2011. It was now just one five-seat constituency. The reduction, he said, meant that his seat would be lost because he had not done enough work in the northern part of the county. He was sorry. I was gobsmacked. It was a body blow just as the campaign began. And Tom had opened the way for Danny Healy-Rae, maybe a graver offence than deflating the Independent Alliance balloon.

Tom was not for turning. We would struggle without him. But we had hopes elsewhere, especially for Seán Canney and Boxer Moran. Meanwhile Fine Gael was running into big trouble with its disastrous slogan 'Keep the Recovery Going', alienating tens of thousands who had never felt any sign of recovery. Throughout the campaign, the disastrous decline of Fine Gael increased the likelihood of a small group like ours holding the balance of power.

That is exactly what happened when the ballot papers were counted on 26 February. Among the major parties, Fine Gael lost 16 to hold 50 seats, Fianna Fáil added 23 to finish with 44. Labour was annihilated, down from 33 seats to 7. Sinn Féin managed to add 9 to end with 23 TDs. The small parties had a bad day. The Greens came back to the Dáil, but with just two seats, the Anti-Austerity Alliance-People Before Profit Group 6, the Social Democrats 3, Renua none, losing all its incumbents, including Lucinda Creighton. Independents had a good result, with unaligned independents taking 17 seats. The Independent Alliance returned six deputies.

We were disappointed that we did not win more seats, but ultimately, all our incumbent TDs held on fairly comfortably. We had received 4.2% of the national vote without a cent of state funding. None of the smaller groups matched us. Renua was wiped out, the Social Democrats managed only to retain their three seats with 3% of the vote, the Greens scraped two seats with 2.7%, while even Anti-Austerity Alliance-People Before Profit came in behind us with 3.94%. We had one seat less than Labour, the state's oldest party.

We had lost one member, Tom Fleming, but had gained two, Boxer Moran and Seán Canney. Both were gagging to go into government, but only on the right terms.

Boxer Moran was possibly the most interesting new TD to reach the Dáil in 2016. He had worked his passage in the normal way. Originally elected as a Westmeath County councillor for Fianna Fáil in 1999, blocked from progressing by the powerful O'Rourke dynasty, he left the party in 2011. With perfect timing, the autumn/winter 2015 flooding crisis propelled Boxer into national prominence. His leadership of a large group of volunteers operating water pumps to stop the Shannon from flooding dozens of houses in Athlone caught the public imagination, both locally and nationally. Pictures of Boxer in his flooding gear, fighting back the rising waters, appeared everywhere. By the time the election came in February 2016, he was 'Mr Athlone', the local man who had gone down, dirty and knee-deep, when his people needed him.

Boxer had a proud secret that he shared with me when I came calling in 2015. I wanted him to run for the Dáil. He confided that he had left school at age twelve. He was dyslexic and couldn't read properly. He was learning, but still had difficulties. He had even been unable to read his scripts when he was Mayor of Athlone in 2013. I reassured him that it wouldn't make a blind bit of difference to us. He would be an inspiration to others in his situation. He was a master of speaking off the cuff and would never need a script. Two years later, after being appointed a minister, Boxer inspired the nation further when he spoke openly about his reading problems. Even more courageously, he told Ryan Tubridy on *The Late Late Show* that depression in his twenties had pushed him into a suicide attempt. Boxer's candidness was unique in Irish politics. The Independent Alliance had delivered a gem.

Seán Canney's career was more conventional. Like Boxer, he had come to the Dáil along the county council route. He was elected as an independent to Galway County Council in 2004, 2009 and 2014. He failed to win a Dáil seat in the 2011 election but topped the poll in 2016. Seán was a chartered quantity surveyor and lecturer at the Galway-Mayo Institute of Technology. He is a strong advocate of reopening the Western Rail Corridor from Galway to Claremorris but will be able to do this only over the dead bodies of the officials in the Department of Transport who regard it as an enormous drain on resources and incurably non-commercial.

It was a chronically hung Dáil. All the small parties and alliances were now in pivotal positions to be part of a government. They could take it or leave it. The result presented the ultimate challenge to the individuals, parties and groups who had never expected to be in a position of facing the responsibilities of power. Some of the far left and the more extreme independents were institutionalised, pre-conditioned to permanent opposition. They were good at it. Others were champing at the bit to reach the negotiating table. There was no doubt where we stood. We wanted to exercise the mandate the electorate had given us. We were up for serious talks.

Suddenly our reforming ambitions had real potential of being achieved. The biggest party in the state was badly wounded. Within a few hours, the civil war combatants would be looking for new allies. We needed to stick together and even behave, for once, with the discipline of a political party or at least as a negotiating team. We determined to support one another in the weeks ahead because our real strength would now be the number of votes we commanded to support a candidate for Taoiseach. Six was a big figure.

Spooked for a moment, I nostalgically yearned for my thirty-five years of carefree opposition. Suddenly, I thought that maybe, in the words of Robert Louis Stevenson, 'to travel hopefully is a better thing than to arrive'. But I put those dark thoughts behind me. Inexperienced dilettantes, amateur politicians, we were now about to broker a Programme for Government with the Blueshirts.

2

The Blueshirts Play Hardball

WHEN ENDA KENNY woke up on Sunday, 28 February 2016, his world had fallen apart. Fine Gael had lost 16 seats in the general election, to finish with a dismal 50. Labour, his coalition partners for five years, had been effectively wiped out, losing 26 deputies to cling on to a grand total of only 7. Fianna Fáil, whom Kenny had hoped to vaporise for ever, was in recovery, gaining 26 seats to 44. Sinn Féin, hated by all true Blueshirts, had won 9 extra seats, to hit a new high of 23. The Greens were back in business with 2 seats. Independents of every hue had multiplied.

Fine Gael Taoisigh had a dismal record of calling elections at the wrong moment. Neither Liam Cosgrave, Garret FitzGerald nor John Bruton had managed to call general elections at the right time. There had never been a Fine Gael Taoiseach who had won two consecutive terms in office. This time, Enda's dilly-dallying over a November 2015 election had disastrous consequences. His delay had opened the door to a Fianna Fáil revival, a Sinn Féin surge and a ragbag of smaller groups. Inside his own party, the knives were already being sharpened. To the leader of Fine Gael, the political landscape post-election must have looked like an anarchy of Enda's own creation. He will have known that he had blown it. Big time.

Fine Gael leaders had a noble tradition of resigning after electoral reverses. Cosgrave announced that he was leaving office on the night of his general election loss in 1977. Garret FitzGerald followed the same route after his 1987 defeat. Michael Noonan immediately fell on his sword when he failed to lead the party to victory in 2002. Only John Bruton declined to take such an honourable course after his surprise loss in 1997, but he was ruthlessly removed as Fine Gael leader by a vote of no confidence in 2001.

Not Enda. The defeated Taoiseach of 2016 may have been shell-shocked by the result but it didn't take long for him to plot his survival. He needed to work fast at new alliances if he was to stay in power. So, the same week, on Friday, 4 March, newly elected Independent Alliance deputies found themselves surprisingly welcome in the Taoiseach's office. The big loser of the previous week's election entered the waiting room to greet us with a broad grin. He told us a few jokes with the relaxed manner of a politician without a worry in the world. He was sounding us out, wondering if we were seriously interested in entering government with him. Or were we just mavericks? We made it crystal clear that we were talking turkey to everyone, but we needed our proposed reforms to be met, our programme to be included in any deal.

We were aware that Enda had, surprisingly, already suggested that he might need to talk to Fianna Fáil as a necessary prerequisite to forming a government. Was he really thinking of dancing with the civil war enemy, despite his denials during the election campaign? We in the Independent Alliance had already agreed to hold talks with Micheál Martin, who was beginning to woo the smaller parties. The merry-go-round was already in full swing.

After our meeting with Enda, we publicly described the talks as 'constructive'. We wanted both major parties to know that we were united, reliable and game for government. We went home for a peaceful weekend, knowing that government formation might be a long process. Enda had 50 Fine Gael deputies. He needed 80 votes to be elected as the next Taoiseach. Even if he received our six, he was a long way from the magic number. Micheál, with his 44 deputies, was even further from the winning line.

I headed off to write a weekly column for the *Sunday Independent*. Obviously the hot topic was the next government. Our meeting with Enda was in the public mind. It was important to inform readers of the mood music at our meeting with Enda without breaching confidence about the details of what had been discussed.

The column appeared. For a day, there was hardly any reaction. I thought little of it. At Friday's meeting we had established a good rapport with the Taoiseach. Not exactly trust, but it was certainly worth pursuing further dialogue.

There had been a degree of tentative goodwill, even bonhomie, at the encounter. Given that he and I had been scrapping in the Dáil chamber for five years, we were not going to become bosom friends in half an hour. More seriously, I had expressed a lingering worry in highly colourful language. In a reference to the Taoiseach in print, I publicly questioned whether our talks with him were pointless because we were potentially dealing with a 'political corpse'. Was he still the leader in charge? Would he be able to deliver? In a single phrase, on that Sunday early in the process, I nearly blasted into kingdom come our chances of governing with the Blueshirts.

There was no immediate fuss about the article. Indeed nothing much happened until after our meeting with Micheál Martin on the Monday afternoon. We emerged from our first joust with Fianna Fáil to report progress to a waiting media. Their interest in our talks with Micheál was of far less concern than the weekend 'political corpse' jibe. They asked me if it was a constructive way to negotiate. Would I withdraw or apologise to the Taoiseach? The incident grew legs. My colleagues Michael Fitzmaurice and Finian McGrath, standing beside me on the Leinster House plinth, gave me support in front of the cameras, but I knew they felt mortified that I had demolished all the goodwill achieved at Friday's meeting.

I had. A few days later when I met Enda, Frances Fitzgerald and other Fine Gael negotiators, the atmosphere was icy. They were hostile down to the last Blueshirt. They were pleasant and accommodating to my colleagues' demands, while pointedly rubbishing mine. They treated Fitzmaurice as a serious player and Finian as a voice of sweet reason. I was beyond the pale.

The strategy was clear. For a short time Enda and his inner circle tried to divide and conquer the Independent Alliance members. Fine Gael quietly arranged clandestine meetings with key players outside Government Buildings. On 15 March, Simon Coveney and Simon Harris secretly met Fitzmaurice and Boxer Moran in Athlone. At the same time, hints were quietly dropped to Finian about the need to appoint a separate Minister for Disability Issues, to be given to a suitable person — with a seat at the cabinet table. Some Fine Gael top brass now claim that Finian was virtually sewn up in the first week, with promises of office and special concessions for his local hospital, Beaumont. They were determined to split the Alliance, picking our TDs off one by one. Stories suddenly appeared in the media that Michael Fitzmaurice was a potential Minister for Agriculture. They were tickling his belly. If they could have prised the rural TDs away from the Independent Alliance, with offers of special arrangements or high office, they would have done so.

The venom I felt shooting in my direction from the Fine Gael hierarchy was potent. More dangerously, it was part of a cunning strategy. On 20 March, the *Sunday Independent* carried a well-informed story headlined 'Kenny moves to kill off Shane Ross's Independent Alliance'. The article opened: 'Taoiseach Enda Kenny has targeted the break-up of the Independent Alliance — whose figurehead leader, Shane Ross, recently described him as a "political corpse" — in a determined bid by Fine Gael to form a minority government… Mr Kenny is understood to be prepared to appoint the Roscommon TD Michael Fitzmaurice, the other titular leader of the alliance, as Minister for Agriculture in what appears to be a personalised attempt to isolate Mr Ross.'

It was an inspired Fine Gael leak. Another bombshell followed: 'The Kerry TD Michael Healy-Rae is also being strongly tipped to take a seat at cabinet as Minister for Rural Affairs in a minority government which would signal the regeneration of rural Ireland.'

The plot was clear. Kenny was playing for the support of the Rural Alliance's five deputies, led by Denis Naughten. He would tempt Healy-Rae with a cabinet seat and lever Fitzmaurice, Boxer and Canney out of the Independent Alliance. He would capture the lion's share of independent rural TDs. If Finian McGrath wanted to join him, he could be the super junior Minister with responsibility for Disability Issues. I would be toast.

After I read of the plan, I invited Simon Coveney to my office, especially because he had been at the hush-hush meeting in Athlone. He protested that there was no plot to undermine the Alliance or any individual. Coveney — as honest as you can be in a political party — and I agreed that we would try to re-establish any lost goodwill. From that point on, the shenanigans noticeably reduced, but my 'political corpse' phrase still rankled with Kenny. Even when I tried to defuse the row with a public explanation and expression of regret, the wound remained. Relations throughout the entire seventy days of negotiations never recovered. We engaged in dialogue with Fine Gael as enemies, not as friends. Mea culpa, I had poisoned the waters. Today I accept that the remark was personally offensive to a decent man on his uppers.

Meanwhile, parallel, not poisoned, talks with Fianna Fáil and others were taking place in less conspicuous places. There were multiple groups, large and small, arranging to meet under cover. I met the newly elected Fianna Fáil TD Jim O'Callaghan in the Goat Grill in my constituency for an initial conversation. He was amiable and neither of us saw obstacles to dialogue. I invited Katherine Zappone to meet me in Buswells Hotel. I suggested that she join the Independent Alliance team in government formation — we would be stronger as seven rather than six. I naively pointed out that a solo run by any of us could be ignored by Kenny or Martin, since both leaders needed blocks of votes to best the other. She listened. She was inscrutable, leaving me in the dark about her intentions.

How innocent I was to warn Katherine about the futility of solo runs. She turned out to be the best solo runner in Leinster House. She wiped all our eyes, backing the eventual winner early on and landing herself the first job in Kenny's cabinet. I had forgotten that she owed a debt of loyalty to Enda as she had been one of his eleven nominees in the previous Seanad. They obviously understood each other well.

Elsewhere, the Rural Alliance was forming. It was an ad hoc group of independent deputies which comprised Mattie McGrath, Noel Grealish, Dr Michael Harty, Michael Collins and Denis Naughten. They were unapologetically demanding benefits for rural Ireland. Sometimes they negotiated in silos, at other times together. Kerry's Healy-Rae brothers, Michael and Danny, met the Taoiseach soon after the election, but alone.

The shape of the initial skirmishes was emerging. The two big battalions were competing to court smaller ones, but simultaneously eyeing each other for exploratory talks. Labour, battered and bruised, punished for five years of austerity, were out of the picture; they wanted to regroup in opposition under a new leader. Sinn Féin and the hard left kept away, scared of the danger of any contamination by association with the traditional parties. All were positioning themselves for another early election, terrified of being caught propping up in office the right-wing Blueshirts or the still disgraced Fianna Fáil. They saw coalition formation talks as doomed or, at best, as leading to a short-lived government. They fled as fast as possible for their comfort zone — the political wilderness. The Social Democrats and Green Party were stumbling about, wondering which way to jump.

The Independent Alliance was determined to avoid the non-combatant space. While the Dáil numbers dictated that some arrangement between the two big parties would be needed if a government was to be formed, it was becoming equally apparent that smaller groups would be essential components of such an administration.

On 10 March, the Dáil was in deadlock. Enda Kenny and Micheál Martin both lost the first round in a vote for Taoiseach. That prompted an outbreak of half a dozen groups or parties talking to one another in isolation. Disjointed dialogues were taking place between the Big Two and the Greens, the Social Democrats, the Rural Alliance, unaligned Independents, the Healy-Rae brothers and the Independent Alliance. It was a jigsaw of small groups with varying ideologies and multiple demands. Saner heads began to see the merit of more structured talks. No wonder the Taoiseach let it slip on his St Patrick's Day visit to the White House that he was dreading returning home. He is reported to have told the Irish Embassy in Washington: 'Bejaysus, I wish I didn't have to go back and face what I have to face.'

At least he was spared having to face the Social Democrats. On 15 March, its trio of leaders – Róisín Shortall, Catherine Murphy and Stephen Donnelly – announced that they were ending all dialogue with Fine Gael and Fianna Fáil; they were going into opposition. Reports were widespread that Donnelly was livid, but impotent, in the face of Murphy's and Shortall's insistence that they would not be joining either of the two largest parties in a coalition. They were instinctively opposition TDs. Harry Potter always saw himself as a minister.

After the St Patrick's Day break, negotiations at last began to take a more formal, structured shape. The Rural Alliance made public its intention to discuss serious government formation with Fine Gael. Simon Coveney told me that Fine Gael wanted to launch round table talks with willing groups or parties in a search for common ground. The first meeting was due on 23 March in Government Buildings. Coveney — the most committed of all in the Fine Gael party to the idea of a partnership government with Fianna Fáil support — took the initiative. We were up for it, but before the all-party talks began came the first split.

Coveney told me that Fine Gael wanted to appoint Kieran Mulvey as independent chair of the talks. On the surface, Mulvey seemed a good choice. A heavyweight, he was chief executive of the Workplace Relations Commission, a master mediator and a highly agreeable individual with charm and great industrial relations skills. He was Ireland's leading troubleshooter. A fixer. Who better to bring together such an awkward group of politicians?

I knew Kieran, but only peripherally. He was a neighbour of mine in Enniskerry. We sometimes met early in the morning in the local newsagent, Windsors, exchanging pleasantries before heading on our merry ways. He was able and likeable, but he was far from apolitical. It was widely known that he had given

Enda Kenny's government significant political support in the campaign to abolish the Seanad as recently as 2013. Enda's referendum to kill off the Upper House had been in trouble. A mysterious organisation called One House, fronted up by Kieran Mulvey, had appeared from nowhere loudly supporting the Fine Gael-Labour proposal. Among other leading members of this outfit were former Fine Gael leader Alan Dukes, former Labour minister Liz McManus and Labour Party councillor Richard Humphreys.

Kieran had launched One House. At the launch he described the Seanad as a 'rotten borough'. The nation's mediator had dived deep into political conflict that day when he proclaimed 'what we say is we're a Republic. One house is sufficient.'

Kieran's involvement in a divisive political campaign was a highly unorthodox move for the man who headed up the Workplace Relations Commission. No doubt it did him no harm in the government's eyes. Two years later, in 2015, Kieran was appointed to the chair of Sport Ireland under Fine Gael-Labour. Without question he was a good chair of Sport Ireland, a fine boss of the Workplace Relations Commission, but the impartiality of a former cheerleader for Kenny in a referendum presiding over coalition talks was questionable. He had patently done the state — particularly Fine Gael — some service. I told Simon that I had serious reservations about Kieran's impartiality.

The idea of appointing Kieran Mulvey was swiftly dropped. Instead, Lucy McCaffrey, the chair of Dublin Port, was proposed and agreed. Lucy was less forceful than Kieran would have been, but she did not carry the same baggage.

Lucy McCaffrey was not born to the job of mediating the noisy proceedings of warring politicians. This genteel chairperson of the busiest port in Ireland was a consultant whose big gig involved her in huge decisions that had a major effect on the nation's travel and trade. Throughout the government formation talks she was polite and patient. She listened, impassive but intent, to the meanderings of politicians with little in common, except possibly their zeal to seize the reins of power. Her task was to keep us talking. The show must be kept on the road until a Programme for Government was agreed. None of the participants was a shrinking violet. Lucy sat at the top table alongside the Fine Gael team that fielded Taoiseach Enda Kenny, Frances Fitzgerald, Simon Coveney, Leo Varadkar, Simon Harris, Seán Kyne and Eoghan Murphy. It was held in a large, elegant room in Government Buildings, easily accommodating the various factions gathered to strike a deal, although we were all kept at arm's length. It was a perfect square of classroom tables, with space in the middle of the room to give oxygen to the egos. Directly opposite Enda's team sat the Rural Alliance quintet and the two Green party representatives, Eamon Ryan and Catherine Martin, flanked by various other independents, including Katherine Zappone and, initially, Maureen O'Sullivan. We in the Independent Alliance took our places on the left-hand side of the room. Opposite us the Healy-Rae brothers held court.

Lucy must have been gobsmacked at the sight of the bruised and bandaged Michael Healy-Rae, fresh from his ordeal of being savaged by a cow three days earlier on his Kerry farm. Beside him sat his brother Danny, resembling an Old Testament prophet and sounding like the prophet Isaiah on amphetamines. They were hardly typical of Lucy's more conventional colleagues in the day job down at Dublin Port. Yet Michael was a real powerhouse in the room. Despite his serious injuries, he was able to hold his own on any subject, national or local. It became crystal clear at the Programme for Government sessions that Michael was a man whose portrayal in the media as a purely pork-barrel politician was nonsense. I knew him well because his office had been opposite mine in Agriculture House for the previous five years. He was famous for working late at night and arriving at unsocial hours in the morning. He always puts Kerry first, but he has an impressive national and global knowledge that he often deliberately hides under a Kilgarvan bushel. Behind the scenes, Michael was pitching to be a minister. And he would have been a good one. As a politician, he has been grossly underrated by the Dublin-dominated media.

Michael's big problem is not his own shortcomings. His problem is Danny. He needs his brother to boost the priceless family brand that delivers two seats in Kerry, but Danny's inane interventions on nearly every subject sometimes make Michael look like a clown by association. It was obvious at the talks that Michael was ministerial material, but Danny was a different kettle of fish. Danny remains an embarrassment that Michael will need to overcome if he is ever to achieve the recognition his abilities deserve. It was widely rumoured that Michael had done a deal with Enda Kenny on the fringes of these talks, but Danny had threatened to walk if his brother even dreamed of supping with the Blueshirt devil. The brand would have been sundered. At the end of the day, Michael was in line for a ministry until he couldn't be sure of delivering a second vote. Danny sank his sibling.

Injured or not, Michael sat through the first day's seven-hour marathon, which covered such worthy subjects as Housing, Jobs, Rural Development and Health. God bless his patience, because he, above all, knew that the real action was on the margins of the talks. His interventions brightened up some of the duller sessions. At one point he upbraided Leo Varadkar for failing to pay attention. He accused the Minister for Health of not being fully engaged. Leo retorted that Michael had spent the day taking phone calls. Michael's underlying message was more subtle than mere political tomfoolery: Leo was distancing himself from the talks because he had an interest in them failing. They were his rival Simon Coveney's project. If they failed, both Enda and Simon would take the flak. The Fine Gael leadership race to succeed Enda was already in full swing.

Leo made the point even more clearly in a later session. After Enda had taken off for another meeting, Leo grabbed his 'Taoiseach' nameplate. In front of dozens of watching eyes, instead of putting it down in front of himself, he handed it to his rival, loudly suggesting, 'Here, Simon you're looking for this,' to the amusement of the onlookers. Coveney dropped the nameplate immediately, responding, 'Look how quickly Leo made a grab for it.'

Even on Day One it became obvious that Lucy's plenary talks were part of a necessary softening-up process. Although the palatial surroundings had added a new status and urgency to the talks, Fine Gael had decided to love-bomb the smaller groups in Government Buildings. We were all invited to lunches, sometimes sandwiches, occasionally hot dishes, between sessions. Each group was allocated a room in the ministerial corridor to use as a place to relax and plot. Ministers were available to assist on any topic, however small. And they were unbelievably attentive to our every need. Finian McGrath was overheard saying that he could not even go to the loo without being stalked by a Fine Gael minister. There we were in the heart of government, embedded in ministerial offices, being fed and watered and with access to cabinet ministers. You could get to like it! That was the idea. Furthermore, each group and each individual could bring along advisers. We were made to feel important. Of course, the Healy-Raes brought Healy-Raes, namely their sister Rosemary, a legal tax expert, and Michael's son, Jackie, a Kerry County councillor.

The conference room and the lunches were packed with advisers, thoroughly enjoying sampling the cuisine and comfort of Government Buildings. An attempt was definitely being made to lure the smaller groups into the Fine Gael nest by offering the taste of temptations to come.

I invited along lawyer Tony Williams to assist with the Judicial Appointments Bill, former Appeals Commissioner John O'Callaghan to guide me through the tax maze, and AIB's one-time internal auditor, Eugene McErlean, whose expertise in the banking system was invaluable. Eugene had blown the whistle on AIB in the early noughties, had summarily been cast aside and had later received a full apology from them.

But by far the most permanent and priceless of my advisers was my parliamentary assistant, Aisling Dunne. Aisling had almost single-handedly steered the Independent Alliance into its unique position on that day, poised for government, but capable of imploding without notice. Aisling was a lawyer with wisdom well ahead of her youthful years, much, much cleverer than her immediate boss but blessed with the good sense to disguise it at all costs. She restrained me from most of my worst possible indiscretions, but only if she found out about them in time. Sometimes she didn't, when I managed to escape her surveillance, as happened when I dropped the clanger about the 'political corpse'.

While the talks were going on with worthy policy papers and dull discussion documents being produced at the plenaries, breakout sessions were being held in adjoining rooms. These were the 'smoke-filled rooms' without the smoke, of course. Lucy's job was high level. No substance was agreed there but plenty of horse-trading was advancing on the margins.

Talks between Fianna Fáil and all the participating parties were still being held, albeit in less salubrious surroundings, but a sense that the Fine Gael event was the only game in town was growing. The trappings of power were on display. And they felt better than the makeshift hospitality of Fianna Fáil.

On 30 March, in the second week of talks in Government Buildings, the discussions suffered a setback. The Greens, professional wobblers at their most courageous, pulled out. Eamon Ryan insisted that he wanted to leave Fine Gael and Fianna Fáil to form a stable government. It was becoming apparent to all participants that there was now only one solution. Fine Gael would have to form a government supported by Fianna Fáil and a few Independents. The Dáil arithmetic suggested that Fianna Fáil must commit themselves to keep a Fine Gael-led government in office, in order for it to survive. Otherwise, the talks were going nowhere and there would be a general election.

Micheál Martin realised this. He was now ready for talks with Kenny and was preparing the ground for a noble retreat 'in the national interest'. We were disappointed at his withdrawal. Our dialogue with Fianna Fáil had been much less adversarial than with Fine Gael. The Independent Alliance had met Micheál on several occasions. He had been accommodating in the earlier days, but the more we met him, the more concerned we were that he might merely be going through the motions. The election of Seán Ó Fearghaíl as Ceann Comhairle in mid-March had already aroused our suspicions that Fianna Fáil was not seriously interested in forming a government. Nonetheless, both Finian and I were well disposed to Fianna Fáil. He knew from his earlier pact with Bertie Ahern and Brian Cowen that when they shake hands on a deal, they deliver. Fine Gael are altogether trickier, even when the signatures are on a document. In addition, we obviously preferred to negotiate with two competing partners rather than with one remaining player. If Micheál walked off the pitch, our leverage with Fine Gael was gone.

For my part, Fianna Fáil had readily agreed to implement several of my most urgent projects, namely the need for judicial reform and the reopening of several of the Garda stations closed by former Minister for Justice, Alan Shatter. They admitted that political patronage should no longer decide who became a judge. They had accepted the need for constitutional reforms, including root and branch changes in the Seanad.

After some amateur theatricals by both leaders, a second failure to elect a Taoiseach in the Dáil on 6 April was followed by a statement from the two largest parties that they would 'discuss how a viable minority government might work'. Decoded, Fine Gael was now the only game in town for the independents. Fianna Fáil was accepting defeat and would explore the benefits of a 'confidence and supply' arrangement.

A third inconclusive vote for Taoiseach was held in the Dáil on 15 April. This time was different. After she had tweeted in the morning that she would abstain, Katherine Zappone voted for Kenny. It was a breakthrough for Fine Gael, but the 52-77 defeat meant that Kenny still had a huge mountain to climb. At this point, apart from his fifty Fine Gael deputies, he had bagged only Katherine and his old friend Michael Lowry. The Tipperary deputy had missed the first vote for Taoiseach to attend a funeral back home, but had publicly committed to supporting him in future rounds. At what price, no one could quite decipher.

Suddenly, a new player appeared on the stage. Enter the President. Michael D. himself was getting itchy. On 19 April, disturbed by the endless instability, he issued a stern warning to the party leaders that he was 'very, very well aware' of Article 13 of the Constitution which gives him 'absolute power' to dissolve the Dáil if the Taoiseach tells him that he cannot form a government. In shorthand, the President was losing his patience with the main players. If Enda came back to him with no government for a fourth time, he might insist on a dissolution. The pressure piled on both Fine Gael and also onto us.

On 29 April, after the predictable hiccups and showboating — much of it about water charges — Fianna Fáil and Fine Gael reached an agreement. Fianna Fáil would support a minority government led by Fine Gael. They would abstain on confidence votes, including budgets. The deal was conditional on Fine Gael securing enough independent votes to ensure the government's survival, with Fianna Fáil sitting on their hands in the Dáil chamber. The magic number for Kenny was 58.

We were back in the game. Fine Gael needed the Independent Alliance to form a government. Kenny was sure of the votes of Zappone and Lowry, with Denis Naughten looking likely to crawl on board, taking his tally up to 53, but he was still five short. He could never rely on Mattie McGrath's crew or any of the left-wing parties. He needed our six en bloc.

A fourth vote for Taoiseach was due on 6 May. It was probably the last chance saloon.

While Lucy McCaffrey had delivered partial agreement on some of the big-ticket items — such as housing, agricultural supports and mental health — many of the thorny issues remained unresolved with less than a week to go. John Halligan had still not secured his primary demand of a Cardiac Cath Lab for Waterford Hospital, being strongly resisted by the HSE. Michael Fitzmaurice was fighting the mother of all losing battles on the bogs, Seán Canney was quietly pushing for the whitest of all elephants, the Western Rail Corridor, and Finian was still struggling for a breakthrough on Beaumont Hospital, even though he was widely believed to have quietly secured the Disabilities portfolio and a promise to sign the United Nations Convention on the Rights of Persons with Disabilities. Boxer Moran had skilfully secured commitments for Athlone, including a pledge that a new Midlands tourist brand, later to be known as 'Ireland's Hidden Heartlands', would be launched by the next Minister for Tourism. I still had big problems with fierce

Fine Gael resistance to the terms of the Judicial Appointments Bill and the reopening of Garda stations, including Stepaside. The six of us met and swore that we would all back one another's demands without flinching. As Michael Fitzmaurice said, 'It's all for one and one for all.'

As Michael spoke those words, there was no dissenting voice, but the silence was ominous. I don't believe I was the only one who wondered if he himself was deliberately preparing to ask the impossible, ensuring that he would get the answer 'No'. Simultaneously, he was the only person on our team who I felt was an undiluted, albeit very effective, naysayer. Did he have the temperament for the hard decisions? And, at the end of the day, did he really expect the rest of us to walk the plank for the Roscommon bogs?

On Tuesday, 3 May, talks resumed in Government Buildings. Paschal Donohoe led off for Fine Gael and heaped on the pressure. Another vote was due for Taoiseach on the Friday. Michael D. was rattling his sabre. We were left in no doubt that if Enda Kenny was not elected, a dissolution of the Dáil and a general election would follow. All outstanding matters should be resolved within forty-eight hours. It was an ultimatum.

Most of us were relieved that the entire process was coming to a head. Meetings were arranged with relevant ministers to resolve the remaining thorny issues. The emergence of Michael Noonan as chief negotiator on the Fine Gael side signalled that this time they were serious. Noonan could make decisions without reference to anyone. Kenny had given him full authority.

The hardest topics still to be resolved included Michael Fitzmaurice's and my own pet subjects. Fitzmaurice had been batting for rural Ireland throughout the nine weeks of talks. Thanks to Boxer Moran, Seán Canney and to him, rural Ireland had won serious concessions, including increased funding for the Sheep Scheme and revisions to the LEADER programme

(EU funding for community-led local development), along with firm commitments on the rural broadband scheme. But Fitzmaurice was different. It seemed he would live by the bog and die by the bog. He was a hard man to negotiate with because his idea of punctuality did not coincide with the readings of any clock on God's earth. Nevertheless, in those last two days Michael Noonan and the relevant minister, Heather Humphreys, broke their backs to accommodate him. For two days, Fitzmaurice wrestled with them both over whether his demands were in breach of an EU directive. One participant in the talks told me that he was constantly looking over his shoulder, back towards Roscommon. At one point he shook hands on a deal with Heather Humphreys, only to return the next day with further demands. The message from his home base was to stay out of government. Right up to the last hour before the vote, Fitzmaurice was holding out for more.

Another source close to the talks with Fitzmaurice insists that they had sorted out all his points of difference, but he was still refusing to accept that the agreement would work. They were convinced by the end of the process that Fitzmaurice had never had any intention of going into government. He had been flattered by Fine Gael's hints to the media that he might be Minister for Agriculture, but his real problem was his constituency rival, Denis Naughten. There was no room for two cabinet ministers from the Roscommon–Galway constituency. Naughten had already done his deal with Kenny and was destined for cabinet. Fitzmaurice, outmanoeuvred by Naughten, was being forced to resume his role as the voice of the militant turf-cutters.

Alongside Fitzmaurice's travails, I was engaged in a pitched battle over the appointment of judges. Both Michael Noonan and the Minister for Justice, Frances Fitzgerald, fought the corner of their lordships from the Four Courts. It is hard to exaggerate how deeply committed Fine Gael is to the esoteric ways of the Law Library. The Blueshirt tradition of 'law and order' has always been accompanied by an almost visceral attachment to the Four Courts. Political protection of the Law Library is a Fine Gael core value. The O'Higginses, the Costellos and the Finlays are all famous Fine Gael families, with strong legal and political connections. In the eyes of many Fine Gael lawyers, a challenge to the ways of the judiciary is akin to treason.

For two days we were deadlocked. Frances Fitzgerald fought a rearguard action, pleading that Fine Gael would *never* allow political bias to affect such a precious democratic pillar of the state as the selection of the judiciary. Perish the thought! She genuinely found the suggestion that Fine Gael would do political favours for friends of the party deeply offensive. In defence of the Fine Gael opposition to reform, she frequently quoted a woman called Jennifer Carroll MacNeill as an authority on the subject. I had never heard of Jennifer, but in June 2016 she published a book called *The Politics of Judicial Selection in Ireland*. I later discovered that Jennifer had been special adviser to both Frances and her predecessor in Justice, Alan Shatter. After popping up as a Fine Gael councillor in 2019, in the 2020 general election Jennifer replaced Mary Mitchell O'Connor as the Fine Gael TD for Dún Laoghaire-Rathdown.

The clock was ticking. Frances was constantly sighing, patently frustrated by my insistence that it needed a full-blooded bill to change radically the way judges were selected. She offered minor adjustments to how the Judicial Appointments Advisory Board operated. Eventually, as precious hours passed, she and Michael Noonan realised that I was deadly serious about a bill setting up a Commission for selecting judges which had a majority of independent lay (non-legal) people and a lay chair.

I warmed to Michael Noonan. He was wise, wily, but, above all, witty. He regularly defused tense situations with humour. He could be hilarious, even at the most stressful of times.

More importantly, he was decisive and navigated us through this dangerous territory. He obviously calculated that judicial reform was a red line for me, as it was. He and Frances conceded the principle that the bill should include the lay chair and lay majority. After advice from the Attorney General, Máire Whelan, I in turn withdrew my demand for the government to have no discretion at all in the selection. Instead, the cabinet would be allowed to select from a list of three suitable candidates for each position.

On 5 May, we were ready to go with the Programme for Government and a vote for Kenny, provided Michael Fitzmaurice settled any outstanding difficulties. And one other minor item was still outstanding: the division of ministries.

The allocation of ministers' jobs was the unspoken unknown. In seventy days, the issue on everybody's minds had never been mentioned. We knew that Katherine Zappone, as the first mover into Kenny's camp, had hit the jackpot. She would be a senior minister. Denis Naughten too was judged a certainty on the understanding that he would keep the Rural Alliance sweet. We were pretty sure that Finian had been promised a post as a 'super junior', with access to the cabinet table. Otherwise, we were full of high expectations. The Taoiseach sent a message that he wanted to see me at around 10.30 p.m. My colleagues and I assembled with Aisling and other advisers during the evening to discuss what we would seek. The consensus was unequivocal: we were in a powerful position. Fine Gael needed us. My riding instructions were clear: without apology, to demand two cabinet seats, two super junior posts and two juniors for the full term of the government. And for good measure, make sure that Enda gave us three Seanad seats. No problem. I was happy.

After the Taoiseach summoned me, I trotted up to his office with a spring in my step. He was alone, but grim-faced. The atmosphere was woeful. No camaraderie or sense of joint achievement surfaced. He soon put a stop to my eager anticipation. He offered the Independent Alliance one cabinet post, one super junior and one junior. Full stop. He dismissed the idea of Seanad seats. They were all gone, presumably in a secret agreement, an unwritten part of the 'confidence and supply' deal with Fianna Fáil.

Was he serious, I wondered? Was this his final revenge for the 'political corpse' wound? Or was it just an opening gambit? I protested that the Independent Alliance would never accept anything approaching this. I waited for him to start compromising. He was not for turning. He reluctantly agreed to meet us all together the next morning, but insisted that the meeting was pointless. He would not be changing his mind.

My colleagues were waiting in another office in Government Buildings. I returned with the bad news. They were stunned. We agreed that we could not accept the offer. All our minds instantly worked out that only three posts meant that three of us would emerge empty-handed. We agreed to meet the Taoiseach the next morning, but the current offer was off the table. It was all over, we felt.

After a short discussion with Aisling, I headed home. Despondent. My wife, Ruth, was still awake. I told her that there would be no government elected the next day or on any other day. Enda was prepared to give us only three ministries, to be divided between six of us. And there were no Seanad seats on offer.

I told Ruth the offer was derisory. There would be another general election. The Independent Alliance would have to vote against Enda. I waited for the sort of comforting sympathy that only spouses can offer after a personal setback.

Ruth Buchanan may be married to a politician but she emphatically, as she often insists, is 'not a politician's wife'. She rarely approves, or disapproves, of what she regards as my political escapades. For some reason, which I cannot fathom, she does not have a starry-eyed view of politicians, Fianna Fáil, Fine Gael, Greens or even independents. An animal lover, if she had the choice of being marooned on a desert island with a dog or a politician, she would undoubtedly opt for the dog.

She is, however, a clergyman's daughter. Her late father, Alfred Buchanan, was the Church of Ireland Dean of Kildare. With such a rarefied pedigree comes an inbuilt refinement and a sense of right and wrong which she has carried with her through thick and thin. She had a protected childhood and never heard the 'F' word until she was an undergraduate. On 5 May 2016, she revealed that she had been a fast learner. She dug deep. Ruth let out an avalanche of expletives that would have made Michael Fitzmaurice, or even Paul Gogarty, blush. Until that night, I never knew the depth of her vocabulary.

The broadside I received after telling her that our ambitions were doomed landed on target. Stunned, I tried to explain it. I pleaded that we were not being offered our rightful quota of ministries; Enda was a vengeful Blueshirt, refusing to share the jobs fairly. Not even one Seanad seat out of the eleven that were in his gift.

I was sinking further and further into the marital mire, hanging myself with every sentence.

'Did you not get your policies put into the Programme for Government?' she asked. 'Have they not agreed to end the political appointment of judges? And even to open your bloody Stepaside Garda Station? All your Independent Alliance colleagues have achieved important policy concessions. What is wrong with you? You have pocketed all those great gains, but when it comes to the jobs, that is your red line. You would ditch your policy gains because you are not all getting plum jobs!' And then the killer. 'I thought you guys stood for an end to cronyism. Now you are putting jobs for the boys before reforms. Tell that to your constituents. Go back in there tomorrow and tell Enda you're on board.' And that is a highly edited version of the outburst.

She was right. I had a sleepless night. Enda may have screwed us on the spoils but we had bagged some significant policy gains. Before the cock crowed at dawn, I had done a complete U-turn.

On the Friday morning I rang Finian and John. I have to admit, I did not tell them the reason for my change of position, but happily we agreed that we should, after all, go into the final meeting with Enda with open minds. Later that morning Boxer and Seán decided that government, even without enough ministries, was better than opposition, the wilderness or another election. Fitzmaurice alone became an outlier.

We were all due to meet in the Taoiseach's dining room early, before we trotted over to have a final, probably fruitless showdown with the Taoiseach.

We gathered in a gloomy mood. Yet even in those final hours before the 'do or die' vote, we enjoyed lighter moments. None was more amusing than fifteen minutes on that last morning when nerves were fraught.

It was 10 a.m. The debate on the vote for Taoiseach was at noon. The Independent Alliance was holed up in the Taoiseach's private dining room, preparing for our last-minute head to head with Enda. Boxer Moran, Aisling and I were there with some of our other advisers. Boxer spotted a bottle of Dubonnet on the sideboard. His eyes twinkled. 'OK, everybody,' he suggested, 'let's have a drink.' The rest of us blinked. He promptly decorated the large table with wine glasses, including at places to be occupied shortly by latecomers. He filled all our glasses with tea and proposed that we tell anyone else joining us that we were having a bit of a party before the vote.

Finian McGrath entered the room, looked around and responded to the untimely celebration with horror in his eyes.

Boxer asked him would he like a drink. He was stunned, declaring that we had all gone insane, reminding us that there was still serious business to do before the vote. He turned to me, aghast, as I swigged back the tea out of a wine glass. Finian was aware that I was, with good reason, thirty years off the gargle. I could see his mind boggling. He could see a portfolio for Disability Issues sinking in an alcoholic aberration before his very eyes. Were months of government negotiations about to be destroyed by a bottle of Dubonnet?

Next, an adviser to one of my colleagues arrived. He saw the rest of us downing the syrupy mixture. His reaction was different to Finian's. His eyes lit up. He grabbed the bottle of Dubonnet, filled his glass, downed it in one gulp and refilled it. Before he could take another drop, we had to confess that we were drinking cold tea. He made me promise him that I would never tell his wife or leak his moment of weakness to the media.

After that light interlude we met the Taoiseach. As we feared, he was not for turning. He was on his way into the Dáil. We could take it or leave it.

We didn't tell Fine Gael at that stage that five of us were inclined to be on board. Fitzmaurice was still deeply opposed and went into a huddle alone with Michael Noonan. In theory, it was all of us or none of us, but that could never hold for a purely local issue. The rest of us gathered with Simon Coveney in the Sycamore Room (so named for the large bleached sycamore table at its centre). We were still in search of another junior ministry. There was less than an hour to go until the noon debate on the nomination of Taoiseach was due to begin. Minutes before midday, Enda paraded down the long corridor leading to the Dáil chamber, his wife and family in tow. The cameras were clicking. That showed confidence. They were there to cheer him to victory.

As Enda headed for the chamber, Michael Noonan told him that Fitzmaurice was likely to jump overboard and that we were looking for another junior ministry. The Taoiseach gave Noonan the go-ahead to throw another job in our direction, if he really had to.

As the Dáil debate gathered pace, we were still horse-trading in the Sycamore Room, although in our hearts we knew the deal was sealed. Noonan was talking to Fitzmaurice but it was obvious he would not agree to Fitzmaurice's demands on the bogs. He had legal advice that the action Fitzmaurice was demanding (the designation of alternative locations for turf-cutting) would constitute a breach of domestic law and the European Habitats Directive. Alternatively, Fitzmaurice sought a direction to be given to the Gardaí not to enforce the legislation against the turf-cutters. Naturally, that too was rejected. Fitzmaurice packed his papers and left the table. He cut a lonely figure.

By this time there was high drama in the chamber. As Fine Gael realised that the independent cavalry had yet to arrive, they began to play for time. They were being forced to filibuster the vote to elect their own Taoiseach! Notes were being brought into the chamber for Enda updating him on the state of play of the talks offstage. I was receiving frantic texts from journalists, asking if the six of us were going to vote for Kenny. Where were we and what was the sticking point? Noonan joined us in the Sycamore Room. At that moment Coveney, the architect of the entire partnership government, offered us a final junior ministry, to revert back to a Fine Gael deputy halfway through the cycle of the government. Crucially, 'halfway' was a point in time which was never defined. We shook hands and headed for the chamber.

The vote was taken shortly after that. Kenny won by 59 votes to 49. Added to his full complement of fifty Fine Gael deputies, he had secured Katherine Zappone, Denis Naughten, Michael Harty, Michael Lowry and five of us in the Independent Alliance.

Four independent TDs abstained. Michael Fitzmaurice was joined by Maureen O'Sullivan and two surprises, Michael Healy-Rae and Noel Grealish. Both Noel and Michael had nurtured expectations of offers of ministries until the eleventh hour.

Noel Grealish had been told to stay by the phone that Friday morning. In his own talks with Kenny, he had asked to be made Minister for Sport. Kenny had declined the request but offered him a junior ministry for Water. Grealish turned down the offer, on the basis that it was a political graveyard. Nevertheless, he was told to wait beside the phone, but it never rang. Grealish abstained. Fine Gael thought they had him in the bag. After the vote, Simon Coveney and Leo Varadkar approached him in the chamber to ask why he had abstained. Surely they had a deal? Still, there was another opportunity. If Grealish voted for the government in the vote on the cabinet later that evening, they would consider scoping out a junior ministry for him. Grealish was in no mood for mockery: 'Do you know the story of the Christmas tree?' he asked. 'There is a lovely box at the bottom of the tree on Christmas Day, and when you unwrap it, there's nothing in it. Don't be making a fool out of me.'

The Dáil adjourned for three hours for Kenny to go to the Park, return to Leinster House and name his cabinet.

In the meantime, a message was sent to us. The Taoiseach wanted to know who was taking the cabinet post, the super junior ministry for Disability Issues and the other two junior positions. The five of us convened hastily.

I had presumed this was a no-brainer. The super junior gig for Disabilities was tailor-made for Finian, the ordinary junior position was for John Halligan and the extra junior could be shared between newcomers Seán Canney and Boxer Moran. As the longest serving member of the Oireachtas in the group, I had, with usual modesty, assumed that the cabinet post would be mine.

Finian had scooped up the super junior job in seconds, with no opposition. John unopposed took the junior post, which was due to revert back to Fine Gael later, but never did. When it came to the cabinet post, I put up my hand. Suddenly, on my right, a second hand rose. Seán Canney held his arm erect for at least ten seconds. The councillor from Tuam wanted to jump straight into the cabinet room! I knew then that I would need to watch my back. There was a quiet hush. Happily, the matter was resolved in my favour, with Halligan immediately stating that the posts should be determined by seniority, thus ensuring that the neophyte Canney was out of the running. It was rapidly agreed that Boxer and Seán would share the final junior's job. They tossed for the first year, a decision that was to cause blood on the floor two years later. Canney won the toss and took the first year.

A message was sent to Enda's office. Within an hour, I was told the Taoiseach wanted to see me. I spent the hour with Aisling wondering what cabinet post he would offer. We had not demanded any particular portfolios because we never knew until the last minute who would be on our team. If Michael Fitzmaurice had been togging out for us, it might have presented problems. He had been eyeing Agriculture or Rural Affairs.

For the second time in twenty-four hours I headed for the Taoiseach's office. This time the atmosphere was certain to be better, but Enda was matter-of-fact, glacial. There was no warmth, none of that 'great to be on the same team' bonhomie you might expect once the arguing was over. He was giving me Transport, Tourism and Sport. I thanked him politely and wondered to myself how on earth he had chosen me as having the necessary skills for that portfolio. Nobody had as much as asked when I had last travelled on a bus or on the Luas. While

I had railed against excesses within the CIE family and fought a crusade to overhaul the M50 toll system, I was still surprised at his choice. Tourism and Sport sounded good, though.

I left Kenny's office, pleased but puzzled. Then the penny dropped. Public transport was on the point of industrial relations mayhem. There would be strikes by the bucketful in the coming months. The minister would be in the line of fire. What a bed of nails, probably a political graveyard.

But there was always the lighter relief, the delights of Tourism and Sport. A second penny dropped. Kenny would appoint a junior minister, a Fine Gael bruiser, to grab all the good news that usually comes from those two sectors. Probably the ebullient Michael Ring, who is an acquired taste, even for the most patient of his colleagues.

Elated nonetheless, I left the Taoiseach's office and immediately bumped into RTÉ's political correspondent, Martina Fitzgerald. She coolly asked me what job I had been given. 'Transport,' I volunteered without hesitation. Within seconds she had put it out on the airwaves.

Half an hour later, I received a stern message from the Taoiseach's office. I had broken protocol. It was the Taoiseach's prerogative to announce in the Dáil the names of his ministers and their portfolios. Until then, new cabinet members should not reveal their appointments to anyone. An apology to the Taoiseach was warranted, but not forthcoming.

There was no healing process on a day when bygones should have been buried. In the Dáil debate that followed the appointments, most of the goodwill for the new government came from the humorous contributions of Micheál Martin and Mary Lou McDonald. After a long session, we were all bussed up to the Aras to receive our seals of office from Michael D. On the bus, I wondered how long this government could possibly last. We may have signed a deal, but there was no love lost between five of the Independent Alliance members and Fine Gael. My own relationship with the Taoiseach was toxic. We had embarked on a joint venture as enemies, not friends. Like many observers, I did not expect the 'partnership' government to last for even six months.

3

A Cabinet at War

'DO YOU REALISE,' I asked Finian McGrath, as we went into our first cabinet meeting, 'that you and I are probably propping up the most conservative government in the history of the state?'

Finian winced. It had undoubtedly flashed through his mind that he was waving goodbye to old comrades, such as another of Tony Gregory's supporters, Deputy Maureen O'Sullivan. I knew it would be strange sitting on the opposite side of the Dáil chamber from Mattie McGrath, Catherine Murphy, Stephen Donnelly and Michael Healy-Rae. Would Mick Wallace and Clare Daly be tearing us to bits from the opposition benches? We needed to make up our minds quickly whether we would be Trojan horses in this political coalition or converts to conservatism. It was not a dilemma we ever really sorted out.

Looking around the table on the first day in cabinet was a sobering experience. Five years of political opposition to Fine Gael might be difficult to transform into instant harmony, but that was not the real problem. The gang in the room contained not a single radical voice. It was a mixture of dyed-in-the-wool Fine Gael families, teachers, privately educated prima donnas and the odd farmer. There was also a sniff of condescension, Fine Gael feeling that they were the natural party of power. They had lost the election but, somehow, were back in office, almost by right. They would tolerate us but would have to hold their noses.

Enda Kenny was originally a national school teacher, but only for a very short time, before he reached the Dáil. His father, then Deputy Henry Kenny, died in 1975. Enda took his seat in the subsequent by-election at the age of only twenty-four. Over his forty years in the Dáil, Enda had never rocked a single boat. He was instinctively on the conservative wing of the party. His father had been a close friend and political ally of Taoiseach Liam Cosgrave, a man whose views were always on the right of the political spectrum.

Enda was comfortable with most of his chosen cabinet, although he had to juggle geographical demands, gender balance, conservatives and liberals in order to reflect fast-moving public opinion. Many of those he chose for cabinet seats were as instinctively averse to radical change as he was. Yet politicians in the 2016–20 government rapidly played catch-up on the social issues of the day. They were often led by opinion polls on uncomfortable topics, dragged unwillingly into referendum campaigns or the Dáil lobbies to approve of progressive legislation.

Part of this conservative mindset was due to history. Apart from Kenny, several others of the 2016 cabinet had fathers who had been Fine Gael deputies. Charlie Flanagan's father, Oliver J. Flanagan, was legendary for his resistance to change of all sorts back in Liam Cosgrave's day. Charlie, Minister for Foreign Affairs in the new government, while showing few signs of inheriting his father's more extreme views against contra-ception, divorce and the entire liberal agenda, had certainly inherited Oliver J.'s rock-solid Fine Gael Laois-Offaly seat as far back as 1987.

Michael Creed, Minister for Agriculture under Kenny and later Varadkar, had also been elected following the death of his father, Donal Creed, whose Cork North-West seat he retained in the family in 1989. Creed was brought up on the family farm in Macroom and appears to have inherited traditional farming values.

The new Minister for Communications, Climate Action and the Environment, independent Denis Naughten also had a pure Fine Gael lineage. His father, Liam, was a Fine Gael TD and senator in the eighties and nineties. After Liam died in a tragic car accident, Denis took his place in the Seanad and a few months later landed in the Longford-Roscommon Dáil seat formerly held by his father. Denis left Fine Gael after a spat with Kenny over Roscommon Hospital, but his conservative Fine Gael pedigree was an impeccable qualification for this cabinet.

Even Simon Coveney, whom Kenny appointed Minister for Housing, had entered politics after the death of his father, Hugh Coveney TD, in 1998, by winning the vacant Cork South-Central seat. The Coveneys are a Cork 'Merchant Prince's' family — an 'old money clan', who are rich as Croesus. Coveney's patrician manner probably owes just as much to his education at Clongowes Wood, a Jesuit secondary school for the sons of the seriously well-off. Simon is a Fine Gael thoroughbred. At cabinet he was solemn, but thoughtful. His privileged background made it extremely unlikely that he would be prepared to challenge the status quo. He never did; he was part of it. He was loyal to both Taoisigh, Kenny and Varadkar. But despite his Fine Gael conservatism, once upon a time he had shown healthy, but sporadic, signs of normality, even flashes of rebellion. In his youth he was expelled from his fiercely expensive (€20,000 annual fees today) school after a spell of drinking and partying in his transition year. Sadly, he did not display a hint of any such unorthodox tendencies in cabinet where he was the most diligent and competent of members.

Five out of fifteen members of the cabinet were sons of former Fine Gael deputies.

Minister for Education Richard Bruton was another Fine Gael toff who had been to school at Clongowes. His father had not been a deputy, but his brother, John, had been no less than Taoiseach. A Fine Gael TD from well-off farming stock, Bruton went to UCD and Nuffield College, Oxford after his time in Clongowes.

Most of the other Fine Gael ministers were privately educated. Leo Varadkar, Minister for Social Protection, was at the King's Hospital School in Dublin and Trinity College Dublin before becoming a doctor, Paschal Donohoe was at TCD before working for the multinational Procter & Gamble, and Tánaiste Frances Fitzgerald went to Sion Hill Convent, Blackrock, albeit a public school, but she continued on to third level at UCD and then the London School of Economics.

Mary Mitchell O'Connor, a school principal, was a runner-in to Fine Gael. She came from an even more conservative background, the Progressive Democrats, a party that finally dissolved in 2009.

Good and able people all of them but, after a single glance at the table, I realised that Finian and I would have an uphill task fomenting revolution in this company. They were to the manor born. Not only were they uncommonly affluent, well-educated and middle class, there was a distinctly tribal feeling in the cabinet room that first day. I surveyed my new colleagues and wondered whether I — a free-marketeer, an ex-stockbroker and an English public-school boy to boot — was going to be the most radical voice in the room.

This was the tribe who had just lost the election on the fatal 'Keep the Recovery Going' slogan. It was difficult to imagine how any of the 2016 cabinet (including Finian, Katherine Zappone and me) had suffered significantly enough in the downturn to know much about the so-called 'recovery'. Worse still, most of the cabinet had been elected by voters who were among the better off. Where was the voice of the unemployed, the working classes, the marginalised, even of the struggling classes who had seen no recovery in their personal fortunes? No attempt had been made to include them at the table. Apart from Finian, was there a member of the cabinet who had ever allowed a trade union official over the threshold of their home into their drawing room?

It was not as if Fine Gael had no voices for the disadvantaged within its ranks. For five years, I was puzzled that they had not promoted a community stalwart, Catherine Byrne, to the cabinet.

Catherine was the Fine Gael deputy for Dublin South-Central. She has a cv which reads like none of the other Fine Gael members of the 2016–20 cabinet. She lives in Dublin's less privileged area of Inchicore. Her primary education was at Our Lady of the Wayside National School in Bluebell. After that, she attended the Holy Faith School in The Coombe, her local area. At third level, she took a City and Guilds Diploma in Catering from Cathal Brugha Catering College and completed a Lay Ministry course at All Hallows, the north Dublin college that has educated generations of priests. She played ladies' soccer at the highest level and previously managed schoolboy soccer teams in her community. Catherine is a rare creature — a community activist who joined Fine Gael. Her father was a Labour supporter, while her brother favoured Fianna Fáil. She was persuaded to join the party by the late Jim Mitchell, one of a dying breed, a Fine Gael TD and an authentic 'Dub'. Her friends were astonished at her choice of party, but she knew Jim from the local youth club where she was a volunteer. He persuaded her to run for the Dublin City Council and she topped the poll in 2004.

After a spectacular result in her Dublin South-West inner city ward, she became Lord Mayor of Dublin in 2005/06. Catherine would be a Fine Gael spin doctor's nightmare because she is a gentle, understated soul who works her heart out in the community and shuns the media. She has been consistently overlooked in the competition for cabinet positions. The Dáil and the cabinet are woefully below acceptable gender quota thresholds. Yet Frances Fitzgerald, Regina Doherty, Mary Mitchell O'Connor, Josepha Madigan and Heather Humphreys have all been given preferment ahead of Catherine in recent years. Apart from Frances Fitzgerald, the other four were elected to the Dáil as recently as 2011 or 2016, long after Catherine in 2007, yet they all leapfrogged her.

In 2016, Enda gave Catherine a junior job as Minister of State for Communities and the National Drugs Strategy. She appeared at the cabinet table on one occasion to give a presentation on drugs policy. Her contribution showed a knowledge of her brief that left junior ministers from other departments who made similar presentations in the shade. Catherine plays soccer, not golf. She lives in Dublin 8, not Dublin 4. She believes in God, not Mammon. She never went to a private school. She is proudly working class, not bourgeois. The cabinet was crying out for her and others like her. Inexplicably, it had none. Fine Gael doesn't really do working-class cabinet ministers.

Even when Leo arrived as Taoiseach, he continued in this vein. He brought Eoghan Murphy and Josepha Madigan to the top table. Eoghan was a pupil at St. Michael's, Ballsbridge, and Josepha, a well-heeled solicitor, went to Mount Anville in south Dublin. Both schools charge around €6,000 a year for day pupils. Two more toffs for the top table.

The cabinet has fifteen members. The chief whip, Regina Doherty, and two 'super juniors', Finian McGrath and Wexford TD Paul Kehoe, also attended. Seated on the Taoiseach's left were the secretary to the government, Martin Fraser, and beside him the Attorney General Máire Whelan, both there in an official, not a political, capacity. Regina sat on the Taoiseach's right. The rest of us were spread around a large oval table. We all had permanent seats. The room is decorated with pictures of Irish republican heroes, including Patrick Pearse (the revisionists have not yet managed to remove him) and Constance Markievicz. Elsewhere, Wolfe Tone, Robert Emmet, even Charles Stewart Parnell looked down on the proceedings. Portraits of all past Taoisigh hang in the corridor outside. The atmosphere in the room itself is a little intimidating, not because of the intellect of the occupants, but because of the formality of the furniture. A small adjoining room offers coffee, tea and fruit to ministers. The dignity of the surroundings was sometimes a little undermined by one of Simon Harris's inelegant discarded banana skins or Josepha Madigan's emptied yogurt tubs lying on the table.

Cabinet meetings rarely lived up to their media billings. Reports of big splits, rows, divisions in the cabinet are often hyped in the press. Not because there are no divisions. On the contrary, they are multiple, but because so much of the business is resolved behind closed doors long before it reaches the cabinet room. The procedures are so complicated and tedious that they must have been designed to ensure that no minister brings items to the cabinet table unless he or she is certain that they will be passed without much friction. The big rows tend to be spontaneous, about politics, not about legislation.

How is this artificial harmony on law-making achieved? Cabinet memoranda, new legislation, matters for decision or notification are all despatched to departments for 'obs' (observations) long before they reach the fifteen ministers. If there are matters of dispute, they are raised at that point. Civil servants then try to sort out any comments or criticisms, in consultation with their ministers. Negotiations are held between departments and, if necessary, are agreed by ministers in dispute at one-to-one meetings. Finally, the finished product is delivered to the minister, who presents it for approval at the cabinet table. I can remember only one occasion when a minister brought a proposal to government and was told to revise it and report back in a week. In my four turbulent years, there was never a vote at cabinet. Delicate matters were usually fixed in advance.

It is during this proofing procedure that the much-maligned special advisers are invaluable. They flag political dangers to the other ministers' advisers. Civil servants and the Attorney General's office can spot the legal and technical pitfalls in the memos, but they rarely see the political perils buried deep in a dense piece of legislation. Aisling Dunne, luckily a lawyer in an earlier life, read all the relevant memos pre-cabinet and rescued me from many minefields.

Consequently, potential disputes on decisions at cabinet were often defused. Government legislation, already micro-managed elsewhere, rarely provoked rows. Big decisions were taken beforehand or on the margins. That was the theory, anyway.

Legislation was one thing. Delicate matters with political sensitivities were dealt with in a completely different, less professional, manner. Political fixers took over. The Programme for Government was based on an understanding that there would be 'no surprises', a euphemism for 'no ambushes'. In the early days there was a surprise almost every week, which often spilled over into a row between the cabinet partners.

Unfortunately, Fine Gael had a funny way of conducting cabinet meetings. They were held at 10 a.m. on Tuesday mornings. At the beginning of our term, all the non-Fine Gael members — Finian, Katherine Zappone, Denis Naughten, Attorney General Máire Whelan, government secretary Martin

Fraser and I arrived on time. We learned the hard way. Fine Gael ministers always held a pre-cabinet powwow, beginning at around 9 a.m. They would invariably troop into the cabinet coffee room at least 45 minutes late, keeping us waiting without any apology or explanation. Sometimes the delay lasted for well over an hour. They treated the rest of us with contempt. Their disdain fuelled the atmosphere of distrust, even hostility, that already existed between the Independent Alliance and Fine Gael.

There were other reasons for this mutual distrust. At an early point in the life of the government, leaks of cabinet meetings were appearing in the media. Enda tried to limit them by insisting that we leave our mobile phones in the ante-room lockers. No one could text, and therefore leak, during cabinet meetings. They made up for it afterwards.

And sometimes, beforehand. An acceptance — even a custom — had developed that cabinet ministers could let the Tuesday morning newspapers and early morning radio know in advance about departmental memos or even legislation they were bringing to cabinet. So RTÉ's *Morning Ireland* would lead with this item and the leaking minister could gain good coverage in advance of the meeting. But, all too frequently, far more explosive material appeared, apparently from a source outside the relevant department. Often it was leaked by one minister to embarrass a colleague in cabinet.

The remedy to leaks was comical. 'Enquiries' were regularly held after individual cabinet ministers blew fuses about their memos, or their contributions, being leaked by colleagues, frequently with a negative spin. Martin Fraser, secretary to the government, would be delegated to find the source of the leak. All departments were asked to investigate. Both Aisling and I often received brief calls from our Secretary General, Graham Doyle, asking if we had leaked the cabinet paper? Not surprisingly, no minister, nor anyone else with access to cabinet papers in any department, was ever believed to have replied 'Yes' to this question during the entire term of the government. No 'Enquiry' ever made any known progress.

The leaks spread beyond the detail of exchanges at the cabinet table. Both Fine Gael and independents in government were believed to have leaked and briefed far more widely against each other in the early days of the partnership government.

From the outset, the temperature was running high between Fine Gael and ourselves, but it took less than a fortnight for it to reach boiling point.

A cabinet meeting was called, unusually and suddenly, for the afternoon of Thursday, 19 May at 4.30 p.m. to formally appoint fifteen ministers of state, including the Independent Alliance members John Halligan and Seán Canney.

It was an odd time to arrange a cabinet meeting. On Thursday afternoons, Leinster House is empty, or emptying, as ministers and TDs head for their constituencies. The agenda had only two items: the appointment of ministers of state and senior Garda appointments (this matter was ultimately postponed). There was nothing on the 'Supplementary Agenda' which usually shows items pending, but which are still awaiting approval to join the full agenda. I was in a bit of a bind because I had a long-standing date as a guest speaker at a dinner in London. I decided to go ahead with the dinner and felt it only right to inform the Taoiseach that I would be absent from cabinet. He did not seem distressed.

Late in the day, I changed my mind and opted to stay for the cabinet meeting. It was a bit early in my life as a minister to be ducking the cabinet for dinners overseas and, more importantly, I owed it to John and Seán to be there on their big day. I told the Taoiseach that I could, after all, attend.

On the day of the meeting, the Taoiseach told me that the

government intended to nominate, without a process, on that same day at the cabinet, someone as a vice president of the European Investment Bank. He did not tell me who he intended for this €270,000 a year job, probably the biggest plum position in the government's gift. I told him that I was unhappy with this arrangement and would have to consult with my Independent Alliance colleagues about how we should respond. He asked me to talk to Michael Noonan because it came under the Department of Finance's umbrella. He knew I liked Michael.

The issue was not raised at that cabinet meeting. I met Michael Noonan afterwards but, unfortunately, he repeated Enda's line that they had a name in mind but refused to tell me who it was. My unexpected presence at that cabinet meeting seems to have delayed their plans.

I smelled one of the most gigantic rats imaginable lurking in the woodwork. I assumed the lucky nominee must be John Bruton or Alan Dukes or some other Fine Gael grandee. Fine Gael were unlikely to allow a salary like that to fall into alien hands.

After I met Noonan, a few weeks of wrangling about the process followed. On 23 May, I wrote as follows to Enda Kenny:

Dear Taoiseach,

Thank you for alerting me to your wish to appoint a specific (unnamed) person directly to the position of Vice President of the European Investment Bank.

I spoke to the Minister for Finance about this proposal after last Thursday's Cabinet meeting.

As I told you, I was uncomfortable with the suggestion and would revert after speaking to my Independent Alliance colleagues. After consultation with them, we are of the unanimous view that this position should only be filled after a transparent, open independent process. It should include advertising the post, followed by interviews to ensure that the successful candidate is properly qualified for this €270,000 a year job.

I trust that you will understand our position. It is one of the fundamental principles of our group that all state appointments should be subject to rigorous, non-political processes.

Best wishes

Shane Ross

He replied the same day:

Dear Shane,

Thank you for your response to a query raised with me. The query related to a nomination by Ireland to enter a process for consideration for possible appointment to EIB as a Vice President and not for direct appointment.

In the context of selecting Ireland's nominee I note and understand your views and am happy to discuss further with you.

Best wishes

Enda Kenny TD

Taoiseach

After much toing and froing between Aisling and one of Michael Noonan's top officials, Ann Nolan, we eventually agreed that there would be a four-member selection panel of the Secretary General of the Department of the Taoiseach, Martin Fraser; the Secretary General of the Department of Finance, Derek Moran; the chairperson of the Policing Authority, Josephine Feehily; and the chairman of the Low Pay Commission, Donal de Buitléir, all establishment figures, but people with good reputations.

The job not only carried a salary of €270,000 but included an 'installation allowance' of €46,000 and a 'resettlement allowance' of €23,000. The cost of travel to Luxembourg and moving expenses were also to be covered. And, just for good measure, the European Investment Bank agreed to pay the favoured appointee's monthly living expenses and another monthly allowance of €911. This was the ultimate gravy train.

The quartet addressed the task in hand. The position was publicly advertised — ten applications were received and five people were interviewed. A shortlist of three of the five was given to Michael Noonan. He chose a man called Andrew McDowell.

Andrew McDowell was not a household name, like John Bruton or Alan Dukes would have been, although there is no evidence that either of these two men were being considered for the job. There would have been uproar if it had been a party grandee, plucked out of the ranks of the Fine Gael hall of fame.

So, who was he? Andrew McDowell was definitely not a Fine Gael grandee, or a celebrity in need of a big job. He was a Fine Gael superguru. An unsung superguru, at that. The public would not know his name. The insiders would know him intimately. He was one of them. Perhaps he should tell us who he is, himself. Speaking to the UCD business alumni magazine in January 2017, six months after he had landed the European job, he explained his great success:

Around 2005 I met Enda Kenny at the airport in Paris on the way back from the OECD. We ended up talking while queuing up at the check-in desk — I expressed some concerns about the direction of the economy. Coming into the 2007 election, when he was looking for an economic adviser, I got a call asking if I would be interested in interviewing for the job. I had never been very active politically, but I saw this as a wonderful opportunity to bring ideas and advice into practice.

I was with Fine Gael from 2007 until 2011, initially as economic adviser. Then I took on a broader role as director of policy to prepare policy positions for the party in every area.

During that period, my worst fears had become fulfilled in terms of the direction of the economy. It was a harrowing time politically, but also a fascinating time for somebody involved in economic policy formation. The challenge couldn't have been greater.

Enda became Taoiseach in 2011 after an election fought on the basis of the five-point plan to restore the country's economic fortunes. He asked me to join him as his economic adviser and programme manager in government and I was there until the end of August 2016. Under his leadership, it's quite evident that most of what was promised and planned in 2011 was delivered in terms of turning the economy around and moving the country out of the bailout.

Andrew McDowell ended up as one of Enda's most powerful advisers, second only to Mark Kennelly, who stayed on until Enda stepped down in 2017. Andrew enjoyed a charmed life.

On 6 July, the day after McDowell's appointment to the European Investment Bank, Fiach Kelly of the *Irish Times* wrote that the new vice president 'has been at the heart of government since Fine Gael assumed office with Labour in 2011 and was one of the key drivers, if not the driver, of economic policy.' He went on to say that 'his influence has extended far beyond pure economics...'

And so it had. I had met McDowell only once, when he was a key negotiator for Fine Gael in the government formation talks. He was exceptionally bright, but he was Enda's man to the letter.

We had got our process, but Fine Gael had got their man. When the appointment finally came to cabinet on 5 July, Michael Noonan asked me not to put it to a vote. In a throwaway remark, he asserted that he had never seen a vote in cabinet in all his years in office. That revealed how much the cabinet itself had been sidelined.

Finian and I felt that we couldn't put it to a vote. We did not like the outcome, but we were snookered: we had agreed to the process. The nomination went through without opposition. I learned a good lesson early on. Cabinet was not a place where open discussions were encouraged. It was a rubber stamp for behind-the-scenes activities elsewhere.

We lost that spat. Game, set and match to Enda. Relations reached a new low. It was difficult to see how this government could last much beyond the summer recess. We were permanently at daggers drawn, enemies not friends, ambushers or ambushed. And there was an even more lethal battle looming, a fight on the most divisive issue in Irish politics, that had been running in the media for several weeks.

Finian McGrath, John Halligan and I were hell-bent on voting against the government in the Dáil. Journalist Vincent Browne had warned that I was about to breach a clause in the constitution requiring that the cabinet acts as a collective. He suggested that Enda should sack me if I did.

The battle already raging was on a bill from Mick Wallace addressing the thorny issue of fatal foetal abnormalities and abortion, a subject that invariably prompted high emotion on all sides. We in the Alliance believed it was an item of individual conscience and that we had an understanding, on these social issues, there would be a free vote. Fine Gael insisted that since the issue of abortion was dealt with in the Programme for Government, we must vote the cabinet line. They believed there was a clear pathway and timeline spelled out in the programme. We had put our names to it. We were not honouring our commitment on the abortion issue. Or so they said.

The argument went to the heart of many issues involving the cabinet itself. The subject of abortion always split cabinets and raised constitutional problems. Free votes were foreign to Fine Gael.

Our view was simple. We respected the right of all deputies to vote on this issue according to their consciences. While Halligan, McGrath and I had a long record of being pro-choice, our colleagues Boxer Moran and Seán Canney were pro-life. We had agreed among ourselves that whenever an issue like this arose, Independent Alliance TDs would happily vote different ways and respect each other's stances. There would be no danger to the government. The Dáil could decide. In the case of Wallace's bill, even Fianna Fáil gave its TDs a free vote.

The Fine Gael leadership was livid. They regarded our position as grandstanding and reneging on the Programme for Government. I have to this day some sympathy for their dilemma. For them, it was countercultural. They had painstakingly navigated an acceptable, albeit vague, path down the abortion tunnel in the Programme for Government that would lead to the removal of the loathsome Eighth Amendment of the Constitution on abortion. It was not easy for Enda Kenny to sell this to his own flock. His party still bore the bruises inflicted by the abortion question on their numbers under his leadership in the previous Dáil. They had lost four anti-abortion deputies, namely Minister of State Lucinda Creighton, Terence Flanagan, Peter Mathews and Billy Timmins. The quartet waltzed off into the sunset, formed the Renua Party and imploded. Issues like abortion, contraception and divorce had inevitably dogged a traditional party like Fine Gael ever since its foundation. To be fair to Enda, despite his deeply conservative instincts, he was prepared to make slow moves towards a giant step, because his reluctant party needed a prudent, gradual approach.

John, Finian and I had little time for procrastination or compromise. Relationships between Fine Gael and ourselves were now so bad that we saw no point in talking to them. This confrontation would be fought out on the floor of the Dáil or in the media. We were squaring up for a fight. We were already increasingly thinking of ourselves, not as part of a government but as the watchdog — or worse, the enemy — within.

Apart from our convictions, all three of us had another genuine difficulty with opposing this bill. It was a carefully laid, political trap. Wallace's comrade and ally, Clare Daly, had introduced an identical bill in the 2011–16 Dáil, when we were in opposition with them both. We had all supported it. How could we now vote against it, only a year later, just because we were in government? We would look like arch-hypocrites, suddenly content in comfortable ministries, selling out at the first opportunity. We were cornered.

Back in 2015, the government had sought the opinion of the Attorney General, Máire Whelan, on the bill. She had determined that it was unconstitutional.

Fine Gael made the first move. Immediately after it became clear that Wallace's bill would come to cabinet and shortly afterwards reach the floor of the House, Minister for Health, Simon Harris, saw the danger. He promptly referred the identical bill to the same Attorney General for an opinion. It was a slick political move for two reasons. First, Harris knew exactly what she would say. Secondly, he must have felt that a declaration by the Attorney General that the bill was unconstitutional would bind us into an unbreakable political lock. It was inconceivable that a member of cabinet would defy the Attorney General's legal advice. Finally, it gave us perfect cover. We could plead that we would dearly love to support the bill, but, unfortunately, all ministers were bound by cabinet decisions and by the Attorney General's opinions.

Instead of taking a conciliatory approach, we took the road of outright defiance. On 28 June, the cabinet sat to decide its stance on this troublesome bill. Finian and I sought a free vote. Wallace must have been wallowing in the divisions he had created. Fine Gael's position on that day was clear: the road to repeal of the Eighth Amendment of the Constitution was through a Citizens' Assembly, an all-party committee and a referendum. The Independent Alliance had signed up for that in the Programme for Government. We countered by insisting that a vote on termination in cases of fatal foetal abnormality was never envisaged.

There was no middle ground. There was anger on both sides. The Attorney General sat through the entire proceedings while we squabbled about the value of her ruling. At one point I dismissed it as 'only an opinion', in a manner that was unnecessarily impolite to an expert. We were deadlocked. Enda adjourned the heated discussion for two days, until Thursday, 30 June.

The following day, Pat Leahy wrote in his column in the *Irish Times*: 'Both sides expect a compromise to be reached. The Independents accept the Attorney's advice, but don't necessarily want to be bound by it themselves. To many on the Fine Gael side this sounds suspiciously like having your cake and eating it.'

Perhaps Leahy was right. He was bolder in his prediction of a compromise, claiming that the consequence of the government not accepting Máire Whelan's advice would be that 'she would have no option but to resign'. That was food for thought.

I did not know Máire Whelan at all well. I had questioned her reappointment by Kenny the night before the cabinet was announced. The Independent Alliance had a clear understanding that we would have a right to 'consultation' with the Taoiseach about the choice of an Attorney General in a partnership government. When I reminded Enda of the matter of this 'consultation', he responded, 'That is correct. I have now consulted with you and it will be Máire Whelan.'

My acquaintance with her hardly stretched beyond seeking a few words of advice on specific legislation when we were both waiting for the Fine Gael mob to arrive late for cabinet. She was a trifle formal, even in these informal pre-cabinet coffee sessions. Refreshingly, although appointed by Enda, she was not a card-carrying member of the Blueshirt tribe. In cabinet, she was impeccably professional. Máire Whelan had a razor-sharp mind, gave her legal opinion when requested and left it at that. I never recall her saying a word in cabinet on anything political; she confined her contributions to legal advice. Her unwillingness to mix it in political exchanges contrasted with reports of other Attorneys General, who waded in behind the government that had appointed them. Máire Whelan may have been a bit distant, but that can be the characteristic of a good Attorney General.

She was impressive, but she was not infallible. Her opinion on a bill carried authority, but we were of the firm view that this matter should be decided by testing in the Supreme Court. If an Attorney General's negative opinion was always guaranteed to kick any bill off the pitch, it left the holder of the office in an all-powerful position. He or she could torpedo a bill on a whim. If Enda had his way on this, all cabinet members would now automatically fall into line without discussion of the merits of the bill.

Another cabinet member and long-time and ardent advocate of a woman's right to choose greatly disappointed us.

Katherine Zappone lined up against us. When it came to the debate in the Dáil, she welcomed the bill and said she agreed with its provisions. However, she accepted the Attorney General's advice that a constitutional change was necessary. Consequently, she was forced to oppose it. We openly wondered how close she had come to Enda after negotiating her plum job in cabinet. Did she feel that she now owed him blind loyalty on all issues?

The Dáil debate saw contributions from independent Clare Daly, Kate O'Connell of Fine Gael and Richard Boyd Barrett of People Before Profit, who had himself lost a baby girl as a result of a fatal foetal abnormality. Kate broke down as she told of her own experience of having a currently healthy five-year-old boy, for whom there had seemed little hope of survival before his birth.

The argument was prolonged because the vote itself was not due for another week. Over the weekend we consulted with approximately twenty-five Independent Alliance councillors at a meeting in Athlone. They supported our demand for a free vote. On the Sunday, John Halligan upped the ante by declaring on RTÉ's *Marian Finucane Show* that he would be voting for Wallace's bill. Late on Sunday, Fine Gael sources were briefing the press that he, Finian and I would be obliged to toe the government line. On Monday, I went on RTÉ's *Morning Ireland* and followed Halligan's lead, stating unequivocally that I would vote for the bill. Finian was already on board. There was now no room for a compromise, an abstention or a fudge.

The stand-off did not last for long. I waited for a call from the Taoiseach, half-expecting to be dismissed after barely two months in government. It was unlikely, since he would probably have been forced to dismiss John and Finian too as fellow ministers, ensuring that the government would fall. During the morning, Michael Noonan and Paschal Donohoe went on the airwaves and made conciliatory noises. At 3 p.m., an official from Enda's office rang me to say that the government would allow a free vote. It was over.

The next day Finian and I walked into the cabinet room content about our victory, but still apprehensive. We were nervous about meeting Máire Whelan, unwittingly caught in the political cross-fire. Like us, she was always at the cabinet at 10 a.m., waiting for the Fine Gael ministers to arrive. At the least, we speculated that there would be awkward moments, maybe argument or sullen-ness from the Attorney General. As we approached the cabinet room, Finian muttered under his breath, 'Do you think she is going to resign at the cabinet meeting?'

When we entered the room, there she was, all alone. It was awkward. Finian muttered that there was nothing personal about our decision not to abide by her opinion.

I was worried. Had we sparked a constitutional crisis? I had seen the steely look in the Attorney General's eyes at cabinet meetings when she was offering legal advice. She had a deter-mination and clarity that I suddenly feared might mask a capacity for cold anger.

We were all standing around the table. Máire Whelan smiled. I cannot remember her exact words, except that she assured us that our stance caused her no anxiety. She was utterly profes-sional. She reminded us that issues like these are often resolved in the Supreme Court. She was totally content with that.

The Fine Gael ministers arrived in, late as ever. They had decided at their pre-cabinet party cabal that, probably uniquely, they would take no position on Wallace's bill. After all the hullabaloo, it was defeated in the Dáil by 95 votes to 45. Even among the Fianna Fáil troops, having been given a free vote, only five of its 43 TDs broke ranks. I winked at Mick Wallace as Finian, John and I passed through the Dáil lobby on his side of the House. It was like old times. We hadn't sold out yet.

The next day Pat Leahy wrote that 'the atmosphere around Government is dreadful'. He was right. A government minister was quoted as saying that 'a Government can't operate like this. Either we get our act together or the Government will simply fall apart.' Our pending demise was widely predicted by politicians and pundits after the fights over abortion and the nomination of Andrew McDowell. We had given Fine Gael a fright, but, in truth, we had equally spooked ourselves. We had unintentionally walked the government to the brink of collapse. Luckily, the summer recess was only a few days away.

The accusations that we had played fast and loose with the conventions of the cabinet and, even more recklessly, with the Constitution, merited a bit more scrutiny. We felt that, if that was the case, the Constitution needed examination and free votes deserved far more latitude.

Certainly, the collision course with Fine Gael was partly our initiative but the conventions around the cabinet caused us concern. They were (and are still) antediluvian and arguably make the top layer of government dysfunctional. The battle over whether the Attorney General's opinion should sink a bill was only the tip of the iceberg. After two months in cabinet, the heart of government seemed to me to be unwieldy, secretive and sometimes acting more like a politburo than a democratic decision-making body. Its proceedings were dominated by conventions, decisions taken on the fringes, a few powerful politicians and absent civil servants.

Finian and I were convinced that Máire Whelan was an honourable woman, but it was worrying, in principle, to think that the opinion of an unelected civil servant could jettison a bill. It was a long-established convention that the view of the government's Attorney General dictated the course of a piece of legislation. Yet top lawyers often disagree. Even judges frequently give dissenting judgements. We are used to split decisions from the learned beaks in the Supreme Court, and many bills approved by Attorneys General over the years have been struck down in the courts.

These guys are gurus, not gods. They are helpful experts. During the debate on Mick Wallace's bill, many lawyers surfaced to insist that it was constitutional. The democratically elected members of the cabinet were apparently obliged to fall in line with the opposite view. The convention and the practice were that all fifteen held the same view as the Attorney General.

Worse still, the opinion of an Attorney General could in theory, one day, be subject to political pressure. The office-holder is the Taoiseach's personal nomination to the President who appoints the Attorney General. He or she is in office at the whim of the Taoiseach. There is little incentive for an Attorney General ever to give an opinion that is embarrassing to a Taoiseach who has such sway over his or her career. It has become custom and practice for the chosen one to be a top lawyer, but often also a party loyalist. That is a bad practice. There are too many historical cases of Attorneys General being active supporters of the party in power or too close to the Taoiseach of the day.

Other bad practices grew over the four-year term. The problems created by cabinet leaks increased. Leaking became the norm. It was said by one cabinet minister, during a government meeting, that the best way for a politician to surface on the RTÉ *One O'Clock News* was to say something highly confidential at cabinet in the morning.

The leaking of cabinet proceedings went deeper than racy tales of feisty exchanges during the occasional cabinet spat. On separate occasions, both Katherine Zappone and Denis Naughten hit the roof about 'colleagues' sending confidential material, which they had circulated to the cabinet, straight to the media, to ingratiate themselves with their pet journalists.

Leaking made the cabinet even less relevant. Ministers resorted to less democratic actions to defeat the leakers. A practice of producing highly confidential items 'under the arm' developed. These were memos for government that none except the relevant minister and the Taoiseach had sight of, until the cabinet meeting commenced. It became acceptable for items with juicy financial information to be delayed by the Minister for Finance, Paschal Donohoe, without notice until the very end of a Tuesday morning meeting. Sometimes the proposal was not even on the agenda. No one could blame Paschal if he needed to protect an initiative from market reaction overnight, owing to a potential leak. Instead, he would painstakingly take us through the detail at the meeting. We would pass it, almost on the nod, often because it was urgent, although we were given no time to examine it beforehand. A bad habit of approving instant, mostly unchallenged, legislation has become acceptable.

Similarly, state appointments often appeared as an agenda item, but no name was provided before the meeting. Charlie Flanagan loved doing this with judges, but it happened with other appointments for fear that the names would appear publicly before the post had been formally filled. The lack of trust was palpable. Cabinet confidentiality has become a distant memory.

An even more sinister development has been the increase in cabinet 'incorporeal meetings' during the Fine Gael years.

The most famous incorporeal meeting in the state's history was the one to pass the state's bank guarantee in 2008. It happened in a major emergency when there was an overnight threat of a collapse of the entire Irish banking system. The finance minister of the day, the late Brian Lenihan, required government approval to give the Irish banks a blanket bank guarantee. Cabinet ministers were called in their beds, some even abroad, to give their consent before the banks opened the next morning. Calls were made by the secretary to the cabinet, Dermot McCarthy, in the middle of the night to gain ministers' approval for this emergency measure. In those days, it was very rare to hold such sudden meetings.

For some reason, incorporeal meetings have become much more frequent in recent times. The 2016–20 government oversaw a significant increase in the number of incorporeal meetings, sometimes passing important legislation or making far-reaching decisions in that way.

Incorporeal cabinet 'meetings' are a misnomer. Nobody meets anyone. An official from the Department of the Taoiseach normally rings the minister's private secretary to alert the minister of the 'meeting' about a matter that requires a decision. The minister is given a time for the call. He is asked to be available.

The first time I was asked to be available for an 'incorporeal', I imagined that this was a video-link meeting being held, instead of the normal face-to-face gathering, because of the difficulties of assembling the cabinet in person at an unsocial or awkward time. Naively, I expected a minister and other colleagues would be at the other end of a telephone or a video link for a discussion or even to take questions.

Alas, nothing of the sort happens in 'incorporeals'. They are a one-to-one conversation. A mandarin from the Taoiseach's department rings around the appointed time and asks if you are happy to approve the sole item on the agenda. There is no minister, no political discussion, no summary of the topic and no presentation. You either approve or you don't. The mandarin makes the calls, tots up the numbers and finishes the entire process in less than an hour.

In recent times the incorporeal meeting has been happening ever more frequently. Out of the 224 cabinet meetings since the formation of the last government in 2016 to 1 May 2020, twenty-nine (13%) were incorporeals. In nearly every case the measure in question has been passed unchallenged, with indecent haste.

What was once a rarity has developed into a more frequent norm. I readily confess to having used the incorporeal route through the cabinet on at least three occasions. When a deadline fell between cabinet meetings, it was becoming a convenience, a backstop in case an item was not ready in time for cabinet. But I could steer measures through without the hassle of being accountable for them. I, like everyone else, had found a way of bypassing the cabinet.

To be fair, one day on a ring-around when I asked the mandarin on the phone if he had certain facts and figures available, he was reassuringly familiar with the details of the cabinet item. He returned with answers to a few other questions later. I approved the proposal. It is a truly ingenious, but profoundly undemocratic, way to ram legislation or decisions through a compliant cabinet.

If the structures supporting the Irish cabinet are flawed, the practices do not encourage scrutiny or accountability. Fine Gael's pre-cabinet get-togethers tended to preordain the conduct of the meetings themselves. Issues any Fine Gael ministers had were normally thrashed out in their internal discussions. In the early days of the government, they anticipated any skirmishes threatened by the non-Fine Gael ministers. Then they trooped into the council chamber with a united front.

Discussion of legislation was undemanding. Rarely did Fine Gael ministers challenge one another on their proposals. When Seán Kyne was first appointed Chief Whip by Leo Varadkar, he frequently queried senior Fine Gael ministers about their legislation. Eyebrows were raised and he soon lost some of his enthusiasm. They constantly bitched to the media about me meddling in other ministers' portfolios, while apparently paying scant attention to my own. From time to time, Charlie Flanagan or Michael Creed would question me on legislation I was bringing forward. Their challenges were almost certainly in retaliation for my multiple sins against Fine Gael. They were enjoying themselves by putting me on the spot.

Few people would take on the Fine Gael heavyweights. Neither Enda nor Leo, as Taoiseach, was ever seriously questioned. The cabinet is by necessity dominated by the Taoiseach of the day. Of the ministers, undoubtedly Michael Noonan held the greatest sway in Enda's final year. It was not just his competence, nor that he was a revered Fine Gael elder. The Finance portfolio defines who is the most powerful minister at the table. He can make or break another department or its minister. Besides, Michael was on a lap of honour, highly respected by his colleagues for bringing Ireland safely through the legacy of the banking crisis. He was also wickedly funny at other people's expense and few wanted to be a victim of his wit in front of their peers. He was the biggest beast around Enda's table.

In the background sat Simon Coveney and Leo Varadkar. Neither was able to exploit their cabinet posts to jockey for position in their leadership battle being fought daily elsewhere. Not surprisingly, Enda did not allot the most populist or powerful portfolios to either potential successor. Simon held the troublesome Housing job while Leo was given the permanently problematic Department of Social Protection. Either might have preferred a ministry such as Jobs, Enterprise and Innovation, traditionally full of good employment news to deliver to the Fine Gael backbenchers. That gig went to Mary Mitchell O'Connor, who was definitely not a leadership contender. Enda was careful not to donate the two principal pretenders to his throne either of the powerful Finance or Public Expenditure and Reform portfolios. Instead, he allotted them to Noonan and Paschal Donohoe. For Noonan, it was now too late for a leadership bid. For Paschal it was too early; he was still a relative newcomer to the cabinet.

Frances Fitzgerald, as Tánaiste and Minister for Justice, certainly had one eye on the leadership. As number two, she might have been expected to exert greater influence on the cabinet than she actually did. Justice produces by far the biggest volume of legislation, but hardly offers a platform for further ambitions. Frances was brilliant at briefing cabinet colleagues on tricky legal legislation, although I suspect some of her counsel fell on deaf ears. No one worked harder than Frances, but, as Tánaiste, she probably punched below her weight politically. Despite her commitment and efficiency as a minister, when it came down to the leadership contest, she wasn't at the races. Part of that was undoubtedly due to the deep suspicion of feminism still running through Fine Gael. They were not yet ready for a woman Taoiseach. I liked Frances and was impressed by her integrity and application. One of my biggest regrets in my entire four years was that I failed to support her when she came under pressure and resigned over the Garda Maurice McCabe whistle-blower scandal. After her exoneration, I again did not speak in support of her in the Dáil. She had been helpful and straight with me in difficult dealings over the Judicial Appointments Bill and deserved better. At one point I was really hounding her to make haste with the bill. Her departure to Europe was a loss to the Dáil of an honest politician. I am not proud of ducking this opportunity to acknowledge a woman wronged because of a reluctance to be too closely associated with Fine Gael.

Frances' successor, Charlie Flanagan, had originally been packed off to Iveagh House. He obviously loved Foreign Affairs. When Leo took over as Taoiseach, it was clear that Charlie did not want to surrender the post to Simon Coveney and take

Frances' post in Justice. He was more cantankerous in cabinet than anyone, even Enda or me at our most antagonistic. Finian and I, to our shame, quite enjoyed getting right up Charlie's nose. Almost a year after the government was formed and when we were on far better terms with the Taoiseach, another row broke out, this time with Charlie.

John Halligan, Finian and I had become genuinely exercised about whether or not Ireland had voted for Saudi Arabia (of all countries) to win a seat on the United Nations Commission on the Status of Women. Charlie refused to say. We pursued him for a reply, including my demand on RTÉ's *Morning Ireland* that he clarify Ireland's vote before a cabinet meeting on 9 May 2017.

Charlie had the shortest fuse in the cabinet. He would explode at the slightest provocation, but normally calm down quite quickly. I could never fathom whether his tantrums were real or contrived. Over the four years we crossed swords about various issues, including his period in Justice when we had to deal with Stepaside Garda Station and judicial appointments. He flipped the lid on dozens of occasions.

This time it was about Saudi Arabia. Apparently, Charlie had totally lost the head at the Fine Gael pre-cabinet meeting. At his worst, he tends to scatter people in all directions.

When Finian and I arrived at cabinet, Enda was in the corridor waiting for us, for a change. We had already flagged a row on Ireland's secret vote for the Saudis. I assumed that the Taoiseach was as furious as Charlie and was about to give us a dressing-down about washing cabinet dirty linen in public. Far from it. The Taoiseach had a broad grin on his face. He hurried us into a side room. 'Get in here quick', he said, 'before he comes in. Charlie's in orbit!'

We hastened into the side room. The Taoiseach told us jocularly that Charlie was up the walls. We quickly agreed a truce for cabinet. Michael Noonan brokered a full peace at the table. Charlie was gagging for a fight, but we agreed at the cabinet meeting that in future all votes of this sort would be flagged to us in advance.

It was around this time that Charlie and I had one of many heated phone conversations. 'You know', he declared loftily, 'I received my seal of office from the President of Ireland' (as though I didn't). He was making the point that I had interfered in his portfolio. And then, in a gratuitous sideswipe, referring to my wife: 'I simply cannot understand how a good Mountmellick woman, Ruth Buchanan, stayed married to you.' Ruth and Charlie hail from the same town in County Laois.

I have to confess, scores of others have wondered the same thing, sometimes upfront, more often behind my back. One similar incident happened back in my Seanad days when I had a spat with Senator Mary White of Fianna Fáil.

I had mischievously expressed a wish in the Seanad that Mary would not get a Fianna Fáil nomination for the Dáil a few days later. The day after the convention, I met Mary in the Oireachtas Library. She was irate, blaming me for her failure to get the nod from Fianna Fáil as their candidate for Dublin South-East the night before. When risen, she was as fiery as Charlie Flanagan at his fieriest. I tried to explain to her that my influence did not extend into the smoke-filled rooms of the Soldiers of Destiny, but she was having none of it. She said she knew I was a friend of P.J. Mara, the Fianna bigwig. I had fixed it with him. And then, out of the blue, 'And how your wife puts up with you, I will never understand.'

'Why don't you ask her yourself?' I replied.

'I don't know her and I don't have her phone number,' riposted Mary.

I called her bluff. 'Here it is,' I said, handing her the number. I was certain she wouldn't make the call.

Mary left the room with a parting shot: 'I'm going to tell her all about you.' I settled down to read the newspapers.

Ten minutes later she returned. 'Well, how did you get on?' I asked. She was swaggering.

'I told your wife what you are like, what you did to me and how impossible you are,' she revealed triumphantly.

'And what did she say?' I asked, confident that Ruth would be loyal to the last.

'She agreed with every word I said and told me that you were absolutely impossible to live with.'

Mary went away a happy woman. A few minutes later Ruth rang to say that she had just received a call from a total stranger complaining about my behaviour and saying that I was impossible. She did not know where the stranger got her number.

'What did you say?' I asked.

'I told her that she was absolutely right. We had a good old bitch about you and she put down the telephone as happy as Larry!'

You certainly need a sense of humour in politics to carry you through all the bloodletting and stress. Charlie Flanagan had a great sense of humour. Like Finian and me, he frequented the Members' Bar, a venue where many wounds were healed.

The cabinet contained a cast of characters with human strengths and weaknesses. Pretty average people, we all suffered from a fair dose of vanity and pride. We all wanted to register public victories and to minimise our defeats. We had all landed in a cauldron where, somehow, we knew we must live together. Strangely enough, I do not believe there were many, if any, personal friendships among the fifteen. Fine Gael were above all else, a tribe, with deeply ingrained loyalties, but few friendships.

The 2016 cabinet was not an ideal body for decision-making. Its make-up was deeply conservative. Its structure allowed power to be vested in very few hands. Its procedures ensured that decisions on most legislation were predestined to pass through without serious discussion. Controversial decisions were decided offstage. The rows tended to be about politics, not policy. Bad habits, like 'under the arm' memos and incorporeal meetings, gave key measures a free pass. Leaks galore guaranteed that most important decisions were made elsewhere. This cabinet's way of operating was a major disappointment and needed reform. It was neither accountable, transparent nor democratic. Nevertheless, these difficulties could have been, and were on occasion, overcome with determination and political persuasion.

4

Pat Hickey's Olympic Downfall

PASCHAL DONOHOE WAS always the most chirpy of ministers. He was one of those Fine Gael guys who had an upbeat word or two whatever the situation. He was my predecessor in the Department of Transport, Tourism and Sport. No one could have been more helpful in the early days when I needed a fatherly figure to advise me on the pitfalls of office. Although he was hardly a father figure to me — he had been a student at Trinity with my son Hugh — he was certainly my senior in cabinet. And he was unusually polite, friendly and shrewd. I am told that he has always held ambitions, formed and openly declared at a young age, to be Taoiseach.

I knew Paschal from right back in our Seanad days in 2007. It was as plain as a pikestaff that the bright spark, the fresh senator from multinational Procter & Gamble, had no intention of hanging around the Seanad for any longer than necessary. Nor did he. Paschal rose rapidly. He was in the Dáil by 2011, a minister by 2013 and, more recently, Minister for Finance. But he never lost the run of himself or his sense of humour.

One Sunday in London, about five years ago, I was having lunch with my family in a chic West End restaurant, The Wolseley in Piccadilly. We were sitting on the balcony, looking down at the revellers below. One of the tables was occupied by a youthful-looking group of bons vivants, who I thought might be a branch of the Young Conservatives.

They were not. To my surprise, in their midst was a familiar face from faraway Dublin Central. Paschal was holding court, as Paschal does. Everyone was listening, as everyone always does.

He never saw me. I said nothing. Two days later when I arrived back in Leinster House, I rang Paschal's number. I was put through to the bon vivant and let him have it with both barrels. Putting on my best broad Dublin accent, I pretended to be a constituent who had heard that he, a man of the people from Dublin's inner city, had been wining and dining in a posh London restaurant. Was he in The Wolseley in Piccadilly on Sunday, I asked? It was a long way from The Wolseley he'd been reared. His constituents, many living in tough circumstances, would be dismayed.

Paschal was, as always, painfully polite and honest, although he did not seem eager to prolong the conversation. It lasted long enough for me to tell him that I, his disillusioned constituent, would never vote for him again.

The next day I met Paschal in the corridors of Leinster House. I asked him by way of polite conversation if he'd had a nice weekend? He volunteered that he had been in London and went on to tell me the story of how he had been spotted in The Wolseley with friends and family. He couldn't believe what a small world it was. Incredibly, he then gave me, blow by blow, a word-perfect account of his telephone conversation with his unhappy constituent.

I nodded solemnly and asked innocently if he'd recognised the constituent's voice. He didn't. I had to exit fast before I collapsed in stitches.

I hadn't the heart to leave him in the dark, so I rang him shortly afterwards to confess. It is to his eternal credit that he regularly tells that story against himself.

I had several helpful exchanges with Paschal in my early weeks in office. He would mark my card about various civil servants and sometimes usefully suggest a few sensible responses to difficult situations. He went out of his way to be helpful.

At one of these casual early meetings, I asked him if, as Minister for Sport, I would be able to go to Rio for the Olympic Games. Paschal replied instantly, 'Not only will you be able to go to Rio de Janeiro, you will *have* to go to the Olympics. It would be embarrassing for the government if you did not go there, especially if we win a few medals.'

It sounded pretty good. Cheering on our national athletes during the daytime and dining in one of those lovely restaurants on Copacabana Beach at night would not be the worst part of the job.

As it happened, my department officials had already been working on a Rio schedule. Both my colleague, the Minister of State for Sport and Tourism, Limerick TD Patrick O'Donovan, and I would go to Rio for around a week each in August. We would share the 'burden'.

The officials told me that I would be accompanied by Assistant Secretary for Sport and Tourism, Ken Spratt. He would be my guide and constant companion at the Olympics. When they said that he would be available to me full-time out in Rio, I inwardly freaked. I didn't know Ken well at the time, but I had an inbuilt dread of civil servants controlling and crowding out ministers. In addition, I couldn't see any reason why I would possibly need a civil servant chewing my ear off while I was watching Irish boxers walking away with a few medals.

When the officials related their Rio plans for Ken and me, I countered by saying that I intended to bring my wife, Ruth, along. You could have heard a pin drop. I saw Ken's eyes involuntarily rise up to the heavens as he turned away from me. I tried to reassure him and the other civil servants that Ruth would pay for every cent of expenditure herself. The state would not suffer any cost.

They froze. They were not happy mandarins. Anyway, Ruth and Ken met at the airport in Rio. There was a bit of a frisson initially, but after a short time they seemed to get on well. I am not sure if the atmosphere was helped or hindered by Ruth's insistence on calling Ken 'Sir Humphrey' (of *Yes Minister* fame) but he took it in good spirits. Both of them had a fine sense of humour, an essential antidote to the series of catastrophes that struck during the Olympic visit. Ken Spratt turned out to be one of the finest civil servants I have ever encountered in public life. His advice was independent, fearless and given after hours of, sometimes agonising, thought. Often we did not agree, so it was left to me to make a final decision. Ken was the ideal minder in Rio: his meticulous attention to detail was priceless in the controversies waiting around the corner and his prudence provided an essential foil to my own inbuilt recklessness.

In mid-July dark clouds began to hover over Rio de Janeiro. The Russian drugs scandal reared its ugly head as the Olympics drew near. Ireland became involved. A letter from the Danish government with an anti-doping pledge was co-signed by the Irish government, but opposed by Pat Hickey, the president of the Olympic Council of Ireland. At the time, Minister Patrick O'Donovan was under serious pressure not to approve the initiative. He consulted with me and I instructed him to go ahead. I sent a message of support to Patrick telling him that there were 'powerful forces at work' against us. Pat Hickey was less than pleased.

Hickey had long been an opponent of Irish sports ministers. He had a fearsome reputation for giving us bloody noses and sending us on our way. His message was clear: sport is above politics. The elite International Olympic Committee (IOC), of which Hickey was a key member of the executive board, was way, way above politics. Hands off, minister.

With barely two weeks to go to the opening ceremony, a fresh row was brewing about whether Russia would be banned from the Olympics for drug abuse. The IOC had to make a decision. Hickey was adamant that a blanket ban was the wrong road to take. On 24 July, the IOC decided against an outright ban on all Russian athletes, despite the evidence of state-sponsored drugs abuse in that unhappy country. The IOC rejected the advice of the World Anti-Doping Agency, following a damning independent report recommending that Russia should be excluded from the Games.

The IOC's softly softly approach to Russia and drugs was hugely controversial. They camouflaged it well and passed the buck brilliantly. They asked all twenty-eight sporting federations comprising the Olympics to make up their minds individually on the Russian question. The conclusion of this canvass meant that Russian athletes could compete, providing they proved, to the satisfaction of the international sporting federations, that they were clean. Dope or no dope, the Russians had crashed through the gates of Rio. Russia's president, Vladimir Putin, must have opened the Beluga caviar that night and raised a glass of vodka to Hickey and his comrades when he realised that he had once again defeated international opponents of Russian doping.

In an interview with Seán O'Rourke on RTÉ that same week, Hickey pooh-poohed his own and IOC president Thomas Bach's perceived good relationship with Putin. He claimed that their links with the Russian leader had been exaggerated and that 'your rival station is branding me in the same category because they think I'm chasing European games in Russia, which I am not, and which has been blown out of the water anyway.'

Four years earlier, at the London Olympics, Hickey had told Vincent Hogan of the *Irish Independent* that he knew Vladimir Putin 'very well'. He went on to boast about 'what a great day at the judo hall with [David] Cameron and Putin. That's my family — you're with friends.'

Hickey was an incorrigible name-dropper. Imagine if he had been forced to tell his 'friend' Putin that he and his fellow IOC board members had banned Russia from the Olympic Games.

In the interview with O'Rourke, he went on grandiosely: 'my job as president of Europe (*sic*) is to unite north, east, south and west and the last thing we want is to go back to Cold War days and the Olympic boycotts that we had in 1980 and 1984. I think this is the best way forward.'

Hickey was referring to his position as president of the European Olympic Committee. Critics suggested that he was getting way above himself. His alleged closeness to Putin was backed up by a powerful, widely used photograph of the president of Russia at a plush Moscow dinner, sitting beside Hickey and his wife, Sylviane. One president breaking bread with another.

Patrick O'Donovan was due to attend the opening Olympic ceremony on Friday, 5 August. Somewhat surprisingly, he did not meet Hickey there. Worse still, Patrick did not meet Hickey during his entire period in Rio. The 'president of Europe' was so far above politics that he did not even grant a minister of state from his home country the courtesy of a 'meet and greet'. Vincent Hogan had put it more delicately four years earlier, writing pointedly that Hickey was a man 'from a country he has essentially outgrown'.

If that was Hickey's attitude, I did not expect to be granted an audience with him in Rio. On Monday, 8 August, Patrick O'Donovan texted me from the Games, insisting that, despite hiccups, all was good. 'Really enjoying it. Everything is going fine. You'll have a great time here.'

If only he had known.

Hiccups included an Irish boxer, Michael O'Reilly, testing positive for drugs the day before the games opened on 4 August and the shock arrest of another Irishman, Kevin Mallon, and his Brazilian translator for ticket touting on the night of the opening ceremony. Two negative stories about Ireland had broken in two days.

The Mallon arrest suddenly turned the focus of unwanted attention on Hickey. Mallon was arrested, banged up in prison and charged with 'providing, diverting or facilitating of tickets for *cambismo*' — the Brazilian term for the illegal resale of tickets.

A bad story became worse when it was revealed that, allegedly, some of the tickets had originated with Hickey's Olympic Council of Ireland. The OCI issued a rebuttal saying that it 'has no knowledge of the two individuals arrested. The OCI has launched an immediate investigation with our Authorised Ticket Reseller (ATR) into how these individuals were allegedly in possession of OCI allocated tickets.'

Back in Dublin, as Minister for Sport, I was under pressure to respond to the series of bad events for Ireland out in Rio. The big question was how we felt about the integrity of the inquiry being set up by the OCI. Ireland's good sporting name was being damaged by the day. Was the OCI inquiry credible and independent? Or was it a whitewash? Was it going to find results? Who was on Hickey's inquiry team?

With developments rapidly moving out of control, I decided to contact Hickey in Rio. On Wednesday, 10 August I texted him: 'Pat, could you please give me a ring ASAP? Shane Ross.' I received no reply that day. More than twenty-four hours later, on the Thursday evening, with a media frenzy building, there was still no sign of a return call. I sent him another text: 'Hi Pat, could you please ring me ASAP? Shane.'

This time he did respond: 'Just called you. I am available if u (*sic*) call me back.'

I did. We spoke, exchanged views and arranged to meet in my hotel in Rio immediately Ken Spratt and I arrived from the airport on the Sunday.

On the same night, Hickey broke cover and took to the airwaves. RTÉ's *Prime Time* broadcast an interview with him with their correspondent in Rio, Philip Bromwell. Hickey was confident and almost avuncular. He had never met Kevin Mallon. He was behaving professionally. He had taken immediate action on the ticket issue. When the OCI had completed its investigation, it would share the outcome with everyone. Current unfortunate events had no effect on Team Ireland. Hickey fully expected the OCI to come out of the report with a 'clean bill of health'.

That was the problem. After hearing the interview, so did I. He sounded just a little bit too confident about the outcome of the OCI investigation.

The president of the OCI had told Philip Bromwell about the composition of the OCI committee seeking answers from the OCI about the OCI. The investigators were to be none other than OCI vice president, Willie O'Brien, OCI general secretary, Dermot Henehan, and the OCI's legal adviser and a senior counsel, Siobhán Phelan.

The alarm bells, which had already been humming, began ringing loudly. The OCI itself was looking into how OCI tickets had come into the hands of Kevin Mallon and other individuals. The temperature was rising by the hour.

On Friday morning on RTÉ's *Morning Ireland*, I expressed severe reservations about the make-up of the investigating committee, saying that 'the problem is that the Olympic Council of Ireland is a player itself'.

At the same time, I wrote to Hickey asking him to ensure that his inquiry was truly independent. Its all-OCI membership was unacceptable. In addition, my letter asked a series of questions about the OCI's arrangements with various ticket sellers. These two items were due to set the agenda for our meeting on the Sunday night in Rio.

The media flagged the meeting as a shoot-out. Ken and I prepared meticulously because the stakes were high. I had been warned by officials not to challenge Hickey. It was a source of pride to him that he had seen off several sports ministers in the past, despatching them with a flea in their ears. My officials had always been averse to confrontation. My instincts were the opposite. Ken Spratt was more cautious, advising prudence, seeking peaceful solutions, not outright war.

Hickey too was preparing. He had taken legal advice on how to conduct himself at the meeting. After his later arrest in Rio, the Brazilian police discovered an email from a legal adviser telling him that 'Shane Ross should be put back in his box'. Hardly legal advice, but it went on to suggest that Hickey could say little, because an Irishman was under arrest and charged with serious offences. He should then emphasise that the OCI was an autonomous body and was carrying out its own investigation. It needed no external input. Politicians should keep away.

By the time we reached Dublin airport on the Sunday morning, every dog in the street who had an opinion on Hickey had given me advice on how to deal with him. Some wanted me to attack him full frontal. Ken Spratt's written advice bluntly warned me not to 'rise to the bait inappropriately, not to be goaded into an inappropriate response…' Ken had not known me for long, but he knew me well!

The flight via London took over fifteen hours. Not the best preparation for a crucial meeting.

We arrived at Rio's Windsor Excelsior Hotel at around 10 p.m. The media were waiting. I promised that I would talk to them after the meeting or, at the least, would issue a statement. Ruth, cool as a cucumber, headed off to unpack and leave a couple of what she undoubtedly regarded as grossly inflated egos to clash. She was looking forward to ten days of seeing the sights of Rio, particularly the 98-foot high statue of Christ the Redeemer, while Ken and I tussled with the ticket tout ticking time bomb.

Ruth was right about the egos. She was wrong about the sights of Rio. The moment that we entered the meeting room, I knew that Hickey and I were not going to part as friends. The mood music was grim. Hickey was waiting with his vice president, Willie O'Brien, a long-time Hickey loyalist who had been on the council of the OCI for twenty years. In front of us sat all that was wrong with the OCI. Older men, in office for far too long, ready to put a politician 'in his box' for daring to challenge them.

After I had opened the conversation with a plea for no confrontation, but for an agreement, I suggested that any inquiry into the ticket-touting events in Rio should be a joint venture between the Irish government and the OCI.

Mistrust surfaced in the first minute. Hickey interrupted me. He wanted the meeting recorded. After a brief skirmish, it was agreed that both sides could take notes. Hickey produced a note-taker. Ken took copious minutes on our side of the table.

Hickey stuck to the legal road. O'Brien parroted the same line. There was a trial going on. They had taken legal advice: Hickey could say nothing. He was not accountable to the Irish government.

I told him that if that was the case we would have to hold our own independent investigation. There was not an inch of give to this suggestion from either Hickey or O'Brien. They were determined to stonewall. I reminded them that the Irish government funded the Olympic Council of Ireland. Hickey responded that our contribution of €200,000 was 'peanuts' compared to the OCI's overall funding.

As the meeting headed towards an abrupt end, I told Hickey that he had left us with no option. If he continued to refuse to give any independents a seat on his inquiry, the government would hold its own investigation. He seemed unperturbed, defiant and uncompromising. There would be no independent member recruited on his watch.

As we moved to leave, Hickey gave us a parting kick in the teeth — our next route, our fall-back had been blocked. He had found out that we had planned to go above his head if he gave us the two fingers. We had made an appointment with Christophe De Kepper, Director-General of the International Olympic Committee, the next day. Hickey gleefully told us that he had been asked to join our meeting with Christophe. We had been outplayed. Round one to Hickey. He rubbed salt into the wound by saying that, in the meantime, he would update De Kepper, so that he would be up to speed with our meeting. The brethren in the IOC had closed ranks.

We could not agree a common statement for the media since I would not pretend that our meeting had been cordial.

There was no common ground. The OCI would hold its inquiry without a single objective independent voice at the table. We would hold our own inquiry back in Dublin.

And then the silver-tongued Hickey changed tack, with a cheap olive branch. He offered to provide me with a car for the entire period of our stay. I declined. He then asked me out to dinner at Italy's exclusive Hospitality House (an Olympic speciality, held in an exclusive beach club) on the Tuesday or Wednesday of that week. I thanked him and promised to let him know if I could attend.

At the door of our hotel, Hickey and O'Brien were greeted by the RTÉ cameras in search of an interview and news of the outcome of the meeting. Ken and I stayed behind and drafted a brief statement.

According to reports, Hickey told the media that we had enjoyed an 'excellent' meeting. He said that 'Mr Ross and I had a great exchange of views. I'm restrained with what I can say because I received senior counsel's opinion two days ago, which is, that while there is an Irish citizen in jail we have to be extremely careful what we disclose.' Kevin Mallon, languishing in jail, was a watertight shield against any questioning by the media.

When Ken and I emerged, we were in the dark about what Hickey had said to RTÉ. Ken, like all good civil servants, melted into the background as RTÉ wired me up. He looked distinctly apprehensive in case I might launch a full frontal on Hickey. I had no idea that Hickey had given the impression that we had just finished a constructive meeting. So I simply told RTÉ the truth: that I was 'stunned' by Hickey's reaction at the meeting. 'We just met a brick wall. I have said all along I don't think the OCI inquiry is credible, because they are a major player in this particular controversy.' I went on to give a very strong signal that the government would now be forced to hold its own inquiry. The OCI had already stated they would not be co-operating with it.

Back home, the opposition gleefully interpreted the show-down as a bloody nose for the minister, an amateur who had been outfoxed by Hickey, just like those ministers who had tangled with the maestro in the past. I had emerged empty-handed. They were right, but there were many more rounds to go. It was becoming apparent that the difficulties ran far beyond the immediate need for an inquiry with at least one member of the panel being independent of the OCI. The OCI itself was the problem.

The next round was our pre-arranged meeting the following day but, before that, we were due to enjoy the boxing.

Ireland's boxers had endured a nightmare Olympics. Unexpected defeats were coming thick and fast, but in the ring on Monday was Katie Taylor, followed the next day by our bantamweight world champion, Michael Conlan. The nation awaited a lift. The rebuff from Hickey would be forgotten. We expected that we would soon be celebrating a victory for Ireland's greatest-ever female athlete, Katie Taylor, against Finland's Mira Potkonen. Katie was a banker.

We headed off for the boxing in good spirits, confident that we would keep our lunchtime date with Hickey and Christophe De Kepper, emboldened by having an Irish victory in our back pockets.

When we arrived at the boxing ring, we met Sport Ireland chairman, Kieran Mulvey, and chief executive, John Treacy, both in hopeful mood. Like us, they were eager to have something to cheer about.

And we cheered and cheered for Katie. But it was not to be. Her loss to the Finn in her opening bout was a sporting earthquake.

About an hour after Katie's shock defeat, we were in the car leaving the boxing complex. I spotted two small, downbeat women wheeling their suitcases along a dusty Rio road. They were all alone and inconspicuous, but I could have sworn they had tears in their eyes. It was Katie and her mother, Bridget, walking disconsolately away from the scene of her defeat. I got out of the car and offered my commiserations. They politely said thank you and took off on foot. Happily, Katie would have many days of triumphs ahead of her.

We were gutted. Blow after blow had hit Ireland in those dark days in Rio.

Ken and I were due to meet De Kepper and Hickey in their five-star hotel at 12.30. We did not hold out much hope for a breakthrough, but welcomed the opportunity to see what narrative had been peddled to De Kepper about the OCI and the ticket touts.

When we arrived at the hotel Hickey, not De Kepper, greeted us at the entrance. After his brazen gatecrash of our encounter, Hickey had now seized ownership of a meeting to which we had not originally even invited him. Quite an operator.

He confidently navigated our passage through the strict security at the hotel, which was to be the scene of his dramatic arrest within forty-eight hours. Their lodgings were a fortress of luxury. It was certainly of a far higher standard than ours, but that is par for the IOC course! I had read stories about these IOC chiefs travelling first class while the athletes sat in the back of the plane.

De Kepper had a temporary office in the hotel. He was more relaxed than Hickey and set the tone for a meeting that had little of the high-octane tension of the night before. He was firm, but friendly. Hickey had obviously briefed him and De Kepper insisted that he trusted the OCI to carry out a thorough inquiry. He was not enthusiastic about our government investigation. This was the Hickey line.

When we came to the crux issue of independence, De Kepper agreed that independence would improve the credibility of any inquiry. And then, giving Hickey his seal of approval, he instanced the 'independent lawyer' already on the OCI investigative panel as evidence of its independence and credibility.

I sensed a stitch-up. Nevertheless, both Ken and I pointed out that the 'independent' lawyer was not, in fact, independent. She was a lawyer, but she was the legal adviser to the OCI.

De Kepper turned to Hickey, who countered that Siobhán Phelan was a senior counsel, who just happened to be legal adviser to the OCI. De Kepper seemed surprised. He said that, after the OCI had got to the bottom of the ticketing row, the IOC would examine all aspects of the case. There was a chink of light. He rapidly reasserted that the IOC would not interfere with the OCI because it was the appropriate body to carry out the investigation.

The tone of the meeting had noticeably changed. Hickey volunteered that he would reflect on the request for independent membership of his inquiry team.

Ken and I sensed a shift and began to quit while we were ahead. But, first, I wanted De Kepper to be left in no doubt that there was a clash coming. The IOC, often accused of considering themselves to be above governments, do not relish unnecessary battles with politicians. I told De Kepper that there was a public demand in Ireland for a credible inquiry. Hickey finally promised to reflect and revert, but he insisted that ultimately the decision was a matter for the OCI, meaning of course, himself. We departed, anticipating possible progress. Did the IOC really want to become embroiled in a row that could now easily be avoided?

Later that day, we witnessed another gallant Irish defeat. I strongly supported my Dundrum constituent, Scott Evans, in his quest for a medal in the badminton. He lost nobly, but one of the most heartening features of his match was the presence in the crowd of a group of Ireland's field hockey players, cheering him on. The hockey team had narrowly failed to qualify for the next round themselves, but were determined to boost the morale of fellow Irish competitors, albeit in other sports.

Meanwhile Sport Ireland chairman Kieran Mulvey, wearing his mediation hat, had taken an initiative. Unknown to me, he met with the OCI later that day. Kieran spotted a way out of the impasse and wanted to broker a deal. He then approached Ken and asked him to meet with OCI vice president Willie O'Brien on Tuesday to discuss.

In the meantime, Ken kept the heat on Hickey by writing a follow-up letter to De Kepper, asking that the president of the IOC, Thomas Bach, be informed about this very serious matter.

Our aim was that Hickey would give in to pressure; otherwise the IOC would begin to regard him as too hot to handle. Perhaps it was working. There was movement.

Back at the Games, there was one last Irish boxing hope the next day when, surely, bantamweight world champion Michael Conlan would deliver the tonic which the nation so badly needed? As everyone now knows, Conlan was somehow judged to have lost the fight against his Russian opponent. Immediately he stepped out of the ring, Conlan took to the airwaves, lost the head and let rip. He lashed out with words like 'cheats' and 'corruption'. I was at the fight, where not a single observer expected a Russian win on merit. Some dubbed it a travesty of justice; others saw the hands of the Russians in a result where one of their countrymen had triumphed. The Games were beginning to stink.

After watching Michael Conlan's fight, I spent much of Tuesday afternoon in Hickey's company. He escorted Ruth and me around the crowds at various medal award ceremonies. We were both photographed with Ireland's brilliant sailor, Olympic silver medal winner Annalise Murphy.

Hickey was at his charming best. We never mentioned the war. He was in his element shooting the breeze with the great and the good, rather than the nobility of the athletic world. Yet one thing alarmed me. He kept his conversation peppered with the royals he knew, constantly introducing me to the odd crown prince or other titled individuals. At one point he said he wanted me to meet someone who he insisted — with awe — was 'the Denis O'Brien of South America'. This was meant to impress. It didn't. At least he resisted mentioning his 'friend', Vladimir Putin. Russians were not flavour of the month outside a very limited circle in Rio.

Hickey's serenity in a crisis and his little affectation that the skirmish we were fighting on ticket touting could be ignored as background noise were impressive posturing. The stakes could not have been higher for him. He would have been well aware that earlier on the Tuesday afternoon Ken and I had met Kieran Mulvey. After a lot of haggling, Kieran had brokered a deal between us and the OCI. The OCI had yielded ground and accepted an independent on their inquiry. I wanted to nominate Ken Spratt. That was a runner. Kieran prepared an agreed text as follows:

> *The Minister for Transport, Tourism and Sport, Mr Shane Ross TD, and the Olympic Council of Ireland (OCI) have agreed that the Minister will appoint an independent person to join the two OCI officers as part of the investigating team in relation to the issue of Olympic ticketing which arose during the Rio Games. It is expected that the investigation will produce a completed report within 6 weeks of the end of the Rio Games.*

It was a major U-turn by the OCI. But Hickey was tricky. Suddenly, he wanted to clear it with his executive, a body never regarded in the past as anything but a rubber stamp. Then there was silence for the remainder of the day.

Pat Hickey dined that night with Kieran Mulvey and John Treacy. By all accounts he was in good form. Italy's Hospitality House was as good as it gets in Rio. He had invited me to the dinner at our meeting on Sunday night, but I had subsequently declined. Little did he know what awaited him in the hours ahead. During that evening Mulvey had asked him several times to close the deal with us. He had agreed, but said he needed to secure the formal support of his executive. Possibly a first.

Events scuppered the deal.

Ruth and I were out for a walk on the pavement alongside Copacabana Beach soon after 7 a.m. the next morning when the lights on my mobile phone began going ballistic. Pat Hickey had been arrested. We were stunned. The reason clearly related to the ticket-touting scandal.

The news was already travelling around the world by the time we got back to our hotel. Ken was outside the front door. He had just committed the worst sin in the civil service bible: he had lost his minister. When he spotted us returning, he was suddenly a picture of visible relief. The Irish ambassador had been in touch; he would be giving Hickey consular assistance.

There was an unexpected pang of pity running through our hearts when we learned that Hickey had been arrested in humiliating circumstances. When arrested in his hotel at six o'clock in the morning, he was in his dressing gown and the police photographs from the scene had been flashed across the globe. His wife was distraught. He was thousands of miles from home and probably being held in bad conditions in a Brazilian jail. There was a question mark around his health.

For Hickey, innocent or guilty, this was a personal tragedy. Twenty-four hours earlier he had been mixing with captains and kings at medal ceremonies. Twelve hours after that, he had been dining with Ireland's top sports chiefs in one of Rio's top restaurants. Today he was alone in a Brazilian jail. We may have been at loggerheads, but I would not wish such a fate on anyone. We awaited news of Hickey from Brian Glynn, Ireland's superb ambassador to Brazil.

The news came. Hickey had been taken to hospital with a heart condition. He had complained of cardiac problems after his arrest and was being medically examined as a precautionary measure.

In the meantime, what was the correct action for a Sports minister and a senior official caught in this upheaval? It was an *annus horribilis* for Irish sport and for many of Ireland's Olympic competitors. Should we stay in solidarity with them and concern for Hickey, now in Rio's Samaritano Hospital, or go home to set up our own independent inquiry in a drive to salvage Ireland's rapidly tanking reputation?

After consultation with Aisling Dunne in Dublin and others at home, it seemed the right course was to return to Ireland. The OCI inquiry was obviously now dead in the water. No organisation could run an inquiry into ticket touting in parallel — or even in competition — while its president was facing serious charges, including alleged ticket touting, tax evasion and money laundering, overseas. We, now more than ever, needed to hold our own independent inquiry to ascertain the facts and satisfy public disquiet in Ireland and scrutiny from overseas.

The opposition were making hay at home. It was open season on the absent minister whom Hickey had sent packing. They condemned Hickey for his arrogance, but savaged me for allowing him to send me away empty-handed. Little did they know that on the day Hickey was arrested, we were on the point of announcing that he had done a U-turn and had agreed to appoint an independent member to the inquiry team.

That was water under the bridge now. Our inquiry had to be established immediately. In the August news vacuum, the saga of Ireland's Olympic Games woes featured far too prominently in the media for all the wrong reasons.

I remembered Paschal Donohoe's words of advice: that it would have been wrong for the Minister for Sport not to go to Rio. I had anticipated a week of medals for Ireland, of pleasure mixed with a modicum of hard work. Instead, I had to tell Ruth that we were packing our bags after just three days in Brazil. She had not even had time to visit the statue of Christ the Redeemer, high over Rio.

Ken made the necessary arrangements. We would leave that night on a long flight through Paris. We would arrive in Dublin on Thursday afternoon. Attorney General Máire

Whelan would be meeting us on Friday to discuss arrangements for the inquiry.

Dublin airport was a media scrum. There was a sense of high drama but the event was an anticlimax after Hickey's arrest. Nothing new emerged. Most questions were about the type of inquiry it would be, whether or not Hickey had put me back in my box, and if I had spoken to Enda.

I hadn't. My Fine Gael colleagues had been conspicuous by their failure to defend me in my absence. One or two of them even mischievously suggested that the entire issue should go, out of my hands, to an Oireachtas committee for examination. Most were silent, thoroughly enjoying my obvious discomfort.

The Taoiseach may have been one of them. We had not met since our early summer spats, but relations had not improved. On the Thursday evening he rang, proposing that I have a good night's sleep, set up the inquiry the next day and report to him. He pointedly suggested that, this time, I listen carefully to Máire Whelan. He was certainly not throwing plaudits in my direction for cleaning up Irish sport.

What could I expect? I had shown little loyalty to my Blueshirt bedfellows when challenging them publicly only six weeks earlier over the appointment of Fine Gael insider Andrew McDowell. Or a few days later when Finian, John and I had ridden roughshod over Máire Whelan's opinion on Mick Wallace's bill on abortion. Now Máire was suddenly back in my life. Ironically, I now needed her legal opinion — exactly what I had dismissed as of limited value only six weeks earlier. The media was not slow to point out that the reckless minister, who had defied the Attorney General, was now beholden to her. Miriam Lord in the *Irish Times* eviscerated me in an article headed 'Shane Ross rediscovers value of AG's advice'. Touché.

And worse: of all things, I needed a willing judge. Given my crusade against the current political process to appoint judges, no beak from the bench was likely to find my approaches to chair an inquiry irresistible. Máire Whelan would be able to deliver the right judge for the job. The boot was now on the other foot. Last month I had rubbished Máire's opinion. This month I needed it. If the inquiry hit the buffers, there was real trouble ahead. It had taken only six weeks for me to get my comeuppance.

I had already sounded out former High Court president, Judge Nicholas Kearns, phoning him before heading for Rio. I asked him if he would be interested in serving as an independent member of the OCI inquiry. He expressed an interest and I promised to contact him, if necessary, over the coming days. I knew little of Nicky Kearns' expertise in this field, but clearly remembered playing cards with him — for high stakes — many years earlier in a poker school mostly made up of well-heeled senior counsel. From memory, he was a better lawyer than a card player.

As the controversy deepened following the showdown with Hickey, Nicky had sent me a text saying that he was watching the story, but advising me to consult with the Attorney General.

On 19 August, Patrick O'Donovan, Ken Spratt and I met in my office in Leeson Lane with the Attorney General, her officials and Department of Foreign Affairs staff to decide the nature of the inquiry. The Attorney General was professional to the last syllable. It was her once derided, but now desperately needed, 'professional opinion' that it should be a non-statutory inquiry, to be carried out by a retired judge. We could appoint the judge as early as the following week when the terms of reference were made public. Máire Whelan was all business, no sign of hostility towards me, nor any detectable suggestion of sweet revenge.

Patrick and I gratefully grasped the nettle. We did not explore which judge should be approached on that day, but knew there was now a whole inquiries industry being staffed by under-worked, retired judges.

Patrick and I held a press conference to announce the posi-tive result of our deliberations. Once again, I received a grilling from the media, puzzlingly antagonistic to my actions over the last two weeks. I reflected that night: why was I getting such stick from the Fourth Estate for the Rio venture? Was it just an ingrained, knee-jerk response to what they saw as my normal arrogance?

It seemed to defy logic. I had done some pretty dumb things in my political life and been rightly denounced by the media. This time, they had portrayed the showdown with Hickey as a contest between an amateur and a professional. They were right. They fired flak in my direction for leading with my chin by publicly demanding concessions from Hickey which had put him in an impossible position. I had left him no wriggle room. I was out of my depth, they said, fencing with a wily fox who had swatted away my predecessors in the Department of Sport.

Yet, after the showdown, where were we? Hickey had already resigned — albeit supposedly temporarily — his posi-tion as president of the OCI. His own inquiry was dead in the water and we were setting up our own fully independent inves-tigation. The OCI had suddenly promised to co-operate with it. A week ago, they were refusing to give us as much as a seat on their own internal probe. OCI reforms were on the way. Were we not winning?

That weekend saw further dramatic developments in Brazil. On 21 August, the Brazilian police seized the passports of OCI representatives Dermot Henehan, Stephen Martin and the dele-gation's *chef de mission*, Kevin Kilty. It also sought the passports of vice president Willie O'Brien and Linda O'Reilly, Hickey's personal assistant, both of whom had left the country in the nick of time the day before. And finally, the court wanted the passport of Football Association of Ireland boss, John Delaney, who doubled as a vice president of the OCI. Delaney had not yet arrived in Rio and, somewhat wisely, decided that it might not be the most hospitable location for him to rest his head at that particular moment.

On 22 August the OCI appointed a crisis subcommittee to respond to the situation in Brazil. It consisted of board members Sarah Keane from Swim Ireland, Professor Ciarán Ó Catháin of Athletics Ireland and Robert Norwood of Snowsports Association of Ireland. In a statement they committed to appoint an international accountancy firm to conduct an independent review of ticketing arrangements in Rio. Its work would begin immediately. Significantly for us, its report would be handed over to the judge chosen by the government to chair the state inquiry into the OCI's handling of ticketing at the Rio Olympics.

Within just eight days, the OCI had changed the guard. Hickey had been disowned.

It was time for us to speedily establish our own inquiry and appoint a judge. I had spoken to Enda Kenny over the weekend and he was keen to see the controversy removed from the headlines. A text had arrived on Saturday from Nicholas Kearns: 'Shane, just in case my name is under consideration for inquiry announced yesterday, must advise that while I was willing to be added as independent member of the OCI inquiry, subsequent events and format now envisaged rule me out for all sorts of reasons, regards Nicky.'

Nicky was not going to tog out. It was back to the Attorney General to suggest a suitable judge. I was beginning to see the merits of Máire Whelan.

I was not disappointed. Within three days, we had scrutinised and approved the qualifications of former High Court judge Carroll Moran. He had hardly ever seen controversy. I immediately asked Aisling to 'Blueshirt proof' him to ensure that he had none of the links to Fine Gael so much enjoyed by many other judges. If Pat Hickey or any of his band of loyalists had been able to suggest that Moran had Fine Gael connections, it could have been fatal. If the judge's report had then favoured the government's narrative, it would have instantly been dismissed as flawed.

Moran never received criticism on that score. Or on any other that we could find. He had been seventeen years in the Circuit Court before serving in the High Court. He had retired a year earlier, in 2015. If any criticism could be levelled at him, it might have been that he had never made any waves. He was solid, scrupulous and worthy. That was exactly what we needed.

Moran's report was due to be finished in twelve weeks. It was delayed by nine months till August 2017 due to the refusal of Hickey, the IOC and other key players to give evidence. The boycott by key figures certainly hampered its progress. Yet it highlighted a shambolic corporate governance regime at the OCI. It pointed out that Hickey ran the OCI himself, merely informing his colleagues of important decisions, rather than consulting with them. It found that tickets assigned for friends and families of competitors were instead, shamefully, allocated by the OCI to authorised ticket reseller, Pro10, to sell on. The athletes' families were shabbily treated. Pro10 was to get all forty-six family tickets for the opening and closing ceremonies. Judge Moran found that the Irish supporters were neglected. His report declared that the OCI had shown 'more concern for the commercial interests of the Authorised Ticket Seller (ATR) than for the interests of the athletes, their friends, relatives and supporters or those of the spectating public.'

Carroll Moran found that the close relationship between Hickey and Marcus Evans, the owner of authorised ticket seller

THG Sports, had continued despite Hickey's efforts to conceal it by suggesting that their contact had ended in 2014.

The report could, quite rightly, not stray into the sphere of criminal activity. It didn't. That was being addressed elsewhere, but Carroll Moran did the state a service. His report was the catalyst for reform of the Olympic Council of Ireland. It exposed one of the most powerful sports bodies in Ireland as being unfit for purpose. It accelerated the reform process that enabled the government to restore funding to the new OCI after we had stopped it, while Hickey's regime imploded. It helped to restore our reputation abroad. We were not looking for blood, merely good corporate behaviour, fair treatment for athletes and transparency. If serious, specific wrongs had been committed, they would have to be decided in another forum. The demand for an independent inquiry had let the genie out of the bottle. We were on the road to reform.

Pat Hickey was released from Bangu Prison after eleven days. He was not allowed to leave Brazil until December, when he returned to Ireland after putting up €410,000 in bail money. This vast sum was raised by a loan to him from the Association of National Olympic Committees of which he was vice president. Luckily for him, the Olympic movement has deep pockets. In February 2020, the full €410,000 loan was written off 'on medical and humanitarian grounds'. Hickey continues to protest his innocence, although few observers expect that, one way or another, his trial in Brazil will ever go ahead.

Hickey's fall from grace is no reason for those of us who crossed swords with him to feel satisfaction. His story is a classic tale of people losing the run of themselves. It is yet another example, so common in Ireland, of the consequences of organisations, banks, companies, sports bodies, and even charities, falling into the hands of one person. The rot inevitably sets in.

Hickey is a Dublin Northsider. He came from modest, but hardly humble, beginnings. He was educated at St Vincent's Christian Brothers School, Glasnevin. He never received a third-level education but went into auctioneering and insurance, establishing a family firm in Dublin's Dorset Street. Little is known of the success or otherwise of his small company, but more is recorded about his meteoric success in navigating the maze of organisations that make up the opaque world of the Olympics. His power base was the unlikely sport of judo, for which he has a black belt. In 1979, he became president of the Irish Judo Association and managed Ireland's judo team in the 1984 Olympics. In 1989, he became honorary life president of the Irish Judo Association. In the same year, at the age of forty-four, he was elected president of the Olympic Council of Ireland, a position he was to hold for twenty-seven years.

Hickey was virtually impregnable as president of the OCI. He quickly realised that the vote of each small sports body, like judo, equalled the vote of the larger ones, like boxing or athletics. He cornered the smaller, poorer, sports federations and ensured that they received adequate recognition and their share of the spoils. They reciprocated by voting him back into power until his downfall in 2016.

His long tenure was not without challenges. In 2001, Richard Burrows, a first-class sailor, a joint managing director at Pernod Ricard and former boss at Irish Distillers, and future Governor of the Bank of Ireland, very unwisely challenged Hickey for the top job. At the time, Burrows was one of Irish business' magic circle, on an enormous salary, a member of all the right clubs and a pillar of smart society. Hickey brilliantly played the role of the small sports' champion against the plutocrat from the mighty Bank of Ireland. The small sports rallied to his cause. He buried Burrows, winning by 27 votes to 10, ensuring that no serious challenge to his position ever arose afterwards.

He was a master networker. He assiduously worked the highest ranks on the elitist Olympic circuit. He was *chef de mission* of the Irish team in Seoul in 1988 and in Barcelona in 1992. After the break-up of the Soviet Union in 1991, he cultivated the smaller Eastern European countries. In turn they, like the small sporting clubs in Ireland, looked after him. The result was his election to the inner circle, the IOC executive, in 2012. In his own words, 'I became very popular in the East.' He reciprocated by single-handedly leading the drive for the European Games which he delivered in the human rights blackspot of Baku in 2015.

Baku was not his finest hour. Journalist Nick Cohen of the *Guardian* was deadly in his criticism of Hickey's involvement. 'This weekend,' wrote Cohen, 'marks a dismal low in the rotten history of modern sport. The Olympics movement is holding the first "European Games" in Baku, Azerbaijan. In theory they are meant to sit alongside the All-Africa, Pan-American and Asian games, and give Europe a continental tournament between the full Olympics. In practice, there's no need for them. Olympic sports already have their European championships.

'But — and you will only understand the seedy imperative that drives a disgraceful tournament when you grasp this — the European Olympic committees do not control the rival competitions. They wanted a piece of the action. And in an effort to find it, Patrick Hickey, the EOC's Irish president, showed how he could move from being unctuous to unscrupulous without pausing for breath as he toured the borderlands of Europe looking for any tyrant with money to spare.'

Cohen continued: 'First he tried to woo the dictator of Belarus. He charmed Alexander Lukashenko and gave the murderous old brute an award for his "Outstanding Contribution to the Olympic Movement". His flattery was in vain. Lukashenko's ill-governed country was too poor to afford the games. So Hickey headed to the mafia state of Azerbaijan, whose ruling Aliyev crime family will spend whatever looted petrodollars it takes to win international prestige.'

Cohen didn't pull his punches. Hickey was soft on dictators and tyrants. Baku was Hickey's vanity project and the odd abuse of human rights by a tyrant or two wasn't going to halt his bid for glory.

Hickey spoke openly and with pride of his relationship with heads of state and aristocrats. He boasted about his friendship with Putin. He was proud of being his special guest at the London Olympics judo competition in 2012. He referred to his 'great friend and mentor' the former OCI and IOC chair, Lord Killanin.

When he was escorting me round the medal ceremonies on that windy day in August 2016, less than twenty-four hours before his arrest, he was full of the hubris that provoked his ultimate demise. He never stopped mentioning his friendship with the royals, the rich and the powerful. It was constantly as if he was saying, 'Look at me, here in Rio, a bigshot on the world stage. The boy from St Vincent's CBS in Glasnevin has made it into the global big time. And nobody seems to recognise it.'

He had confronted Irish sports ministers before. He had loathed Fianna Fáil's Jim McDaid and successfully defied him on an accreditation issue at the Sydney Olympic Games in 2000. In 1999, he had publicly fought with Fine Gael Minister Bernard Allen over who should distribute sports funds.

Pat Hickey was a difficult character for a minister to confront. He was an egotistical cog in a very influential wheel, the IOC, which considered itself to be above politics. He confused the trappings of power, brought about by lashings of money, with power itself, brought about by a popular mandate.

On 31 August 2017, the OCI met in Dublin. Following the publication of the Moran report, it voted unanimously not to reinstate Hickey. The organisation that he had built up into a powerful force on the Irish and international stage had turned its back on him.

5

Gaffes Galore

'CAN I BORROW your mobile?' my grandson Ed asked me one Sunday lunchtime in June 2019. I don't really approve of computer games, but I am not yet hardened enough to refuse simple requests from grandchildren, so I willingly handed over the gadget. I knew Ed's form. He was occupied for the afternoon.

After lunch, I glanced over at him, lovingly. My other five grandkids were well sorted watching sport on the box, playing the piano, or running around in the garden. It was a contented scene. I glowed with pleasure at the sight of such a happy occasion.

In the late afternoon, we went through the ritual, slightly formal farewells. Ed thanked me and returned my mobile. Everyone left for home, laden with half the uneaten chocolate puds or meringues.

I settled down with the dreaded Sunday newspapers, in no hurry to read them. It had been a bad week, but at least it had ended well, within the bosom of my supportive family, all thankfully oblivious to the trials of being a minister.

First, I decided to check my messages. All week they had been bearing bad news, so I switched on the mobile. The screenshot had vanished. Gone was the shot of two of my grandkids which I had carried around fondly and dewy-eyed. Instead, I was confronted by the sight of myself.

Unfortunately, the screenshot was a picture of the minister in a rather unlikely situation. There I was, beaming down at a scene from the Bible. Shane Ross was a priest at the virgin birth. There he was, the baby Jesus, laid in a manger. The three kings and the cattle were looking on.

As a technophobe, I had no idea how to remove the image. The wretched thing was stuck there mocking me for days. Eventually, I had the courage to show it to someone. Aisling removed it with a disapproving silence.

If I could have got hold of my suddenly less-than-beloved grandson Ed at that moment, I would have multiplied his lexicon of profanities on the spot. Even the babes and sucklings knew what had been happening that week. The Minister for Transport, Tourism and Sport had been out at Dublin airport chasing the limelight courtesy of Katie Taylor.

I had been caught red-handed, nakedly seeking a photo op with Katie, stalking her around the arrivals hall. Social media had gone wild. Suddenly I was being Photoshopped into the moon landing, in the White House with Donald Trump, into the boxing ring with Muhammad Ali and at the Open Championship at Portrush with Shane Lowry. The wits in the Dáil bar were having a ball superimposing me into any big event in the history of the universe. There were unflattering comparisons with former Taoiseach Charlie Haughey, when he jetted off to Paris to be photographed with Stephen Roche after he had won the Tour de France in 1987. Certainly, Haughey never got the same slagging as I did.

It was well deserved. Katie, a heroine of mine since her career began, had become the undisputed lightweight champion of the world, beating Delfine Persoon in Madison Square Garden. The inevitable question arose. Should she be given a hero's welcome at the airport? I was as keen as mustard. Her flight was due in Dublin airport early on the Tuesday morning, 4 June. I asked

Minister of State for Sport, Brendan Griffin, if he would like to join me in the greeting, but he had engagements in Kerry.

Airport homecomings for sporting icons were usually a public relations penalty kick. I had greeted returning footballers from the Euros in 2016, the triumphant women's hockey players from the London Olympics in August 2018 and Team Ireland off the plane from the Special Olympics in Abu Dhabi in March 2019. They liked the recognition, and they deserved it. And believe me, I didn't mind the limelight. Ireland was in the middle of a sporting golden age. Good news events were rare in my Department of Industrial Strife and Stress, so Katie Taylor's victory was an opportunity to celebrate.

There was always a potential downside to the airport jamborees. I was in danger of being the worst in the world if I did not meet every Irish sporting hero returning from an overseas success. In truth, nearly all our sportsmen and sportswomen are wonderful ambassadors for Ireland. Besides, in this case the Lord Mayor of Dublin, Nial Ring, was mischievously volunteering to compete for the privilege of formally welcoming Katie home. The independent councillor from the inner city had announced that he would be 'thrilled' to host something in the Mansion House 'if Shane Ross doesn't give her the recognition she deserves'. Ring went on, 'Women like Katie and our own Kellie Harrington (whom the Minister ignored and I stepped in and organised DCC to give a civic reception) are blazing a trail and we need to recognise and acknowledge their amazing achievements.'

I would certainly have been damned from a height if I had ignored Katie. So I trotted out to Dublin airport on the Tuesday. I had to go airside to welcome the new world champion before she came through to meet the fans. As I waited, I recalled how private she was, how reluctant to have any homecoming at all. My team in the department had been chasing her for months to honour her at a private lunch. We had twisted her arm. An airport staffer told me that there was no chauffeur-driven car waiting for Katie's arrival, not even a taxi. Her own car was sitting in the long-stay car park.

I was in an exuberant mood, relishing the prospect of greeting Katie and enjoying a media bonus. I met her and her mother airside where both politely said they remembered the dark day we had met on the street in Rio after her shock defeat there.

And then we hit the waiting crowd. It was an unforgettable moment. Instead of bowing out after a few pictures, I behaved like a teenager with an idol in tow. I stuck to the hero of the day like a limpet. Was I conscious of the cameras? You bet I was, determined to feature in the pictures with Ireland's most successful sportswoman ever. It was a golden, unmissable opportunity, never to be repeated. I also had my civil servant-approved congratulatory script ready to deliver when Katie was able to pause for breath.

Never before in the history of political public relations stunts has an Irish politician been battered by a bigger boomerang. It was totally self-inflicted. Social media went berserk. The story became how the minister gatecrashed Katie's homecoming. A whole industry of memes sprung up overnight. It certainly gave friend and foe infinite openings for their creative juices. They took the mick unmercifully, but fortunately most of the memes were happily humorous.

In truth, my behaviour was pretty shameless. It was a mega-gaffe. Even my grandchildren kept their heads down, but at least one of them sounded a firm warning on my screensaver.

It was not my finest hour.

Pride comes before a fall. It is the oldest rule in politics.

On St Patrick's Day 2018, I was fortunate to have bought three tickets for one of Ireland's greatest sporting moments:

the Grand Slam rugby match against England in Twickenham. It was billed as a tough away fixture against the old enemy. To attend was the opportunity of a lifetime. To win would be unmitigated paradise.

Paradise arrived on St Patrick's Day. We beat England 24-15 in freezing wet weather. I decided to head to the airport after the match. The high jinks on the plane back to Dublin were all good-humoured. On the aircraft I took a bit of harmless ribbing from strangers for various ministerial lapses. Par for the course from a group of victorious rugby supporters.

The next day I was booked to meet Ireland's Grand Slam team at a celebration in Dublin's Shelbourne Hotel. I am not so sure the winning squad were as keen to meet the minister as much as the minister was to meet them, but that is the price they pay for being sporting celebrities. Politicians want to meet you, and to be photographed with you. I am an incurable sinner in that department.

The Shelbourne was a low-key reception. I greeted captain Rory Best off the bus. We held the Championship Trophy aloft. He did his painful duty of being photobombed by the minister.

No media was present at the reception. Keeping my eyes open for a photo op, I spotted Johnny Sexton and Rob Kearney sitting quietly on a sofa, glasses in hand. The last thing they wanted was for a wandering minister to disturb their quiet moment of private glory, but that is what those unfortunate conquerors got. They knew what was coming. I swear they looked sideways as I approached. We had been talking of the Grand Slam triumph for only a few seconds when I popped the question. Johnny Sexton, never a candidate for a career in Iveagh House, sighed out loud.

Wearily, the heroes of the day before stood and posed for the mandatory picture. As it happened, happily for the two lads, I had little time to linger. I needed to hotfoot it to the FAI football awards at the RTÉ studios that night. Another opportunity beckoned for some favourable media coverage. I was on a roll.

Under a bit of pressure, I headed for Government Buildings to change into a dinner jacket. But in haste I decided to post the picture of Sexton and Kearney — with me in the middle of course — on Twitter. It was too good a chance to waste. These guys, the toast of the nation, had just won the Grand Slam. So I hurriedly took to Twitter and sauntered into the FAI gig knowing that any media coverage of the FAI gig would be a bonus.

Every Irish fan must now know what happened. By the end of the evening the swagger had left my step. When I stepped out of the FAI awards, my mobile was hopping. Ken Spratt, the department's top sport official, was ringing.

'Minister,' he opened politely. That was enough. I instantly knew this was serious. First it was a Sunday night, not a normal time for a civil servant to call but, far more ominously, Ken called me 'Minister' only when Pat Hickey had been arrested or when the world was about to cave in. He respectfully asked if I had been doing my own social media that night.

My heart sank. 'Minister,' he went on, 'you put up a tweet of you, Johnny Sexton and Rob Kearney. Unfortunately you got the wrong Kearney. You said it was Dave, not Rob. We have been trying to contact you for hours to correct it. The reaction on social media is, er, very active.'

I decided to read the tweet again. There it was, 'Congratulations and welcome home this evening to superstars Johnny Sexton and Dave Kearney.'

On my arrival at the department, I had made a rule never to swear in front of civil servants, but I nearly broke it that night. As rapidly as I could, I turned to the Twitter account. The tweet was providing endless enjoyment to celebrating rugby fans all over Ireland and beyond. I watched as the number of comments on social media leapt by the minute. Ken had suggested that

I take down the tweet, but I didn't know how to remove the wretched thing. Laboriously and in a cold sweat, I deleted it under instruction and put up an amended tweet. I was attempting damage limitation. It was too late. The howler had taken off. Rob Kearney himself had already decided to respond, extremely wittily to boot, 'You're welcome, Leo,' adding fuel to the already blazing fire.

My second tweet read: 'Oops! Wrong Kearney!! Last tweet said pic was Sexton and Dave, but it's Rob. Kearney replied, "Thanks, Leo!" Touché. Congrats again.' But my attempt to take control did little to quell enthusiasm online for my faux pas.

So happy was Rob with his handiwork that he even followed it up with another gentle jibe. Two days later, he announced that he had signed a new contract for Leinster and the IRFU until November 2019. This time he took to Instagram with a timely dig, 'Delighted to have signed on with @leinsterrugby and @irishrugby until November 19 — lots done, more to do!! Cheers, Dave.'

It was great craic, but it threw more petrol on a fire I was frantically trying to quench.

There was no quenching this one. It was an inferno.

It was the sort of gaffe the tabloids love. On the Monday morning, a headline appeared of such skill that it later won the 'Headline of the Year' award. On the front page of the *Irish Daily Star* appeared possibly the most brilliant piece of word-juggling of the 2018 sports season. Blazoned across the cover of the tabloid were the words 'CHILLY WRONG KEARNEY' beside the picture I had posted of Sexton, Kearney and me on Twitter. It was a fair cop. Journalist Keith Falkiner and headline writer John Mitchell clearly had a lot of fun with it. So did the nation.

The Members' Bar is the Holy of Holies in Leinster House. Deputies and senators go there to plot, and sometimes to escape the eagle eyes of the media and the public. Unlikely alliances are formed there over lunch or a pint. Secret deals are struck. There are dark corners in one annex where deputies can be hidden from sight.

Over the years a potential trip to North Korea was cooked up in the Members' Bar. Despite the furore it caused, that is almost as far as it ever went. When in Opposition from 2011 to 2016, Finian McGrath, John Halligan and I had long spoken of our desire to visit that troubled peninsula. I was fascinated by the last hard-line Marxist state, still closed to the rest of the world. John Halligan had tenuous links to North Korea through his mentor, Seán Garland, former president of the Workers' Party. Finian, as a follower of Castro's Cuba and Che Guevara, would probably carry street cred in a Marxist regime. Similarly, he had frequently promised to organise a trip for us to Havana to observe the joys of Castro's rule. More frequently, we spoke with curiosity of going to North Korea's capital, Pyongyang. All such talk was restricted to the three of us in the Members' Bar. It was an entertaining secret daydream which stretched the bounds of reality to the limits.

No such secrecy applied in the Leinster House public café next door. It was a danger zone where public, press and politicians met. I regularly went in there for breakfast. One day in November 2017, I was just leaving after bacon and eggs, muesli and fruit when the Sinn Féin TD for Waterford, David Cullinane, called over to me, 'Where's Halligan?' I had a good, jovial relationship with both John and David Cullinane, rival Waterford deputies.

'I think he's on his way to Thailand,' I responded, adding jokingly: 'The longer John spends out of the country, the less difficulty we'll have with the weekly votes.' (We regularly jested that it was best if John was travelling for Ireland at the time of crucial votes in the Dáil.)

'What's he doing out there?' Cullinane asked.

'Dunno. Anyway, he'll be able to prepare for our trip to North Korea while he's there.'

Cullinane asked if we had plans to go to North Korea, to which I replied, almost casually, that the three amigos — John, Finian and I — were considering a jaunt out to see Kim Jong-un.

I must have taken leave of my senses. I looked at the man opposite Cullinane at the table. To my horror, I saw the smiling, triumphant face of Senan Molony, political editor of the *Irish Daily Mail*. I fled without even acknowledging Senan. He had a scoop. It was my first big blunder, of many.

True to form, Senan Molony worked the phones that day. He rang John, Finian and many others, including the Korean Embassy in London. John and Finian innocently confirmed the story. They gave good reasons why a peace mission would be helpful: we were a neutral country; independents could help a peace process. We had welcomed at least one cultural visit to Waterford from North Korea already. Others, like the Dáil's rent-a-mouth, Fine Gael backbench TD Noel Rock, responded to Senan's call with words of unhelpful advice.

Next day, the splash on the front page of the *Irish Daily Mail* read: 'HALLIGAN PLANS PEACE MISSION TO DISARM KIM. Dáil team hopes to "reduce tension" in North Korea.' Senan Molony's story was accompanied by two large photographs of John Halligan and Kim Jong-un. Inside the paper, all three of us featured.

There was almost instant pandemonium in the Department of Foreign Affairs. I spoke to Minister Simon Coveney, who was far from amused with all three of us. Apparently, at least forty foreign embassies had already phoned Iveagh House asking if there had been a change in government policy. Were three ministers really heading for Pyongyang on a 'peace mission'?

In a normal administration, we might all have been sacked on the spot. But the loss of three ministers would have ended the life of the Varadkar government. Neither the Taoiseach nor the Tánaiste had been kept in touch with our supposed plans. In truth, we were still only kicking around the idea. Until my big mouth opened up.

Over the weekend we were savaged by the mainstream and social media. On Monday, 6 November, the Taoiseach was asked about it. He was characteristically calm, merely saying that there would be no government mission going to North Korea. He then qualified the statement by insisting that 'I am not the keeper of any of my ministers, so if they wish to travel to North Korea, I am not going to send anyone to stop them at the airport, but certainly it won't be a government one.' He did not sound as though he wanted us to book return tickets.

Halligan insisted that it was intended as a cultural tour, a formula that had broken down barriers in the past. I tried to point out that it was a table tennis team that had, in 1971, ended the Cold War between the United States and China, but there was an avalanche of hostile opinion crashing down all around us. The media was almost unanimously hostile, some calling for our heads. Our less adventurous Independent Alliance colleagues, Boxer Moran and Seán Canney, were not amused. We were in retreat, but still standing and managed to survive the weekend.

As the next week opened, another blow landed. It emerged that John Halligan's department had lost an employment case taken by an interviewee for a job. The woman had been asked inappropriate questions and the Department of Business, Enterprise and Innovation was fined €7,500 by the Workplace Relations Commission. Unfortunately, the man who had put the wrong question to the woman candidate was none other than the minister himself. John had asked the prospective candidate to become his private secretary if she was married and had children.

There was fury in the Dáil. All parties joined the lynch mob. Brendan Howlin pressed the Labour button of outrage, Fine Gael TD Kate O'Connell was 'disgusted', Fianna Fáil's equality spokesperson, Fiona O'Loughlin, called John's remarks 'deeply offensive'. He was being battered all round.

Tánaiste Frances Fitzgerald formally apologised to the woman on behalf of the government. Everybody was distancing themselves from John Halligan. The reaction was particularly cowardly because he was in Thailand. Some were looking for blood. Fine Gael was not helping, hanging John out to dry.

Hypocrisy emerged everywhere. John had certainly made a mistake and he admitted it. He insisted with his apology to the woman that his only interest was in providing flexible hours for those who needed them. He was a good employer, as any of his former staff will testify.

More importantly, anyone who has known John for more than twenty minutes will be aware that he hasn't got a drop of sexist, racist or sectarian blood in his body. He has championed women's rights, a woman's right to choose, LGBTQ rights, feminism in all its forms, and has a genuine respect for people of all genders. He has even led the battle for transgender rights in the Dáil. Any time I travelled to his Waterford constituency, the visit was always notable for the flock of women surrounding him in his office, in his constituency work and in his social life. John is a magnet for women, based not on flirtation but on recognition that he is someone who is fearlessly on their side.

The rats were leaving the sinking ship. So I was delighted that RTÉ's *Prime Time* rang that Thursday afternoon, when John was taking such pressure. In his absence in the Far East, would someone be available to defend him on the programme? He had shouldered the brunt of the blame for my North Korea gaffe and was now being pilloried for a mistake that was no resigning matter. John had walked through hot coals for me in tight situations in the previous eighteen months. The former Workers' Party TD was my closest ally in the Dáil. It was payback time from the stockbroker to the Marxist. I took the *Prime Time* slot, insisting that John would be staying on. So were Finian and I. His was not a hanging offence. He went on to be a very fine minister of state. He knew the value of loyalty.

The North Korea trip was called off. The three amigos cheated the gallows.

They have thin skins, these Shinners. At least, some of them do.

Imagine handing a piece of propaganda on a plate to a Shinner. Worse still, imagine not expecting them to make full use of it.

During my time in the Dáil, I have had remarkably good relations with Sinn Féin. It was one thing voting the same way as them while we were all in opposition. It was another matter entirely to keep good lines of communication open with the parliamentary party when in government, especially when I was in partnership with the Shinners' bête noire, Fine Gael.

Sinn Féin behaved far more reasonably than Fianna Fáil when it came to putting reforming legislation through the Dáil. They agreed that there were flaws in the judicial system and supported my pet project, the Judicial Appointments Commission Bill. Fianna Fáil opposed it down to the last beak on the bench. Furthermore, I could never have advanced my bill on drink-driving without the responsible support of Sinn Féin. In both cases their votes carried the legislation through the Dáil and Seanad. I have enjoyed a good relationship with Mary Lou McDonald ever since we had both sat on the Public Accounts Committee in the 2011–16 government.

As a minister, I never expected Sinn Féin to pull their punches of course, but I also hoped that they would consider legislation on its merits rather than milk every bill for naked political advantage. Most of their TDs did.

Early in my term, I broke a Fine Gael taboo by regularly receiving delegations led by (or including) Sinn Féin TDs and senators. These included Gerry Adams, Pearse Doherty, Jonathan O'Brien, Pádraig Mac Lochlainn, Martin Kenny and Imelda Munster. I even enjoyed good relations with Martin Ferris, who had been sentenced to ten years for smuggling arms to Ireland on the *Marita Ann* in 1984. In 2016, one of its new deputies was Gerry Adams' running mate, Imelda Munster, the former councillor from Louth.

Imelda Munster gave me a pain in the head. I was aware that in 2016 exceptional talent wouldn't be essential for a successful result in the Louth constituency as Gerry Adams' running mate. Adams would carry a candidate over the line on his coattails. Gerry duly delivered a second Sinn Féin seat in the Dáil. Behold, the mighty Imelda.

Imelda, Sinn Féin's Transport spokesperson, was the least challenging opponent I ever encountered as a minister in Dáil Eireann. Independent Deputy Clare Daly would turn me upside down and inside out; Fianna Fáil's Transport spokesman, Robert Troy, occasionally drew blood; former Labour, then independent deputy Tommy Broughan was a wizard, who sometimes left me standing on road safety; Catherine Murphy was thorough where I was shallow; but give me Imelda any day. When Imelda rose to speak, a minister could relax. She picks a bit from her Sinn Féin brief and then begins to ramble all over the place. Her musings on the various transport industrial disputes were straight out of the trade unionist Dermot O'Leary School of megaphone solutions. When she was stuck (which she regularly was), Imelda would launch into a mantra that I was hell-bent on privatising the state's transport companies. I could take a breather in the certain knowledge that no one believed her. And no one was listening.

My Imelda experience reminded me of former UK Labour Chancellor Denis Healy's remark about debating with his opposite number, Sir Geoffrey Howe, Foreign Secretary in Margaret Thatcher's cabinet. The clever Chancellor observed that it was 'like being savaged by a dead sheep'. It was usually best to swat Imelda away. She provided the breathing space to prepare for the next question.

One morning in March 2019 I was going through my umpteenth Imelda experience. A trifle bored, maybe even tired and irritable, I decided to have a go. Imelda had been her usual self, complaining that I was incompetent, unable to do my job and blind to the sensitivities over the 'Green Card' issue. She threw in the kitchen sink, bemoaning my absence from a recent Transport Committee meeting and sarcastically thanked me for attending the Dáil given my work commitments! And finally, she hoped that I 'didn't have to miss my elevenses!'

It was one of her better efforts. Unfortunately, she had trivialised a serious Brexit problem, namely what would happen if motorists crossing the border with Northern Ireland were required to carry green cards as proof of insurance. For once I rose to the personal bait, playing straight into Imelda's hands.

Rounding on her, I began by pointing out that when the same issue, green cards, had been raised by her colleagues Aengus Ó Snodaigh and Pearse Doherty the previous evening, they were 'mature, sensible and constructive'. I continued confidently, 'As I said, I thought that what they were doing before the Deputy came in last night — and she was late again today — was something very constructive. They were representing their communities.'

I warmed to my theme of comparing her efforts with those of her more credible Sinn Féin colleagues, provocatively adding that they were 'like thoroughbreds in a horse race'. And then turning to her, fatally, I became intoxicated by the eloquence of my own analogies; 'and you came in as you normally do, and you're like a donkey in the last race, at the last fence. You upset the whole apple cart.'

The Leas-Cheann Comhairle, Pat "the Cope" Gallagher, called on me to use parliamentary language. Imelda seemed unruffled, claiming that if 'the minister wanted to be personal to mask his own overall incompetence, that is fine. I can take it.' But she couldn't. She added, at her most profound, 'He is a disgrace.'

The Leas-Cheann Comhairle asked me 'to forget about donkeys'. Imelda seemed content. We went on for another twenty-five minutes. Imelda made several inane interruptions over that period. There were no demands for an apology, but I smelled trouble. I saw Imelda's opportunity before she did. The 'D' word was a big blunder.

When I left the chamber, I met the government's deputy press secretary, Catherine Halloran. 'How goes Donkeygate?' she asked mischievously. Suddenly I realised. She told me that the incident had taken off. Social media was in full flight and the Sinn Féin trolls were working up a frenzy. I had handed Imelda a weapon to beat me with. When I arrived back in my office, Aisling simply sighed supportively. She knew it was not important, but it was another own goal.

Imelda Munster was never the fastest on the uptake. It was not long, though, before she grasped the potential for a bit of media attention. She demanded an apology. After she had returned to the world of Sinn Féin, she had discovered a dose of outrage. In a statement she accused me of name-calling in the chamber. She seized the moral high ground, asking 'what message does this send out to other women who may have an interest in getting involved in politics? I believe that Minister Ross should apologise for his distasteful remarks.'

Others joined in. Imelda alleged that the remark was something I would never say to a man. She was milking it.

She gave an outraged interview to RTÉ's *Drivetime* and, no doubt, to others.

I was determined that this gaffe was not going to be followed by the usual token apology. I would have preferred to apologise to Danny Healy-Rae for offending his vintner supporters. I swore it would never happen. I had called many people much worse. I was sorry all right, sorry because I had made a blunder by rising to the bait of an amateur like Imelda. An apology to the most hopeless parliamentarian in the Sinn Féin pack would be the ultimate humiliation. No way.

Unfortunately, I received a more mature message from a man thirty years my junior. Leo Varadkar thought I should kick the issue off the pitch. He was not disapproving, but he felt it was just efficient politics to bury the spat before it got legs. Otherwise, it would linger for longer. Frothing at the mouth, I sent out an apology to RTÉ.

Adams' running mate responded by demanding that I apologise in the Dáil chamber. She wrote to the Dáil's Committee on Procedure asking to have the 'donkey' dig removed from the record. The clerk wrote to me asking me to consider it. (Over a year later, I have not yet replied. The equine comment remains on the Dáil record.)

The seventeenth of November 2018 was possibly one of the greatest games of all time for Irish rugby. A historic 16-9 victory for Ireland over New Zealand at the Aviva Stadium was our first ever victory over the All Blacks on Irish soil.

The atmosphere at the Aviva was euphoric. Jacob Stockdale scored the only Irish try in the forty-seventh minute. The All Blacks never went over the Irish line, the first time in twenty years they had failed to score a try. We dreamed openly about maybe even winning the World Cup in Tokyo in 2019. Who was going to beat us now? After the game, even the normally circumspect IRFU blazers were showing real confidence. There was hubris in the air. I was a small part of that hubris. Roaring and screaming with all the other supporters, I wanted to savour the moment. This was history in the making. My insatiable ego demanded that someone record that I was part of the winning party. So I asked our IRFU minder (the IRFU always delegated some poor sod to mind the minister at the matches) to take a photograph. The minder obliged.

As usual I tweeted the picture of myself, among a jubilant crowd, hands clenched in joy, sending congratulations to the team, successfully preserving the moment for my grateful electorate to see the minister sharing in their celebration. After all, photo opportunities can work. When the nation is united behind a sport, whether it is GAA, soccer, rugby or athletics, there is no downside to joining in. Even though Rob Kearney was again playing for Ireland on that glorious November evening, I had no hesitation. Nothing could go wrong this time. I nearly broke my thirty-year-old pledge to abstain from the dreaded drink. It was the Sabbath, so there was less opportunity but the whole nation was on steroids. My tweet would ensure that I could bask in the team's glory.

No Irish rugby supporter had a care in the world. It was a wonderful time to be Minister for Sport.

On the Monday morning I detected a few strange looks when I arrived in the office. Ushers in Leinster House looked at their feet when I passed them in the corridors. The staff in the Members' Bar looked a little embarrassed when I appeared for coffee. I knew something was wrong. Had someone died?

Eventually I asked Aisling on the phone. After boasting to her about having been to the greatest rugby match of all time the evening before, she told me, 'The picture you tweeted from the match. Your fly button was wide open. It's all over the papers and trending on social media.'

Where was the hole in the floor? Thank God I was alone.

I could only imagine what had happened. I looked again at the tweet. A cursory look told me that there it was, the minister with his fly open. Worse still, out of the opening had popped his tie or so it seemed. It looked a bit strange, all right.

My long-suffering staff must have dreaded coming into work on Monday mornings to see what antics I had been up to over the weekend. They would have to field the emails, the social media and the press queries. Even members of the public rang about the fly button saga.

There were further press queries. I resolved to tough it out. Besides, after the initial reaction, I realised it would have been hilarious if it had happened to anyone else.

Yet such howlers seemed to stick in the minds of one or two watchful politicians. They file them in their minds in case of need. No lesser man than the Taoiseach had occasion to refer to it, all of fourteen months later.

Campaigning for the general election in Cork with David Stanton TD, Leo, somehow, managed to slip it into a conversation, reminding the attending press of his coalition colleague's mishap. Leo was trying on a tie in a clothes shop in Cork, as Leo does. Chattering away to the media, cameras flashing, microphones turned on for his tour of Cork, he casually mentioned that he must not make the same mistake as another minister did with a tie. He prompted the question as to who that minister was. And what was his mistake? Hugh O'Connell of the *Irish Independent* obliged: 'Who was the minister?' Hugh asked on cue.

Expressing surprise at the interest, the Taoiseach replied helpfully, 'Shane. You saw that surely? His tie was coming out of his fly. He posted it on Twitter. He didn't quite realise it. Ha ha.'

The attending media laughed loudly. Leo never forgets! Hugh helpfully posted the Taoiseach's harmless humour on

Twitter and put it up on *Independent.ie* headed 'Leo Varadkar recalls photo of Shane Ross' tie sticking out of his trousers.'

I have news for the Taoiseach. I have news for Hugh. They should have looked a little closer at the picture. No tie came out of any fly that Sunday. Or any other day. I had merely removed my jumper as the atmosphere at the Aviva became uncomfortably warm. I had tied the jumper around my waist and over my tie which surfaced below the jumper.

Lots of journalists got plenty of fun out of the picture, even if they didn't look very closely at it. If they had, it might have spoiled a good yarn. I have been a journalist for a long time. In their shoes, I guess I would have milked it dry.

I was in a rare, but hardly serious, pickle. There was no escape, short of a correcting statement. Imagine a minister issuing a press release denying the stories that either his tie, or anything else, was protruding from his fly button. An explanation would soon have had to follow, insisting that his fly button had been closed all evening and… It would have been absurd. It was time to button something else, this time my lips.

The story was of no consequence. Sometimes we become a little too self-important. A large number of people, including the Taoiseach, had a good laugh. The government didn't fall. And, for once, the gaffe-guzzlers got it wrong.

Unfortunately, I have a bit of form when it comes to buttons. Buttons of another sort tripped me up badly. No politician in Leinster House knew how to turn a sweet victory into a defeat like I did.

On 18 January 2018, I had been fighting to change the drink-driving laws for over a year. Initially it had been hard enough to persuade the cabinet to agree, while an obstinate opposition in the Dáil was initially intransigent. The passage of the bill is a tale of filibusters, late-night sittings, personal abuse, but finally of patience rewarded. In the end we broke the Rural Alliance

TDs' filibuster, we defeated the publicans and vintners lobby, and we shamed Fianna Fáil into abstaining. For once, moral persuasion worked. On that cold Thursday in January, the bill passed its crucial second stage. The end was in sight.

Up in the public gallery the victims' groups, totally out of order, but understandably overjoyed, applauded. They had won the day. These brave citizens had sat through hour after hour of the Healy-Rae brothers and Mattie McGrath mouthing gibberish to talk down the clock. After Catherine Murphy had introduced a closure motion, the bill passed second stage by 85 votes to 8.

It had been a marathon. There was clapping from the Fine Gael benches. Even better, Danny Healy-Rae was moaning like a baby. I was in jubilant mood, crowing over the opposition.

Suddenly someone looked at the voting screen on the wall of the Dáil chamber. With undiluted pleasure, opponents pointed out that I had voted against my own bill. I could not believe it: they were right. I had pressed the wrong button. The jibes started flying across the chamber. I was red-faced.

I pretty regularly pressed the wrong button in Dáil votes. I am colour-blind and cannot tell the difference between red (tá) and green (níl) when voting. I was fortunate that I normally had the honest helping hand of Labour's Jan O'Sullivan or even Brendan Howlin — sitting beside me in the chamber — to correct me if I was about to make a mistake. That day I pressed the wrong button and proceeded to prattle on to whomever was good enough to listen to me in my moment of minor triumph.

The need to correct the mistake was apparent. The jeers rose from the ranks of the Rural Independents. A few fellow travellers in Fianna Fáil joined in as I approached the Clerk of the Dáil to make the change, all perfectly transparent. Other deputies do it regularly. No fuss is ever made about it.

The newspapers had a ball. On a day when I might have

At the Dublin v Mayo GAA All-Ireland Senior Football Final 2016. Shane Ross (Dublin) and Enda Kenny (Mayo) slug it out before the game. The result: a draw, but Dublin won the replay by a point.

Shane, as best man, with his wife Ruth Buchanan and Eamon Dunphy at Eamon's wedding in 2009.

Shane with Rachel Murray at the Special Olympics World Games in Abu Dhabi in 2019. Gymnast Rachel won a bronze medal for her combined routines in rope, ribbon, ball and hoop.

The photobombing of the season. Shane shamelessly basks in the reflected glory of undisputed lightweight world champion Katie Taylor after her triumphant return from Madison Square Garden, New York.

Celebrating Ireland beating the All Blacks in November 2018. The minister's tie is emerging from under the jersey around his waist, but not, as some media sources suggested, from somewhere else!

Winner of the 'Headline of the Year Award' 2018. The *Irish Daily Star* lampooned 'Shame Ross' for mixing up Rob and Dave Kearney in a tweet.

Leo's cabinet. President Michael D. Higgins hosts the new Taoiseach's first cabinet meeting in Áras an Uachtaráin. Missing from the photograph is Katherine Zappone.

Minister for Justice (and garda stations) Charlie Flanagan makes a surprise pre-cabinet presentation to Shane Ross. The plaque is an image of Stepaside Garda Station as it was soon to be, when restored to its former glory.

Kerry TD Danny Healy-Rae being challenged by Victims' Group members outside the Dáil on the day that the Road Traffic Bill was passing through the cabinet. Both Leo Lieghio and Julia Patton lost children in tragic road accidents. Deputy Healy-Rae said he didn't believe driving after drinking three glasses of beer caused any crashes.

ROINN AN TAOISIGH

Charlie

Can we go ahead with Farrell Simons & Hughes? & Defer Costello. for Kennedy a week.

Shane

I Need a Woman Can't go with 3 men!

Note passed across the cabinet table: Charlie Flanagan replies to Shane Ross's request for yet another delay in the appointment of Charlie's selected judges. Charlie replies: 'I need a woman. Can't go with 3 men!'

At Arbour Hill Boxing Club, Dublin, announcing the 2017 Sports Capital Grants. Minister of State Brendan Griffin watches as a young member of the club, Kalvin Keenan, lands a painful punch.

Fallen sporting power houses: Pat Hickey (centre), former president of the Olympic Council of Ireland, shares a joke with former FAI chief John Delaney and his partner, Emma English.

Irish football fans: grandchildren Tom (left) and Edward Webb join Shane beside the Little Mermaid before the 2017 Denmark v Ireland game in Copenhagen. It was a 0–0 draw.

John Halligan, Shane Ross and Finian McGrath at the Independent Alliance launch in 2015.

Shane and Aisling Dunne at the White House after a World Anti-Doping Agency conference in Washington in 2018.

Dancing in the afternoon: 'You're a rascal' said a surprised Democratic Unionist Party leader Arlene Foster as Shane Ross tried to coax her onto the dance floor in Leitrim's Ballroom of Romance in February 2019.

expected recognition that this bill had finally been passed, I took buckets of abuse! Not for the first time, a milestone of significance was overshadowed by headlines blaring out that a minister had voted against his own bill.

Such tomfoolery, even about such trivial matters as buttons, inevitably gives rise to witty headlines or even funny Twitter posts. On this occasion, my favourite by far was from a Mr Dominic Plant who posted a picture of my old friend, North Korean president Kim Jong-un. The caption read 'Shane Ross, no come to Korea, no touch buttons'.

'Ministers congratulate Dominant on her assured dominance which led to long deserved gold.'

Yes, that really was the boggling headline on a press release despatched from my office in September 2018. Any punter or journalist would be forgiven for being puzzled. Many were.

Who in God's name was Dominant? Dominant was a creation, who accidentally popped into the sporting ether at the World Rowing Championships in Plovdiv, Bulgaria. She was an Irish competitor to boot. Dominant won a gold medal.

On the Friday afternoon, before they left the office, the Sports division of the department had prepared messages of congratulations to Irish rowers, in anticipation of possible medal wins for the O'Donovan brothers, Paul and Gary, on the Sunday. They did the same for a brilliant, but lesser-known, Irish rower by the name of Sanita Puspure. All angles were covered, whether any of them won gold, silver or bronze. Different draft press releases were ready to go, whatever the result.

There's many a slip between cup and lip. A press release concocted on Friday can pass between many hands by the time it reaches the media on Sunday. During those forty-eight hours, gold medal winner Sanita Puspure had been transmogrified into 'Dominant' Puspure.

The O'Donovans duly won gold on the Saturday. They received the recognition they deserved from public, politicians and press.

On the Sunday, it was Puspure's turn to take gold. The following extraordinary press release went out:

> Minister Ross said: 'Yesterday we thought nothing could top the performances of Paul and Gary O'Donovan in the lightweight men's double sculls at Plovdiv. But today we saw a performance of great tenacity and assurance as Dominant Puspure dominated her rivals in a brilliant, single sculls final. Puspure has long deserved this gold. The celebrations in Cork will be mighty tonight and rightly so.'

'Dominant' was bad enough but to insert the 'dominated' word into the headline as well was sinful, compounding the error.

No doubt about the 'mighty' celebrations in Cork, but the laughter in Dublin was even mightier. No media outlet could resist highlighting the excruciatingly awkward mistake made by, guess who? Me again. The same old minister who had mixed up the Kearney brothers, who was to misname Shane Long as Shay Given, who misprinted athlete Thomas Barr as Thomas Barry, was true to form. This time it was not a mistake of identity. It was donating to Sanita Puspure an unusual Christian name.

How did it happen?

Blame RTÉ, although it was certainly not their fault. Immediately after Sanita won her gold, our national radio station put an item online with a picture of our victorious rower. The RTÉ headline read 'Dominant Puspure powers to world gold for Ireland'.

Someone in my office read the RTÉ headline, hurriedly drafted a press release, assuming from the headline that 'Dominant' was the winner's first name.

The wretched release was hardly out for a minute before journalist Gavan Reilly pounced. He tweeted gleefully: 'A statement from Shane Ross congratulating Sanita Puspure on her success at the Rowing World Championships. RTÉ's headline refers to "Dominant Puspure" and Ross (or his ghostwriter) apparently thinks that's her ACTUAL NAME.'

Helpfully, Gavan pasted a copy of the offending sentence on Twitter. Within minutes it had been retweeted by over 500 punters and been 'liked' by over 1,500. A correction had already been sent out from my office, but it was too late. The genie was out of the bottle. It went viral. The mistake was too good to be true.

We were jinxed. The print media happily ran with the error. Once again, a gaffe had become the story. *TheJournal.ie* could not resist it, quick off the mark, 'Shane Ross press release congratulates "Dominant Puspure for gold medal"... But that's not her name.'

The *Irish Times* was more circumspect: ' "Admin error" blamed for gaffe in Shane Ross statement on medal win.' But the knife was still inserted with relish. Nobody could blame them. It was as good as it gets. Some wags suggested that there was a highly infectious gaffe virus sweeping through my office. Suddenly, others in direct contact with the minister had been afflicted by the blunder bug.

The victim was not the minister. I was certainly accountable, but not likely to suffer sleepless nights at the vicissitudes of the comments on social media. It was not a new experience. But what of poor Sanita? She had been caught in crossfire caused by a ministerial boob.

I thought of apologising to her, but decided against. I soon discovered more about Sanita Puspure than I had known hitherto. Sanita had won the World Championships despite a background of personal stress and adversity that would have left others in despair. Her father-in-law had died earlier in the year, just after the European Championships, which she had missed because of illness. Worse still, she had learned that her sister, Inese, had been diagnosed with cancer. In an interview with Paul Fennessy of *the42.ie*, she insisted that she derived new determination from her beloved sister's illness. She had immense strength of character. Parallel with her journey to the top of her sport, she had been obstructed, but not thwarted, by serious family health issues.

Sanita Puspure was a brave woman. I felt acutely embarrassed that my mistake inadvertently might have distracted from her fantastic achievement. She had every right to be furious at such an unprofessional, clumsy intervention. Her answer to my concerns came in the same interview. She was asked about the 'infamous press release in which Minister for Sport Shane Ross, or at least his representative, wrongly believed her first name to be "Dominant".'

It was an invitation to a hero to have a rant. I fastened my seat belt. She responded. 'I actually did see it as a positive. We were laughing away about it. Never in my mind was there a thought of: "Oh my God, that's so embarrassing." It was like, well fair enough, they did use that word a lot during the commentary, so I can't really blame him for that mistake. It did attract a lot of publicity as well, and it was funny.'

I was flabbergasted. Here was a great Irish world champion with a sense of humour. She did not take herself too seriously.

I never met Sanita until the Irish Times Sportswoman of the Year award 2019 held in December in the Shelbourne Hotel. A few weeks earlier she had returned to Latvia to be with her sister in the last stages of her battle with cancer. For the second year in a row she had won the World Championship in the single sculls. Consequently, she was competing for the Irish Times award with, among others, global giant Katie Taylor and

Róisín Upton, the hockey player with the fractured wrist bone who put Ireland into the Tokyo Olympics in a sudden-death play-off against Canada.

I would have been happy with any of them winning. I did silently wonder if Katie Taylor would relish the thought of standing on the stage with me if she had won the prize. I wouldn't have blamed her.

Katie was spared the pain. Sanita won the award. It was an honour to share the platform with her at the end of the ceremony. No one deserved it more. As 2019 closed she had truly earned the 'Dominant' title.

6

Pork Barrel Politics

THERE HAS NEARLY always been room for one oddball in the Dublin South constituency. For years it was a five-seater, regularly embracing in its arms the latest 'flavour of the month'. Then an ungrateful electorate would unceremoniously spit them out at the next election. It invariably took a terrible revenge on its ministers for failing to live up to high expectations.

The most spectacular example of the oddball was Eithne FitzGerald, the Labour Party candidate in the 1992 general election. Labour had swept into government in the 'Spring Tide'. Eithne, wife of economist John and daughter-in-law of Taoiseach Garret, received 17,256 votes, the highest total in the country. She was instantly made a minister of state by Tánaiste Dick Spring, under the Fianna Fáil Taoiseach, Albert Reynolds. At the next contest in 1997, she tanked, lost her seat and over 11,000 votes, with a tally of just 6,147 first preferences.

Anne Colley, daughter of Charlie Haughey's arch-rival George Colley, took a seat in 1987 when the Progressive Democrats were enjoying their day in the sun. Sadly for her, too, the sun shone for only one summer. She lost out in 1989.

Others to come and go included Roger Garland, in 1989 the first Green Party candidate ever to reach the Dáil, but he was rudely despatched in the 1992 election.

Ministers who suffered the same fate are legion. Eamon Ryan, another Green, seemed well settled for a seat for life in the constituency following his re-election in 2007, but after his spell as a minister in the ill-fated Fianna Fáil-Green partnership from 2007 until 2011, the electors gave him the boot.

In 2016, Labour's Alex White and Fine Gael's Alan Shatter, who had both been short-lived ministers in Enda Kenny's government, were given their P45s. But perhaps the most spectacular exit from Dublin South was RTÉ celebrity and Fine Gael TD, George Lee. The constituency welcomed him like an economic messiah in the 2009 by-election, but were cheated of the chance to kick him out. George stayed in Leinster House for only nine months. He did not like what he saw, made his excuses after less than a year, didn't even wait for a general election, resigned, created a vacancy and left the Dáil, going straight back to RTÉ.

I was the most recent of the oddballs. As an independent, I was lucky that it was 'Independents Day' when I was first elected with 17,075 votes in 2011. I was the latest fad. After being re-elected in Dublin South's successor, the smaller Dublin Rathdown three-seat constituency in 2016, I was made a minister. I had opted for the graveyard shift.

And the graveyard did not let me down. At the 2020 general election, my first preference vote plummeted from 10,202 in the smaller Dublin Rathdown constituency in 2016 to 3,419 in 2020. Despite my well-documented high opinion of myself, I bit the dust.

Why is Dublin Rathdown the most volatile constituency in the country? Why does it so readily welcome fresh, unconventional blood, only to bid us all farewell so impolitely?

In all its various shapes and sizes, Dublin Rathdown has always been mainly a leafy suburb of south Dublin. Originally in its five-seater form of Dublin South, it stretched north-south from the River Dodder in Clonskeagh to the Scalp on the Dublin border with County Wicklow at Kilternan. East to west it started with Stillorgan on the N11 through the ultra-posh Foxrock to Knocklyon in west Dublin. It had a population of 140,543. It included such well-populated areas as Dundrum, Mount Merrion, Churchtown, Ballinteer and Stepaside. It was more middle class than most other Dublin constituencies.

According to the 2016 census figures, the new, smaller three-seat constituency had a population of 94,472. It had below average social housing (4.7% against 8.4% in the rest of the nation), while more of the inhabitants (66.7%) claimed very good health as opposed to the rest of Ireland (59.4%).

But it was in the area of 'Types of Occupation' that Dublin Rathdown differed most from the other thirty-eight constituencies in the state. A whopping 31% had professional occupations, against the rest of Ireland's average of just 17.3%. Moreover, 11.6% of them were 'managers, directors and senior officials' against 7.4% elsewhere. The unemployment figure was only 3.5% while the national average was 7.1%.

The age profile was a little older than the rest of the country. There were fewer people describing themselves as Roman Catholic (67.8%, compared to 78.3% nationally). Significantly more of the residents in Dublin Rathdown had a third-level education, or even above, than in the rest of the country (51.4% versus 28.5%). These were the electors who regularly returned the oddballs to the Dáil. They were well educated, had better jobs, were in better health, were slightly older and more settled.

There is more than a ring of prosperity about Dublin Rathdown. There is even a ring of bourgeois genteelness about the residents in the large, often gated, properties of Mount Merrion and Clonskeagh. Their main worries are consistently their property tax and their inheritance tax liabilities.

Traditionally, it has been a Fine Gael stronghold. At times, when it was a five-seater, Fine Gael held three seats. In the glory days of the legendary Professor John Kelly in the seventies and eighties, he was accompanied to the Dáil by two Fine Gael running mates. Kelly was reputed to do little constituency work but sailed into the Dáil on his reputation as a brilliant orator and a fine parliamentarian. He was both.

But the arrival of Séamus Brennan for Fianna Fáil in 1981 signalled a new, highly competitive constituency where there were no longer any seats to be taken for granted. Dublin Rathdown was not to remain as a comfortable fiefdom for members of big-name Fianna Fáil families like Niall Andrews, son of War of Independence and civil war hero Todd Andrews. Brennan and his later running mate, Tom Kitt, carved out two safe seats. Fine Gael continued to win two, as of right, without working the area in the same way as the two Fianna Fáil grafters. Brennan and Kitt captured the west end of the constituency of Churchtown, Dundrum and Ballinteer, while Fine Gael cleaned up in the well-heeled residences of Mount Merrion, Clonskeagh and Stillorgan. There was often, then, a fifth seat available for the flavour of the month or even a Labour candidate.

I knew only a little about the constituency when I decided to stand for the Dáil in 2011. I had been brought up in Stepaside, so had a close connection with that area. I knew that there was at least one vacancy because George Lee had flown the coop and Tom Kitt was retiring. Fianna Fáil was in turmoil and likely to lose one seat, if not both. I was aware that the area often took a punt on complete newcomers, like Lee, or Anne Colley or the latest Green to arrive on the scene. I hadn't done an hour's local political work in the area in my entire life, but I hoped the national mood was in tune with my political agenda.

The initiative worked. Like Eithne FitzGerald in 1992, I topped the poll in the 2011 election, but was well aware of the fate of she who had gone before me. Fianna Fáil was wiped out, with the Green's Eamon Ryan departing behind them. Fine Gael took three seats while Labour's Alex White held on to his.

I was determined not to be a one-term TD, swinging in on a mood like the others and being ejected when the citizens of Dublin South switched their allegiance, as they almost always did. There was only one way to do that: follow the example of the late Séamus Brennan and work your butt off in the local area. If that meant a dramatic change from my previous life as an independent senator, so be it. It was time to accept that all politics was local. Denigrators call that 'pork barrel politics'. I realised that if I was going to retain my seat, I had better not loftily disdain the idea and turn my back on my home turf.

I spent my first year in the Dáil finding out about the constituency and the workings of the Lower House. It was a time of great austerity, giving much fodder to opposition deputies in protest mode. Cutbacks were imposing hardship on every citizen and every constituency. Mine was more prosperous than most, but the imposition of water charges and property taxes was almost universally unpopular. The International Monetary Fund held the country in a chokehold. The Fine Gael-Labour government was taking unpopular decisions at the behest of the IMF.

Luckily, I was well positioned: of the five deputies in Dublin South, I was the only one in opposition. There was one Fine Gael minister (Alan Shatter), two Fine Gael backbenchers (Olivia Mitchell and Peter Mathews) and one Labour minister, Alex White. All were compelled to defend government policies that included higher taxes and expenditure cuts.

After my first year in the Dáil, I set to work single-mindedly on the constituency. I began spending evenings at local sporting events and residents' association meetings. I went to community centres, country markets, and took time to find out the issues the local people were anxious about. Some evenings, I would knock on people's doors to meet and greet. There was rarely a burning local issue. The citizens of Dublin Rathdown were not the unhappiest punters under the Fine Gael-Labour coalition.

Suddenly, out of the blue, on 6 December 2012, the Fine Gael Minister for Justice, Alan Shatter, announced that he would be closing over one hundred Garda stations throughout the country. It was part of the cutbacks at the time and an integral piece of the latest fad, known as 'smart policing'. To his credit, Alan was way above the pork barrel politics for which I was preparing. He refused to make an exception for Stepaside, one of the busiest stations in his own constituency.

The decision provoked a popular rebellion. The revolt was initially led by Stepaside business leader Des Kennedy, by the proprietor of The Step Inn John McCluskey, and by other local chieftains. Two brave local Gardaí, Pat Cullen and Ultan Sherlock, courageously took up the cudgel in opposing the move. Kennedy started a petition, which quickly garnered several thousand signatures. I met these local activists a few days after Shatter's announcement and we soon joined forces. A strong group of Stepaside stalwarts set to work on stopping the station's closure. We gathered many of the local civic leaders and decided to hold a mass rally. It was set for Sunday, 3 February 2013.

The rally brought around two thousand people onto the street of a small County Dublin village. They came from every estate in the area on a cold Sunday afternoon to protest against a decision that failed to recognise the sharp rise locally in burglaries and other crimes. This was a growing and populous area on the edge of the M50, offering rich pickings for burglars. The residents felt deserted, helpless. At that rally, national politicians, with no vested interest in the area around Stepaside, joined us. Independent TDs Catherine Murphy, Finian McGrath and Mattie McGrath stood shoulder to shoulder with Stepaside residents on local farmer William Richardson's trailer. We swore that we would not tolerate the closure.

After the meeting we dispersed peacefully. Alan Shatter issued a statement that day insisting that there would be no special treatment for his own constituency. His statement closed with the words: 'I am determined, as Minister for Justice, that the resources of our Garda Síochána are used in the best, most effective and efficient way possible. I believe that we are fortunate to have, in Martin Callinan, an excellent Garda Commissioner who is doing a good job in bringing about the modernisation and reform of An Garda Síochána and I support him in his work.'

Shatter and Callinan were joined at the hip.

Stepaside Garda Station closed a few weeks later, in March. We had lost the first round.

A year after the closure, in March 2014, due to ongoing allegations of his treatment of a Garda whistleblower, Martin Callinan's position became untenable. He resigned. Seven weeks later, in May, Alan Shatter followed his favoured Commissioner into the wilderness. The fight to reopen Stepaside resumed, because the residents refused to give up. As their local TD, I joined them in battle to reopen it. The other TDs, Alan Shatter himself and Labour's Alex White, favoured its closure. Olivia Mitchell and the late Peter Mathews were lukewarm, but were tongue-tied as government supporters, until Peter left Fine Gael.

I seized the much-maligned pork barrel mantle with enthusiasm. A local cause célèbre had been delivered. The locals never wanted or would have allowed me to drop the crusade to reopen their station, once the beating heart of their community. They depended on me to voice their despair in the Dáil. When it came to the 2016 general election, they rightly flexed their muscles. Which candidates, they asked, would stand up and support the case for reopening the station if they were elected to the Dáil? A public meeting was called for a Sunday after-noon during the campaign. All the candidates turned up. To his credit, Alan Shatter defended his position. He maintained that it was an operational decision by the Commissioner, which he had to follow. Alex White took the same line. Shatter even claimed that my promises to fight to reverse the decision were 'seriously misleading'.

Alan Shatter, Alex White and Peter Mathews lost their seats, while Olivia Mitchell retired. Negotiations for government formation opened. Rightly or wrongly, I made it clear on day one that a priority for me was to see not only that the Stepaside station should be reopened, but that there should be a review of the closure of all 139 Garda stations.

Fine Gael tut-tutted. The second session of the plenary Programme for Government talks had just ended. Enda called me over. 'You really can't be bringing up issues like local Garda stations at these talks,' he said. 'You should be concentrating on national issues.'

I swallowed hard in disbelief. Enda understood more than anyone the value of local issues. In the 2002 general election, he himself had been trounced in his home Mayo patch by Fine Gael party colleague Michael Ring, the ultimate pork barrel politician. Enda barely scraped home, just 87 votes ahead of another Fine Gael colleague, Jim Higgins, who was eliminated on the eighth count. Ring stole most of the Fine Gael vote because of his tireless work for the local constituency. That is how Irish politics works.

What surprised me was Fine Gael's attitude to my demands. It was somehow beneath the dignity of anyone involved in the talks to mention such a squalid thing as a local injus-tice. Did anyone seriously expect an elected TD to turn his back on his commitments on the day he was elected? How could I, asked Fine Gael members disdainfully, a TD from a middle-class Dublin constituency, behave like the Healy-Raes? There was a hint of condescension, a suggestion that I should know better.

I didn't. Eventually realpolitik ruled. The reopening of Garda stations was included in the Programme for Government, thanks once again to interventions from Michael Noonan and Simon Coveney. Both saw that I had made a solemn promise to bring Stepaside's case to the table. They also saw that Finian McGrath had demanded a cystic fibrosis unit for his local Beaumont Hospital, that Boxer Moran was seeking a tourism brand for the midlands, that Seán Canney wanted a review of the Western Rail Corridor, and that John Halligan had to produce a second Cath Lab for Waterford Hospital. All of us needed to deliver to our constituents or face cries of betrayal.

Besides that, it was Independent Alliance policy that the closure of all 139 stations at a stroke was a mistake. The closures had saved little money, had led to a feeling of neglect and fear in rural, isolated communities and the supposed 'smart policing' to replace stations had not been implemented. To Fine Gael, the merits or otherwise of the closures were irrelevant.

Although the reopenings were agreed in the Programme for Government, the problems were only beginning. Attempts were made at every stage to thwart the promises made. Not by Enda Kenny. He was a dealer par excellence, intent on driving a hard bargain but determined to deliver once he had signed his name on the dotted line. And not by Leo Varadkar. The resistance to the reopenings seemed to come from hidden hands within both the Department of Justice and the Garda Síochána.

The Programme for Government never actually mentioned Stepaside by name. It committed the new government to a review of all Garda stations by the Policing Authority. On page 98, the Programme was quite specific in its commitment to a single action:

As part of the review we will launch a pilot scheme to reopen 6 Garda Stations, both urban and rural, to determine possible positive impacts that such openings will have on criminal activity, with special emphasis on burglaries, theft and public order. This will be initiated within two months.

Sceptics insisted that I had tailor-made the terms of reference for Stepaside, so that the review would inevitably recommend that Stepaside station was one of the six chosen for the pilot scheme. In a sense they were right: the inclusion of 'burglaries, theft and public order' pointed the review towards Stepaside. Burglaries had sky-rocketed there, partly attributable to an enormous population increase. That was precisely why the station's closure had been such a daft decision. Equally, another five stations with similar crime patterns would reopen. The other stations ultimately selected were: Rush, Dublin; Leighlinbridge, Carlow; Donard, Wicklow; Bawnboy, Cavan and Ballinspittle, Cork.

In addition, the Programme for Government specified that the review should 'take into account … station closures since 2012.' It was a long haul from there to 9 March 2020 — seven years after the closure — when the station finally reopened. The entire process was a salutary lesson in the weird workings of government, the civil service and the arms of the state.

My principal point of contact on this issue was the Minister for Justice, Frances Fitzgerald. Like Enda, Frances was a professional. She understood that this distasteful deed had to be done, but there was an expression of sniffy disapproval on her face whenever she was forced to engage on the squalid subject. It was vintage Fine Gael. She held her nose and got on with it.

There were inexplicable delays in the production of the Garda report on the reopenings. Excuses were multiple for twelve long months. I hounded poor Frances for the entire year. She often looked pained when she saw me approaching. We had two points of troublesome conflict: Stepaside and the Judicial Appointments Bill. I gained the clear impression that she was caught between irrevocably opposed servants of the state and me on both issues. I pestered her night and day. She delivered the Garda Commissioner's Second Interim Report in June 2017, which finally recommended that the Stepaside station be reopened. A day later she had left Justice, handing over the Augean Stables to Charlie Flanagan.

Charlie Flanagan was one of the most difficult individuals I have ever dealt with in public life. He is a Blueshirt to the last drop of his blood. As a lawyer, he was the wrong choice for Minister for Justice. The Justice department needed reform and Charlie is no legal reformer. He is as happy as Larry with the legal status quo. Understandably, he deeply resented my continual ventures into his portfolio. One day, when he was in one of his tantrums on the telephone, he let rip at me. 'I received', he boomed, 'my seal of office from the President, you know,' and went on to upbraid me for my frequent interference. From time to time at cabinet, out of pure mischief, he would launch a grenade in the direction of my department. That was Charlie: combative, argumentative, explosive and very, very human. Although I could not help liking him personally, I was dreading dealing with him on Stepaside. And I was right.

My response to the announcement that the Stepaside station was now officially chosen as one of the six in the pilot scheme was probably over the top. Carrying a banner around the village was not a popular move anywhere outside the immediate locality. It antagonised some in Leinster House. The Public Accounts Committee (PAC), dominated by opposition politicians, decided to hold a few sessions in which they would examine the process. Nothing material was revealed, but it gave Alan Kelly of Labour and PAC chairman, Seán Fleming of Fianna Fáil, a chance to revive the pork barrel charge. Even Catherine Murphy of the Social Democrats was critical of the decision, a strange stance for the woman who had bravely stood alongside me on the trailer at the well-attended protest when the station was being closed three years earlier.

More damaging than the political attacks was the evidence of Assistant Commissioner Pat Leahy at the PAC sittings. Pat, a local who had once lived in an estate just outside Stepaside, told the Committee that reopening the station was not his 'top priority'. Pat drew blood. He had street cred, not only as a local resident but as the Assistant Commissioner for the Dublin Metropolitan region. His remarks gave fuel to all those opposed to the project.

Still, luckily, the die had been cast. There was no going back. But there were delays by the dozen. First of all, the station was occupied. There were tenants in the building. It was their home. There was a homeless emergency and a housing crisis. The Office of Public Works (OPW), now in charge of the building, was understandably reluctant to give the tenants notice to quit. Visions of Richard Boyd-Barrett, Ruth Coppinger and a few other socialist deputies occupying a building owned by the state in protest against evictions hovered over the project for months. Nothing could be done until the tenants left. Happily, they were eventually rehoused satisfactorily.

The next delay was because of various surveys of the building. The Gardaí had specific requirements that carried a heavy price tag. The OPW was unwilling to pick up the tab. A tug of war between the two further postponed progress.

And then — disaster — the station was riddled with asbestos. The project itself was again called into question. There was a killer on the premises. The OPW began to question whether the building was suitable for a modern Garda station. There were rumours that the site might be abandoned. At one stage Charlie Flanagan, unhelpfully, but gleefully, told me that I would have to settle for a Portakabin.

All the time, pressure from local residents was intensifying. Political rivals in Stepaside were demanding to know more about the delay. Their TD and minister had failed them. They spun a yarn that the station was never going to open and that they had been led up the garden path. Many of those who had joined the push for the reopening late in the day were now whispering with relish that it was doomed and it was my fault. We were now well into 2018. Two years in the life of the government had passed and the station was still closed.

But all was not lost. Kevin 'Boxer' Moran had replaced Seán Canney as Minister for the OPW. Boxer was key to the project and was determined to see the station open — he understood how important it was. I could pick up the phone to Boxer and ask him the state of repair of the building, the cost of improvements and the timeline. One dark day he came to me to say that the old station was hardly fit for purpose. It would take millions to convert. We might be better to build from scratch in the car park at the back. He wondered would I go and have a look at a 'modular' building in Garda headquarters in Dublin's Phoenix Park.

So, on a sunny afternoon in 2018, I trotted out to the Park with Boxer. We inspected the 'modular' building, escorted around by acting Garda Commissioner Dónall Ó Cualáin. It was a sparkling, purpose-built office on two levels with apparently everything necessary to operate a Garda station. It could be moved in large parts into the car park in Stepaside. It would be assembled there in a short time. I was grateful for the tour, but wanted to reserve judgement.

It began to occur to me: if this purpose-built station was placed in the car park, where would the cars park? What sort of an operation was really being planned for Stepaside? Was I being suckered?

News of the 'modular' proposal leaked out. Alan Shatter emerged from the wilderness and thundered against it. He indulged himself, accusing me of 'bombastry and faking' and misleading voters. I had promised them 'bricks and mortar' and was 'giving them a prefab'. I had engaged in fantasy politics with the people. He went on: 'I don't know whether anyone has analysed how many Gardaí are going to occupy a modular building that occupies four car parking spaces. It will be just about big enough to provide two toilets and a washing facility unless what is proposed is for some public toilet to visit.'

Alan was over the moon.

Happily, Boxer dropped into my office soon afterwards. The old station was back in the frame. It would be expensive, maybe €1.5 million, but it could be done. A grown-up station needed room for a fleet of Garda cars. A decision would soon be made. The modular building was a non-runner.

In the middle of all the delays, Charlie Flanagan arrived at the cabinet early one Tuesday morning. I saw him approaching me and braced myself for our ritual pre-cabinet row about the latest judge to be appointed or vetoed. I was psyching myself up for the skirmish. Our cabinet colleagues were scattering in all directions to avoid being caught in the crossfire. Charlie was armed with a strange plaque in his hand. He called us all together and made a surprise presentation to me. On the plaque was a beautiful, specially made image of Stepaside Garda Station as it would look, in all its glory, when the works were completed. He had specially ordered it for me. And the image was accurate; when the station was finished it was built to the exact specifications as they appeared on the plate.

Pictures were taken by amused ministers.

My constituency rival, Josepha Madigan, looked less than amused. That was the best part.

The Blueshirt from Laois with the short fuse had a big heart, a generous spirit and a great sense of humour. We had many heated skirmishes to come in the months ahead, but Charlie had a wonderful knack of putting our quarrels into proportion. Laughter was a great leveller.

The old station building was approved, but progress was still tortuously slow. Planning permission was needed to change the front door; a new roof was necessary. There was red tape and a need for Gardaí to volunteer to move from their current posts into the new station. For obvious reasons, I was keen for the building to be opened before the 8 February date of the general election. It missed that date by a month. I turned up at 7 a.m., the minute it opened, on Monday, 9 March 2020. It was a great day for a community, which had been under siege for too long. Job done. If that is pork barrel politics, long may it continue.

Assuming Stepaside was living proof that I was a pork barrel politician, the events in Wesley College in the heart of the constituency, in 2018, proved that I was hopeless at it.

Sports capital grants were a paradise for the veteran political pork barrellers. Traditionally, they were dished out by governments in an outrageous manner to their favoured sporting clubs. Constituencies of sports ministers invariably emerged with generous grants to their own local clubs and schools. In 2018, Wesley College eagerly wanted one.

The system was scrupulously fair. The application process was beyond reproach. There was an equitable method of allocation, with various weightings, and a slight bias in favour of clubs in disadvantaged areas. Civil servants marked the applications, somewhat severely, but no one ever suggested that there was any funny business in that part of the process.

After the civil servants had finished their scrupulous work, they forwarded the results, ranked in order, to the junior and senior sports ministers. And then the fun began. Many ministers in the past had changed the ranking order, increased the points awarded to local clubs or made other changes. This was often done under the cover of 'local knowledge', a subjective weighting much loved by politicians, but unknown to public servants. Politics was alive and well in the allocation of sports grants. Civil servants disliked the system for that reason. A lot of their work could be overturned at the stroke of a political pen.

I resolved that there would be no political interference in the process on my watch in the Sports department. I was very happy, as were all TDs, to help applicants fill in the forms or to advise them of the weightings, the points system used and how points were awarded. Since I visited my own local sports clubs every weekend, often receiving scores of questions about the best way to apply for these grants, it would have been folly to be unhelpful. I made it perfectly clear that I could not influence the civil servants' independent marking, any more than any other Dáil deputy.

That attitude was anathema to several clubs and politicians. The nodders and the winkers still surfaced, in the expectation that I would be able to do something for them when the big day came. They wondered what was the point of having a minister in their bailiwick if he wouldn't divert a few bob in their direction?

I disappointed them. The system was not perfect, but it was the same for everyone. Despite efforts to make the application process simpler, a large number of the applications were still adjudged to be invalid for minor reasons, like not including original documents, however peripheral they were to the application. The forms were so complicated that they often defeated the efforts of many otherwise worthy applicants. If the system was flawed, it was not on the side of generosity.

Wesley College in Ballinteer applied for a €150,000 grant for the resurfacing of a hockey pitch. They were joined in their application by YMCA, a local hockey club. Plenty of other clubs in my constituency applied. Some were successful, others were not.

Dublin clubs had always seemed to enjoy an advantage because the grants were given out on a per capita basis, a method that the public servants felt was the fairest. The number of applications from Dublin clubs was smaller, in proportion to the large population of the county, than their equivalent in other counties. On occasion there were excess funds for Dublin, which in turn were redistributed to other counties. As a result, Dublin actually did badly per capita. Per club, they did well.

Almost every weekend, while attending constituency events, I met members of local sports clubs. I was besieged with questions about the sports grants, as were all TDs from Dublin Rathdown. I always advocated that the club apply. I offered to help them complete the complicated forms, which sometimes brought applicants down at the first hurdle. I met applicants from other parts of Ireland and tried to help them too. I met clubs from Tipperary with Mattie McGrath, from Westmeath with Boxer Moran, from north Dublin with Tommy Broughan; indeed probably anyone who asked. They never received any hint from me that they had an inside track, but got plenty of advice on how to maximise their chances. My constituency team was available to help any of the clubs in Dublin Rathdown. They had been trained in the pitfalls.

The assessment process took months but when the officials eventually sent me the final rankings for my sign-off, I was flabbergasted. Wesley was invalid. So was the biggest and best-known GAA club in my constituency, Kilmacud Crokes. It was going to be embarrassing for me to give these two the bad news.

The Kilmacud Crokes failure was a shock. The local club, a household name, had failed in a bid for a sports grant. It had thousands of members. My local political opponents would lacerate me — a Minister of Sport in the constituency failing to 'fix' a sports grant for a big club in the area.

Kilmacud Crokes bit the dust. So did Wesley.

Closer to home, the application of St Columba's College, in the constituency, was also ruled invalid. My father had been on the school's board and both my children had been pupils there. I had done nothing to influence the process for St Columba's, nothing for Kilmacud Crokes and nothing for Wesley. What hopeless sort of a pork barrel politician was I?

I took a deep breath and signed off on the final list, exactly as presented to me. Not a single word was altered.

Kilmacud Crokes accepted its fate, but Wesley went ape. They reined in local politicians and expressed their dissatisfaction in no uncertain terms. Their application had been judged to be invalid on the grounds that they were a private school. They rightly pointed out that they had never been told that private schools were excluded. Nowhere was such a reason for disqualification written on the application form. Wesley threatened to seek a judicial review. Two other private schools outside the constituency took a similar position. They too had been given no indication that private schools were invalid.

We were on the back foot. It was put to me that Wesley might have a good legal case. Other unsuccessful applicants were beginning to complain too, maybe with justification. It did seem to be an onerous process, with little recourse if an outcome was thought to be unfair. After lengthy discussions, I approved a proposal that all invalid applicants would be allowed to appeal, provided I had no involvement in the process and that no official who had marked an original application would be judging the same club's appeal.

One hundred and forty-nine clubs appealed. Thirty-five were successful. Wesley College was one of them. In mid-March 2018, I signed off on the list of successful appellants, again without any interference on my part.

And then I committed a mortal political sin. In an outburst of relief, I tweeted that I was 'delighted to confirm that @ wesleycollege has been granted €150,000 as part of Sports Capital Programme. The funding will ensure the resurfacing of the hockey pitch and will benefit the school as well as @ YMCAHC.'

All hell broke loose. The tabloids went berserk. Headlines galore appeared, all saying pretty much the same thing: 'Private School in Sports Minister's constituency awarded €150k grant after appeal.' The controversy ran for several weeks. I appeared on RTÉ's *Sean O'Rourke Show* and at the Oireachtas Committee on Transport, Tourism and Sport to put up what the *Irish Times* called a 'Spirited Defence of Grant to Wesley College'. Among my greatest critics on that day was Fianna Fáil's Robert Troy, who lambasted me for the grant and wanted to know whether due process had been followed. I was forced to point out that Deputy Troy had made eight representations asking me to give favourable consideration to eight of his local clubs!

More amusing was the confession from Fianna Fáil's Kevin O'Keeffe TD that he had written an 'application for a club that didn't even apply'. The pork barrel was alive and well.

The truth is that the purity of the process was impeccable. Not a comma was changed, but there was a deeper problem. Wesley College was entitled to its grant under the criteria for applications, but Wesley is a school where well-heeled families send their children, paying fees of as much as €15,850 a year for seven-day boarders. Should people from such privileged backgrounds be given government grants, while others in less fortunate circumstances struggled? We recognised this injustice in the next round by changing the weightings further in favour of clubs and schools in disadvantaged communities.

Sceptics in Leinster House and a few of the media dubbed the Wesley debacle as a 'stroke'. They concluded that the grant might have gone down badly outside Ballinteer, but that I was a local hero. Nothing could have been further from the truth.

The Wesley episode was a big vote loser. The publicity probably cost me a whole bag of votes. Ballinteer was a stronghold for me, but the ordinary people of Ballinteer were my supporters, not the posh parents of the pupils in Wesley. On the whole, they probably voted for the Blueshirts. They had a ready-made candidate in Neale Richmond, a former pupil at the school. My own supporters, the less well-off citizens of Ballinteer, were puzzled that, according to the newspapers, I had landed €150,000 for such a privileged school. They were disbelieving when I insisted that I had not done so.

I was all in favour of constituency pork barrel politics, but only to look after those in need, not the privileged. The media savaged me for favouring the constituency. The ordinary constituent denounced me for helping the elite. It was a double whammy.

There was trouble afoot. After the Wesley row, my constituency team took an opinion poll. It showed that the independent vote in the most volatile constituency in the country was in decline. The seat was now under threat.

I decided to double-down on the pork barrel politics. We needed a constituency office, a presence in the area that gave me a more visible profile, more advertising, a regular clinic every week and a campaign of knocking on residents' doors whenever the time allowed.

We probably had a better constituency squad than any of the other candidates, but the parties started with a far more solid base vote. Despite my position at the top of the poll on two successive occasions, I was acutely aware that ours was a soft vote of disillusioned Fianna Fáil supporters of the late Séamus Brennan, combined with a big floating vote in search of the latest oddball! But I was no longer seen as an oddity or a rebel. I was part of a government that had not delivered. And a minister to boot. Many were saying that the Independent Alliance had sold out to the Blueshirts.

The only route to salvation seemed to be to massively increase the volume of constituency work. One of my favourite activities was attending the local sports events — whether GAA or football — at weekends. That was a pleasure, witnessing volunteers at their best, but it was not enough. The constituency team was keen that the candidate should be out and about more. It is harder when you are a minister, with cabinet duties, late Dáil sittings, the odd trip abroad and meetings with other ministers and state agencies. Still, several times a week I hit the doors. It was always enjoyable, whatever the response, but provided a useful, under-the-radar mission to assess the views of constituents.

And then the radar rumbled me.

On Christmas Eve 2018, I had one of my bright ideas. I escaped from my handlers, donned my Santa hat and high-viz jacket and decided to wish Happy Christmas to some of the residents of Ballinteer. I knocked on about thirty doors. With one or two exceptions, the response was good, although many were surprised that a government minister was door-knocking a few hours before Christmas with a Santa hat on.

Mission Santa Hat seemed to go really well, so I resolved to do the same on New Year's Eve. That had a similar response. I couldn't wait until Easter.

Then, on 9 January 2019 RTÉ's Joe Duffy came calling. They were doing an item about a cabinet minister dropping around alone, in the dark, to old people on Christmas Eve.

An elderly lady had phoned in to complain. She made one or two good points. It was dark, it was scary. A whole debate followed. Listeners phoned in, some in strong support of my mission, others outraged. I rang into the programme to defuse the simmering row. However, an effort to work quietly, unnoticed, in a festive mood in the constituency, had backfired.

Joe Duffy even mentioned the 'pork barrel' accusation. Sometimes it is a bit difficult to counter the charge that TDs are never seen by ordinary citizens, outside election time. When you do appear, you are condemned as a 'pork barrel' politician. I plead guilty.

So how come, after all the constituency work, the successful return of Stepaside Garda Station to the area, the busy constituency office, all the doors knocked and other highly visible constituency activity, I went belly up in the general election? There are lots of political lessons in the 2020 Dublin Rathdown contest.

First, it is becoming increasingly difficult for an independent candidate to be elected in Dublin. In a three-seat constituency, it is practically impossible for an independent to finish in the first three places. It means beating three out of the five established parties of Fianna Fáil, Fine Gael, Sinn Féin, the Greens and Labour. At the last election, the only independent TD elected in the whole of Dublin was the hard-left former 'People Before Profit' member Joan Collins, in the Dublin South-Central four-seater, although technically, she was a member of the 'Independents 4 Change' party. Joan scraped in, taking the last seat on the final count. She has since formed a new party called 'Right to Change', leaving not a single independent from any Dublin constituency, out of a total of forty-five possible seats, now in the Dáil.

Second, social media is increasingly important. I was brutal on social media. Although I have 55,000 followers on Twitter, most of my high-profile mistakes surfaced or gained oxygen there. I goofed badly with my Kearney brothers' blunder in a rugby-mad constituency. Other hostages to fortune on Twitter were picked up by the mainstream media, which increasingly depends on social media to feed its frenzy for stories. The trolls had a field day with Wesley's sports grant and the Katie Taylor gaffe. There is no doubt that fewer votes would have been lost if I had stayed away from Twitter.

The constituency team and I went into the general election with high expectations. We had a great group of canvassers and we enjoyed the unwavering support of former Councillor Seamus O'Neill throughout the election. We never foresaw the rise of Sinn Féin, who nearly took a seat in a middle-class constituency traditionally hostile to them. We expected to be fighting it out for the last seat with Shay Brennan, son of Seamus. Instead, Fine Gael took two seats, the only place in Ireland where they made a gain.

Dublin Rathdown is basically a middle-class, conservative Fine Gael constituency. On a good day, the party would have a sporting chance of two seats out of three. Their success this time was in pulling two out of three on a bad day nationally. Neale Richmond and Josepha Madigan split the vote equally — at 15% each — ensuring that they squeezed two seats out of three with only 31% of the vote. It was a brilliant performance by them.

Towards the end of the campaign, we could feel our seat slipping away as voters became polarised. The rise of Sinn Féin was spooking many of the more prosperous voters. The issue on the doorsteps switched to Sinn Féin or not Sinn Féin? Fine Gael successfully plugged away with that message. It was a good strategy. Many of those fearful of Mary Lou's crew deserted us and headed for the safest of havens — the Blueshirts.

Much of the protest vote I had garnered in the two previous elections landed in the Shinners' laps. It was hard for a sitting minister to hold on to a protest vote for four years. In the final week, I found myself calling to middle-class houses, with two cars in the driveway, in Stillorgan. Some of them openly declared for Sinn Féin at the doors. Conversely, others were scared, rallying to the group seen to be most likely to stop them: Fine Gael.

When the votes were counted, I received a disappointing 3,419 votes. Catherine Martin of the Greens, who topped the poll, won 8,958 and was elected, alongside Fine Gael's Neale Richmond and Josepha Madigan. The real surprise was the performance of Sorcha Nic Cormaic of Sinn Féin, a reluctant candidate, who nearly took a seat. Pork barrel or not, Dublin Rathdown kept its record of sending its ministers packing.

7

Drink Drivers Divide the Dáil

'SHANE ROSS', ROARED out the familiar figure on my Twitter feed 'is one of the biggest scumbags in Irish politics.'

A cheer went up from the crew of noisy supporters egging on the speaker. The man's voice was rising to an excitable pitch as it continued: 'Tonight Shane Ross is on the scrapheap of Irish politics.' More cheers from the loud crowd gathered around him. 'He ruined rural Ireland.' And the figure finished with a flourish: 'I said I'd do anything to bring that man down and tonight the good people of Dublin took him out of it.'

Michael Collins, the west Cork deputy, was in fiery form, savouring his re-election in February 2020. He was entitled to celebrate in private with his own people. No doubt Michael would have preferred that the clip had not found its way on to social media, but his words were a great line on the night to his army of supporters.

Michael and I had crossed swords on drink-driving. He had been an opponent of my Road Traffic Bill in the 32nd Dáil because it automatically put anyone drinking and driving, over the legal limit, off the road. His view was not news to anyone, but I did not know until his victory speech that it had been his ambition to take me out of Irish politics.

A quick look back at a text exchange we enjoyed less than two years earlier suggested that the sworn opponent of drink-driving restrictions was far from a sworn political opponent. We had swapped warm New Year greetings for 2018: 'Many happy returns 2u and ur family Shane,' wrote Michael. By then, the bill that supposedly offended Michael so much was within three weeks of completing its passage through second stage in the Dáil.

Ten months earlier, in February 2017, the cabinet had approved my proposed controversial Road Traffic Bill. Michael did not favour it, but he was hardly vociferous about it. Indeed, six months after the matter had entered the public arena, he, and he alone, eagerly hosted a ministerial visit from me to his Cork South-West constituency.

We had only rarely had any conversation about drink-driving, but he did refer to it in an aside in another text, after I had gently upbraided him on another matter. Michael had failed to support my Judicial Appointments Bill at second stage. His reply was amusing, but certainly not personally hostile. On 7 July 2017, he texted:

Hi Shane, Sorry 4 late text just out of metn. I know you're disappointed about my decision today. I spoke to ml&dannyrae b4 d vote&we had concerns dat i spoke to u after about. On the drink driving if I support dat bill shane der will only b one difference between me and my name sake general Michael and dat is whatever gang shoot me in west cork if i vote dat bill deyd b proud to give der names to d guards as dey wud b deemed national heros. Rural Ireland in west cork is furious about these proposals and having two brothers fighting tooth and nail 2 keep der pub doors open I cant support it in anyway shape or form. On any other votes going forward on the judiciary i will vote with u and mattie and u have my word on that. Tell mattie crack d whip from now on. Lukn forward to ur visit in west cork soon i hope. regards Michael.

(For the record, despite his promise, Michael later voted on the opposite side to me on the Judicial Appointments Bill on all occasions when he was present in the chamber.)

A few weeks later he was effusive about my visit to his west Cork kingdom, again texting privately, 'I could keep you a week in West Cork with the amount of people who are lukn 2 meet u. But dats gud news. Lots of projects and ideas going on in west cork.'

And then, on 22 August, the morning of the visit, 'the phones non-stop since 7.30 in a positive way re ur visit. Michael.'

His brother, a publican, and Michael himself met me in Bandon. We had a wonderful day, organised to Michael's time-table. He was delighted to parade the Minister for Transport, Tourism and Sport around from Kinsale to Bandon to Schull. He was a charming host. During the day, I enjoyed a bit of good-humoured banter with his brother and himself about the Road Traffic Bill, but no more.

After I arrived home late that night, I received the following text from Michael. 'Tks Shane. No need to thank me 4 lunch u fully deserved lunch and a lot more tday. It was gr8 that the people of west cork see first hand the work you do and they showed there appreciation in the welcome they gave you. Looking 4ward 2d nxt time. Regards Michael.'

Michael was right. The west Cork welcome was mighty.

How did the visiting minister who received such a warm reception become Michael's hated 'scumbag' on whose grave he was dancing in February 2020? Indeed, Michael was not only dancing on the grave, he was even boasting that he was the undertaker!

I am loath to enlighten him, but today there are many competitors vying for that accolade. No other commentators have credited Michael with a ministerial scalp. Most, somewhat uncharitably, insist that I dug the grave myself! The 2017 Road Traffic Bill seems to have fractured more friendships than any other piece of legislation seen in the Houses of the Oireachtas in recent years.

On my way home from west Cork that night, I dropped in to meet my then friend, Mattie McGrath, at his invitation. He escorted me around a few locations in Cahir. Once again, the people were warm and welcoming. Mattie did mention the plight of the publicans when we passed a couple of pubs that had recently closed down. He was as delighted as Michael to shepherd a minister around the local clubs and hostelries. He even persuaded me to visit a wobbly bridge in Aherlow in deepest Tipperary, badly in need of attention. We were greeted in the dark by local people with torches, seeking immediate funds to repair the damage. Not long after I failed to deliver the local goods for Mattie, he took a more strident, far more personal, turn against the Road Traffic Bill.

The bill had been conceived one day in the Department of Transport when an enlightened senior civil servant, Ray O'Leary, was talking me through the drugs-driving legislation initiated by my predecessor, Paschal Donohoe. Somehow, he dropped into the conversation, as subtle civil servants do, the fact that there was a loophole in former Minister Noel Dempsey's Road Traffic Act 2010. It had allowed first-time drink-driver offenders who were over the legal alcohol limit to escape disqualifica-tion. If a driver's reading was between 50 mg (Dempsey's new lower limit in 2010) and 80 mg, the former limit, per 100 ml of blood, he or she could settle for three penalty points and a fine, instead of a period of disqualification. It was more than a loophole, it was a 'Get out of Jail' card.

It seemed unbelievable. Some drinking drivers were escaping the penalty of disqualification. As Dempsey himself had said at the time, it was a 'yellow card'. More mercy was being given to the drink drivers than was being granted to their victims. The reason for this extraordinary concession in the 2010 Road Traffic Act was the hyperactivity of one of Ireland's most powerful lobby groups, the Vintners' Federation of Ireland (VFI). Initially, Noel Dempsey's bill had intended that the lower 50mg limit should apply to everyone, but rural TDs, under severe pressure from publicans and vintners, extracted a major concession. First-time offenders with alcohol levels of between 50mg and 80mg could escape the driving ban, merely receiving three penalty points and a fine — the same penalty as for failing to yield at a yield sign. The vintners lobby won. Dempsey, undoubtedly a genuine reformer, had bottled it after a Fianna Fáil backbench revolt.

Aisling Dunne and I set about closing the loophole and reforming the law. It seemed a simple task. We wanted to ensure one simple result: everyone found to be driving over the existing limit would be off the road. Never has a punishment been more suited to a crime and it would send a clear and unambiguous message: drink-driving is a serious offence. A short bill would do the trick. There would not be much opposition, apart from the publicans. Or so we believed.

Aisling is from a generation that is often shocked by tales of the recklessness of drivers in the nineteen-eighties and nineties. I am from an age group, many of whom had been guilty of madness on the road in their youth. We had drunk too much and driven under the influence. The offending culture is often wrongly dismissed as history, but when I regaled Aisling and others with stories of our insanity behind the wheel, they were totally disapproving and often disbelieving. Aisling researched the figures. The big eye-opener to us was that the drink-and-drive culture had never fully died. Drink-driving was back on the rise.

My press adviser, Carol Hunt, played a priceless role in sending the message about drink-driving out to a wider public. Carol worked passionately with the Road Safety Authority and the victims groups, starting well behind, but moving public opinion behind them over several months. She was pivotal in persuading the Labour Party to back the bill and abandon Alan Kelly's pro-vintner stance. The message for the media was clear: tolerance of drinking and driving should be banished, as part of a culture indulged by a previous generation.

Thirty years earlier I had been a heavy drinker. In those distant days there was heavy drinking in the Dáil bar, where I spent far too much time. Boozing took place morning, noon and night. Today, I could tell tales about household names that would shock the nation. They could do the same to me, so a balance of terror still exists. *Omertà*. Maybe in the next book.

Some close to me insist that I was definitely an undiagnosed alcoholic. It was an unproven charge, but I realised in sober moments that I had a problem. So in 1985 I gave up alcohol and haven't touched a drop since. Having abused drink myself in the past initially made me feel guilty about penalising others for doing exactly the same thing in 2017. But I knew the damage alcohol could do and that I myself could have caused a death from being blotto at the wheel. Now in a position to save lives, I could either turn a blind eye or I could work to change the law.

There were occasions during the battle to enact the legislation when my past arose. Richard Downes asked me about it on an RTÉ *Prime Time* programme. I admitted that I had been an offender in times gone by. Charges of hypocrisy followed. The vintners were whispering in the ears of journalists that I had been a big drinker in my youth, forced to give up the gargle, on a bogus mission of mercy because I could not handle the demon myself.

Although the vintners were traditionally believed to have stronger links with Fianna Fáil, they had spooked my Fine Gael colleagues with equally energetic lobbying. By the time the measure reached cabinet, both the Licensed Vintners' Association (LVA) and the Vintners' Federation of Ireland had done their homework. The VFI had written to every publican asking them to raise their opposition to the bill with their local TDs and senators. They began to exploit their links and milk their network. Their tentacles stretched into nearly every village pub in rural Ireland. They had political connections that reached far beyond the Mattie McGrath and the Michael Collins brigades. Members of the cabinet were lobbied fiercely.

The politics of alcohol were not just intense at cabinet level, they hit closer to home. My own minister of state, Fine Gael's Patrick O'Donovan, was no fan of the legislation. He was frequently asked by the media about the reforms and often failed to give a wholehearted endorsement. He wanted to see convincing 'evidence' of the need for the bill, a thinly disguised code for his determination to see it evaporate. Patrick's brother is a publican, owning O'Donovans pub in Bandon, Cork.

The general scheme of the bill was drafted by enthusiastic civil servants. It was approved collectively by Enda Kenny's ministers on 14 February 2017 and, predictably, sent to the Joint Oireachtas Committee on Transport, Tourism and Sport for pre-legislative scrutiny, expected by some to be buried there, never again to see the light of day. The chairman of the Transport Committee charged with examination of the bill was none other than Fine Gael's Brendan Griffin. Brendan, from Kerry, was a former publican in the Castle

Inn, Castlemaine and was thought not to favour the bill. My guess was that Kenny had despatched the scheme of the bill in Brendan's direction with clear riding instructions not to hurry it along. (In a strange quirk of fate, later in the year when Leo Varadkar took over as Taoiseach, O'Donovan was replaced by Brendan as my minister of state. Brendan and I could have had a stressed relationship if he had not been such a constructive problem-solver, intent on compromise before confrontation, on friendship before friction.)

As expected, there was no sense of urgency from the Oireachtas committee. Two months later, it called in the sworn enemies of the bill, the VFI and the LVA, to offer evidence. The VFI's chief executive, Padraig Cribben, accused me of 'misleading the public'. He insisted that the bill would not 'contribute to saving one life'. The committee agreed to meet again, but unhelpfully, not for yet another month.

Soon afterwards, we got a break. On 14 June, Leo Varadkar took over from Enda Kenny as Taoiseach. A supporter of the bill was now in command. Brendan Griffin became a minister of state in my department and Fergus O'Dowd, a supporter of the bill, became chair of the committee.

We were in business. The bill was soon back at the cabinet table, but in the intervening months more powerful political opposition had been given time to mobilise. The Vintners' lobby had been hard at work. It could count on big-hitters among Fine Gael's ministers. The bill was consequently on a knife edge when it came to counting the numbers in the cabinet. On 10 July, the night before it was due back at cabinet for government approval, I texted several Fine Gael ministers who were opposed to the bill, including Michael Creed, Heather Humphreys, Paul Kehoe, Michael Ring, chief whip Joe McHugh and independent Denis Naughten. At the same time, I contacted two friendly Fine Gael faces, Frances Fitzgerald and

Paschal Donohoe. Paschal was fully behind the measure, but was unable to be at the key cabinet meeting.

I knew that the Taoiseach (now, thankfully, a supportive Leo rather than a lukewarm Enda) was onside, yet feared that his own reluctant troops might force him to shelve the bill. I received no reply from Michael Creed or Denis Naughten. Michael Ring was a lost cause. Heather Humphreys texted: 'Thanks for your text, Shane. As you know I can't help saying what I think!! Chat in the morning.'

Joe McHugh, to whom I had appealed, pointing out the alarming number of road deaths in Donegal, gave a similar reply: 'chat in the morning'. Paul Kehoe's response was identical: 'will have chat in the morning re bill.' You'd swear they had all received a midnight briefing from the Vintners.

The last person these three wanted to 'have a chat with' in the morning was the Minister for Transport. The chat never happened. But you can be sure they chatted to one another.

Frances Fitzgerald gave the only positive reply: 'yes, will do' promised the Tánaiste. And she did. Paschal said yes, but he would be in Brussels.

The omens were not good, but it was 11 July, my birthday. I had hopes of a gift from Leo.

The cabinet debated the bill in full. It was a rare event, a robust meeting with lively discussion and even a few moments of spontaneous passion, with opposition from all the usual suspects. I was nervously counting the numbers as the argument progressed. It was touch and go. Rural ministers Charlie Flanagan, Heather Humphreys, Denis Naughten, Michael Creed, Michael Ring, Paul Kehoe and Joe McHugh were all, in various degrees, critical of the measures.

At the end of the discourse, the Taoiseach looked around the room and confided that he didn't think that taking votes in the cabinet was a good way of operating. He said he had counted the numbers around the table and the bill should go ahead. It was a close call. No one uttered a word of dissent. The bill was through another hoop. Next stop, the Dáil.

The bill had landed most political parties in turmoil. Fine Gael were not alone in being divided. While Fianna Fáil had started as opponents of the bill, their opposition was softening a little, but the numbers were not in our favour. Some rural Fine Gael TDs, including Hildegarde Naughton (Galway West), Peter Burke (Longford-Westmeath) and Pat Deering (Carlow-Kilkenny) were seeking a free vote, as were my own colleagues in the Independent Alliance. The Labour Party was divided. As the summer recess began in 2017, we were lagging behind.

Yet we had vocal, growing support from other quarters. Outside the two state bodies, the Road Safety Authority and the Garda Síochána, we had two other powerful allies, whose crucial role in the fight for the bill merits more than an acknowledgement. One ally was not surprising, the other was an unexpected bonus.

Unconditional support came from the noblest advocates of them all: the victims' groups. The families of road victims, who had suffered most, were lining up behind the bill. They carried a moral authority that was difficult to challenge. They had nothing to gain from the passage of the bill, except that it might ensure that others did not suffer the same pain as they themselves would endure for the rest of their lives. There are few higher callings than that.

The victims' groups had struck up a good relationship with the RSA and the Gardaí. As part of their 'Crashed Lives' campaign, shown on RTÉ, the RSA had made a deeply moving video of the agony of Gillian Treacy, a bereaved mother with a superhuman bravery that is difficult to describe in words. Gillian had lost her four-year-old son, Ciarán, when the car she was driving was hit by a drunk driver. She herself had been horrifically injured in the same crash. Somehow, she had found the courage to broadcast a message against drink-driving, describing her own emotional grief and physical pain in chilling terms. Her devastating experience, movingly told by her on television, had shocked the nation. Her mission and message about drink-driving had a powerful effect on public opinion at a crucial time.

Gillian was part of the Irish Road Victims Association (IRVA), a group led by Donna Price, another woman who had suffered a personal tragedy of unspeakable sadness. Donna's eighteen-year-old son Darren, an inter-county footballer, died in March 2006 as a result of a collision with an articulated lorry outside Tyrrellspass, Co. Westmeath. Donna set up IRVA in 2012 to provide bereavement counselling for victims' families and assist them in Garda investigations, inquests and legal proceedings. It hosts an annual event to mark 'World Day of Remembrance for Road Victims'. Ever since Darren had been killed so unnecessarily, Donna has devoted much of her life to the cause and prevention of road accidents.

Donna, Gillian and other wonderful women and men, like Susan Gray and her Promoting Awareness Responsibility and Care (PARC) road safety group, joined the campaign. During the summer, they rang TDs, they lobbied Fianna Fáil's Micheál Martin and Robert Troy, their transport spokesperson, they contacted the Labour parliamentary party members, where Deputy Alan Kelly was fighting a rearguard action to beat the bill. According to the *Irish Times*, Kelly had been among an all-party group of local TDs who met the vintners in Tipperary as early as March 2017. At the meeting, local Independent TDs Mattie McGrath and Michael Lowry, with local Fianna Fáil TD Jackie Cahill, joined Kelly in lining up four-square behind the vintners. It was sad to see Tipperary TDs taking their lead from the vintners, particularly as the county consistently had one of the highest number of road deaths.

The vintners may have been fast out of the traps, but the victims' groups quickly caught up. While the well-heeled professional lobbyists were nailing down the TDs by putting them under fierce local political pressure, the victims' groups were winning over public opinion. They held vigils outside Leinster House and lobbied deputies from all parties. They wrote letters, made calls, were interviewed on the media and held individual meetings with Oireachtas members. Donna Price even led a group of members to meet Deputy Timmy Dooley in the Fianna Fáil tent at the 2017 ploughing championships in Screggan, Co. Offaly. Those whom they approached in the RSA tent at the same championships would have needed hearts of stone not to be persuaded by the sight of Donna holding a photograph of her late son Darren, one of 187 framed pictures of road victims on display.

Some did have hearts of stone. When IRVA were holding a vigil outside Leinster House, Danny Healy-Rae approached them and appallingly insisted that 'two or three glasses' would not be the cause of road accidents.

While the Healy-Rae clan, Mattie McGrath and Michael Collins continued with their callous opposition to a life-saving bill, another heart-rending victim, Cork farmer Noel Clancy, was campaigning for a non-drink related change in the driving laws.

Noel's wife and daughter died in 2015 when their car ploughed into a flooded ditch after being hit by another car, driven by an unaccompanied learner driver. It happened on a blind junction. Noel's wife Geraldine and daughter Louise were drowned, unable to escape, trapped in a car because the doors were jammed.

Like Donna Price, Susan Gray and Gillian Treacy, Noel resolved to save others from agonies similar to his own. He joined Susan Gray and independent TD Tommy Broughan in seeking to insert an amendment on unaccompanied drivers into the 2017 Road Traffic Bill.

Noel campaigned night and day for a change in the law, making it an offence for the owner of a vehicle to allow an unaccompanied driver to use it. The so-called 'Clancy Amendment' also allowed a Garda to detain a vehicle if the driver was an unaccompanied learner. I promised to introduce it, but it was initially delayed in the Attorney General's Office. Noel was rightly impatient. Eventually, I was able to bring it as an amendment to the Road Traffic Bill at a late stage. Despite opposition from the usual quarters, it was eventually inserted. This change would never have been achieved without Noel Clancy and the support of PARC. People are alive today because of his dedication to the memory of his wife and daughter.

The other major ally in promoting the bill was a great political surprise. While there were splits in Fianna Fáil, Fine Gael, Labour and my own Independent Alliance on the issue, one party stood firm. Twenty years ago, it might have been difficult for me to write this, but Sinn Féin alone showed a commitment to road safety that was unyielding, and impervious to the pressures of the vintners' lobby or the myth that the bill was an attack on rural Ireland. Sinn Féin not only supported this measure, a government bill, but, unlike Fianna Fáil, they did not try to exploit Fine Gael divisions on the issue. Furthermore, when they were needed for votes, they were always present.

The others who were ever-present at the debates were, again, the victims' groups, sitting in the public gallery. They were there throughout the lengthy filibusters orchestrated by Mattie McGrath, the Healy-Raes and Michael Collins. My most abiding memory of that eighteen-month saga is the constant presence of the bereaved watching every move, bewildered by the filibuster, wondering if it would ever end.

I shared their anger. While it is part of a minister's job to take the flak from the opposition, much of the filibuster was reduced to personal abuse, not quite of the Michael Collins 'scumbag' variety, but not far from it. Michael Healy-Rae was not guilty of this, but others in the obstructionist camp never stopped. Mattie McGrath was particularly personal. I pretended for months that it was water off a duck's back.

Suddenly, one evening in May 2018, following months of time-wasting abuse, I cracked. After a few hours of being harangued in the chamber by Mattie and his gang, I headed into the Dáil café for some peace and quiet. In front of me at a table I spotted Mattie, the man who had taken weeks out of Dáil time and cared nothing for the plight of the victims' groups in the gallery. I flipped my lid. According to the *Irish Times* and to numerous other media outlets, I accused Mattie of being 'a bollocks' and even 'an out and out bollocks'.

The report went on that 'Mr McGrath is said to have stood up to argue with Mr Ross, but was restrained by his daughter, with whom he was eating at the time.' It continued, 'Another member of the rural Independent Group, Michael Collins, was also present.'

It was an unseemly spat. Road safety is a subject that rightly inspires anger and passion but should not prompt such undignified outbursts. Unfortunately, I reluctantly feel obliged to confirm the accuracy of *Irish Times* journalist Fiach Kelly's story to the last letter, even to the last expletive. It was so accurate that I cannot imagine where he and all the other media, which covered it, heard it. Certainly not from me.

Despite my intemperate outburst, the opponents of the bill had been reduced to filibustering because the Dáil arithmetic had moved against them. The victims' groups campaign had landed several punches. The public was undoubtedly now on our side. The vintners were in retreat and Fianna Fáil was, as ever, reading the signals and looking for an honourable exit. Robert Troy did not want to be lumped in the same bracket as Danny Healy-Rae and Mattie McGrath. Fianna Fáil had a difficult withdrawal to navigate.

The first big test had been the vote on second stage of the bill in January 2018. It turned out to be an overwhelming victory, 85-8 in favour. Fianna Fáil, after all their posturing, ducked the issue and abstained. Fine Gael, albeit subject to the party whip, voted in favour without a single deputy breaking ranks. Labour voted 'Yes', with Alan Kelly conveniently missing the division. The Independent Alliance voted four out of five in favour. Boxer Moran, originally an opponent, had suffered a personal tragedy when his own brother was killed in a car accident. After speaking with the victims' groups in the tent at Screggan, he decided to vote 'Yes'. Seán Canney, despite reservations, abstained.

If there had been a free vote six months earlier, we would have been defeated by a distance, but a big swing in public opinion beat the vintners, stiffened the backbones of the Fine Gael backbenchers and spooked Fianna Fáil. It didn't spook the eight militant opponents of the bill. Mattie McGrath, the two Healy-Raes and Michael Collins were joined in the 'Nil' lobby by Michael Fitzmaurice, Michael Lowry, Clare Daly and Mick Wallace.

The filibuster awaiting the progress of the later stages of the bill remained a further hurdle, but in the meantime, off the Dáil stage, two vacancies arose on the board of the Road Safety Authority. I asked my officials to advertise and recruit at least one director with personal experience of road safety advocacy. The independent selection process went ahead, including interviews, without any interference from me. I do not know to this day who applied. But it was a sweet moment when I was asked to sign off on the appointments of Gillian Treacy and Donna

Price, both from IRVA. Two brave road safety campaigners were now directors of the RSA.

That was January. The filibuster continued until May. Eventually, Deputy Catherine Murphy, no lover of the guillotine and even less a lover of the government, moved a closure motion. Sinn Féin, who were equally vehemently opposed to the use of the guillotine, were fed up with the antics of the four main obstructionists. The game was up. The filibuster was brought to an end by a Dáil decision. Even the Left had endured enough.

The Dáil finally passed the Road Traffic Bill 2017 on 6 July 2018 by 75 votes to 8. Fianna Fáil, originally opponents in deference to the vintners, becoming abstainers at the bill's second stage, voted in favour of it at the final stage. Never has a party in recent memory made such a dramatic change of position on a controversial bill, in hot pursuit of public opinion. Alan Kelly was consistent; he went missing again. Seán Canney moved over to our side with Fianna Fáil.

The last hurdle was the Seanad, the scene of many long battles in the past. A full debate, or even a repeat of the Dáil delays, was feared.

We were in for a surprise. A bill that had taken a year to be put through the Dáil, passed second stage in the Seanad within an hour! Attendance was low. All the remaining stages took an equally short time to complete. The disinterest was chronic. Everyone was suffering from 'rural victimisation' fatigue. Fianna Fáil, bruised by the experience, wanted to see the back of the entire episode. There were not enough senators in the chamber to force a vote at any stage. The bill was completed on Tuesday, 17 July 2018 and six days later was signed into law by President Michael D. Higgins.

The 'Clancy Amendment' was commenced on 22 December of that year, three years to the day after the death of Noel's wife and daughter. The Department of Transport, the RSA, Aisling, Carol and I marked the occasion with a dignified, but pleasant, lunch with Noel and representatives of the victims' groups, the true heroes of the Road Traffic Bill battle.

On 19 June 2019 it was an honour to accept an award in Brussels that recognised the sacrifices made by so many, including Noel Clancy. The European Transport Safety Council chose Ireland as the winner of its Road Safety Performance Index trophy for 2018. It was the year we beat the filibuster, strengthened the drink-driving laws, introduced the Clancy Amendment and put two advocates for road safety (Gillian Treacy and Donna Price) from the victims groups on the board of the Road Safety Authority. At last we seemed to be making progress.

8

Judges Defend Four Courts Fortress

ON 15 APRIL 2020, a sensitive memo appeared among our cabinet papers. Minister for Justice, Charlie Flanagan, wanted to appoint a new President of the High Court. There was a vacancy being created by Peter Kelly, an efficient, capable judge, who was due to reach the retirement age of seventy two months later, on 18 June.

An advisory committee would be set up to make a recommendation. Charlie would be given three names and bring one to cabinet. The committee was to consist of the Attorney General, Séamus Woulfe, the Chief Justice, Frank Clarke, with a lay member in the chair. The lay member was still to be confirmed. She turned out to be Jane Williams, the chair of the Top Level Appointments Committee (TLAC), which appoints people to senior civil service positions. As far as most cabinet members were concerned, she might as well have been the Queen of Sheba.

Jane had done a couple of these judicial gigs before. So had Séamus and Frank. The drill was that they looked first for applications (expressions of interest) from sitting judges and senior counsel, examined them and made a recommendation to Charlie.

It was open to the trio to hold interviews. They never did. They felt it was enough to read the written offerings from each of the candidates on why they should be the preferred choice, then have a chat and make a recommendation.

The practice was unsatisfactory because it was lacking in transparency. It was far too cosy. Two lawyers, with inside knowledge of all possible candidates, would be able to make a rapid choice. The procedure emerged only under the guidance of Justice Minister Frances Fitzgerald, in a gesture to satisfy my campaign for judicial reform, because previously there had been no process at all for these senior appointments. This experiment offered little comfort.

It was under this system that the current Chief Justice, the President of the Court of Appeal, the Presidents of the Circuit Court and the District Court had been picked. And, in my opinion, that was the trouble.

This time there was a hiccup. A funny thing happened to this process on the road to the presidency of the High Court.

On 22 May another memo appeared in our cabinet papers on the same subject. There was a sudden change of plan. The Chief Justice, Frank Clarke, had cried off. The new cabinet memo intriguingly revealed that this inexplicable change was 'to ensure no perception of any conflict of interest'. No reference was made to what on earth that conflict of interest might be.

At that cabinet meeting, Charlie Flanagan elaborated. He now had a new advisory committee. He wanted the President of the Court of Appeal, George Birmingham, to take Frank Clarke's place on the advisory committee, which would now comprise the President of the Court of Appeal, the Attorney General and the chairperson of TLAC. Or George, Séamus and Jane.

Being sceptical of all things judicial, I smelled a rodent. At the cabinet meeting, I asked Charlie to tell us what exactly was the conflict of interest issue that was worrying Frank Clarke so much that he had to pull out? He stonewalled. I persisted, asking what conflict existed that would not equally apply to his proposed substitute George Birmingham? Who had chosen George to replace Frank on the committee? If Frank knew all the candidates, George would surely know them as well? I wondered whether there was a business interest somewhere, or a personal relationship. Charlie offered no explanation. Inexplicably, judges, unlike others in powerful public positions, do not have to declare their business interests. They should.

It was an uneasy moment at the cabinet. Unusually, the Attorney General, Séamus Woulfe, intervened. He tried to assure the cabinet that the reason Frank Clarke had withdrawn was in case a 'crank' might attack his bona fides. He insisted that Clarke was just showing what he called 'an abundance of caution'. Séamus Woulfe volunteered that there was nothing sinister because 'I know all the judges to some extent' and 'I know all the candidates'. He was unwittingly identifying one of the serious problems surrounding lawyers appointing judges; they all know one another. The reason for the Chief Justice's sudden withdrawal was as clear as mud. And it was not going to be shared with the cabinet.

The temperature was rising. The Taoiseach stepped in to defuse the situation. Leo suggested that Charlie should have a private word with me outside the cabinet room. I settled for that.

That evening, Charlie told me the reason behind the 'no perception of any conflict of interest' riddle. It did not include the possibility of a 'crank' appearing on the scene, as Séamus Woulfe had suggested. I thanked him, but I was not happy. Such cloak and dagger exploits increase unease among the public about how judges are chosen. The name of Judge Mary Irvine was already travelling around the corridors of the Four Courts as odds-on favourite for the job.

At 7.29 a.m. on Thursday, 4 June, Charlie texted me. Charlie likes making early morning calls. They can be a bit disorientating. 'Quick call?' he requested. When he pitched it in that casual manner, I knew we had a problem. He presumably hoped he would wake me from my slumbers and I would agree to anything. I didn't get back to him.

At 9.07 a.m. he texted again: 'hoping to speak to you'. When he was at his most humble, it was time to sup with my longest spoon.

He wanted to put Mary Irvine's appointment to the Presidency of the High Court through cabinet. I sent him a reply saying: 'Cannot agree this appointment. We agreed interim govern-ment would not make appointments of this sort. Sorry. Shane.'

Charlie responded: 'We cannot leave it vacant especially with massive Covid case backlog.'

With Charlie, there was always a reason.

I asked him to delay the announcement. He initially refused (as Charlie usually did), but relented (as Charlie generally did). So the item did not appear on the cabinet agenda that week. Behind the scenes, Aisling had been speaking to the Taoiseach's chief of staff, Brian Murphy, who, surprisingly, also felt that the announcement should not be delayed for too much longer.

Despite my protestations, the appointment of the President of the High Court resurfaced at cabinet, the next week, on 12 June. Fine Gael seemed determined to fill the vacancy before it handed over the reins of government.

Charlie brought in the item underarm, meaning that no advance notice was given to the cabinet. Few other ministers (bar one or two insiders) had received the nominee's name before the meeting. Judges' names are normally simply bounced on a compliant cabinet to be rubber-stamped.

Charlie proposed Mary Irvine. Had I not spoken, the appoint-ment of the new President of the High Court would have gone through cabinet on the nod. The elephant in the room — Frank Clarke's withdrawal from the advisory committee — was never mentioned. No one in the cabinet, bar me, wanted to ask anything about the process.

There is no question that Mary Irvine is a fine judge. She is ultra-efficient, an important talent for someone organising the High Court list. She is obviously highly thought of by the Chief Justice. She had already received preferment under Frank Clarke's stewardship, not only being appointed to his Supreme Court in March 2019, but also as his personal choice for chair of the key new Personal Injuries Guidelines Committee of the Judicial Council in November 2019. Observers were curious about why Mr Justice Kevin Cross, a man with years of experience in this speciality, was excluded from the seven-person committee, but the choice was at the absolute discretion of the Chief Justice. Cross was seen by many as too pro-claimants.

There were several questions needing to be asked about the process. This one simply did not add up to a transparent, open appointment. I had heard the name Mary Irvine long before the process had properly begun. There was a mysterious need to ensure that there should be 'no perception of any conflict of interest' from the Chief Justice who withdrew. There was an underarm, last-minute cabinet memo.

I asked Charlie Flanagan a few questions. It was a chance to find out what went on behind these tightly closed doors when insiders pick judges. The questions were aimed at probing whether the process is far too cosy, that it is a place where insiders pick insiders, where Law Library influence meets political patronage.

How many 'expressions of interest' were there, I asked? Were there any interviews? How many names were proposed to the minister? How often did the committee meet? Why was the memo underarm? Had the personnel changed midstream following Frank Clarke's withdrawal? And finally, had Fianna Fáil and the Greens given their approval? (The new government was soon to be formed.)

The Attorney General again stepped in, putting his best foot forward to assist the Minister for Justice, who was not on the advisory committee:

There had been twelve expressions of interest: one from the Supreme Court, two from the Court of Appeal and nine from the High Court.

There had been no interviews. None.

Three names had gone up to the minister, unranked in order of preference.

The minister had brought only one name to cabinet.

Fianna Fáil and the Greens were not going to oppose the appointment.

There had been two meetings of the advisory committee to select the candidates. It was not clear if any were held before Frank Clarke's departure.

Suddenly my hackles were up. How come there were twelve candidates, but not a single interview had been held? Did Séamus Woulfe and Judge George Birmingham know all twelve of the interested parties so well that it was unnecessary to meet any of them and ask questions? Conversely, surely Jane Williams, the independent, non-legal chair, would not know all, or indeed any, of the candidates? Surely she would want to interview at least three of the twelve? She didn't call in even one of them. Why not? Surely that would give her a better chance of forming an opinion independent of George and Séamus?

Jane Williams should be a very important part of the selection process. She was totally different from the other three legal players, the Minister for Justice, the Attorney General and the Chief Justice. The other three had qualities in common. All, undoubtedly people of integrity, had strong past or present associations with Fine Gael. All three were lawyers. Jane too has strong legal connections because she is married to David Sanfey, a former senior partner of one of Ireland's most established legal firms, A & L Goodbody solicitors.

George Birmingham, who replaced Frank Clarke on the advisory committee, had been deeply embedded in Fine Gael during his early days as a barrister. He was on the Fine Gael national executive in 1976 and became a member of Dublin Corporation for Raheny in 1979. He was elected a Fine Gael TD in 1981 and, greatly favoured by Taoiseach Garret FitzGerald, was made a minister of state from 1982 to 1987. He lost his seat and returned to the Bar in 1989, becoming a senior counsel in 1999 and a High Court judge in 2007. In April 2018, he became President of the Court of Appeal.

Séamus Woulfe was not a front-line Fine Gael star, like George, but is, by nature and by practice, a Fine Gael foot soldier. He has been particularly active as a Fine Gael member and a branch secretary in Dublin Bay North. He is a strong supporter of his local Fine Gael TD, Richard Bruton, with whom he served in cabinet. He lives in Clontarf in the former constituency of his co-committee member, George Birmingham. They know each other well. Séamus sat on the advisory committee that selected George for the presidency of the Court of Appeal, yet felt no need to recuse himself. That committee also held no interviews.

Charlie Flanagan, the Fine Gael Minister for Justice, who received the list of three names from Séamus, George and Jane, is a lawyer and a Blueshirt to the last drop of his blood. He is as loyal to the legal profession as he is to his party.

These were the selectors.

It is worth pointing out that George Birmingham was only the first 'sub' in this peculiar process. Chief Justice Frank Clarke was the first choice. His withdrawal was peculiar because in the past he had happily served on such an advisory committee. Indeed, he had been a member with both Jane Williams and

Séamus Woulfe on a notable occasion. In April 2018, when the contest was held for the presidency of another court, the Court of Appeal, Frank played his full part. He did not declare any 'perception of any conflict of interest'. The result of the contest in that case was the appointment of George Birmingham.

Séamus Woulfe, Frank Clarke and Jane Williams recommended George Birmingham for the presidency of the Appeal Court. Charlie Flanagan approved and brought his name to cabinet. Quite a merry-go-round.

On that occasion Frank could reasonably have opted to recuse himself from the process, but he didn't. Frank and George had a similar pedigree. Both had been members of Fine Gael before becoming judges. Frank was fully committed to Fine Gael when, upon leaving secondary school, he joined Fine Gael and commenced canvassing for former Fine Gael Minister Jim Mitchell in Dublin South-West. He was on the liberal wing of the party and wrote speeches for Garret FitzGerald. Frank even stood unsuccessfully for the Seanad in 1983 on the Cultural and Educational Panel. He came 21st of 22 candidates, securing just seven votes.

More interesting still was Clarke's commitment at the time to one particular TD. Frank was election agent for a Dáil deputy, and later minister, by the name of George Birmingham.

None of this is any longer widely discussed. Nor does it make either Frank or George a bad judge, which neither is. But it does give rise to two questions: is the process of choosing judges fair and transparent? In other cases, could it possibly be subject to political influence?

There is no suggestion that Mary Irvine was not qualified for the important post. She obviously is. Nor, unlike all other players bar Jane Williams, is she identified with any political party. The question mark in this instance hangs over the process, not the result. The power to exclude is as potent as the power to select. Would any of the nine losers in this instance have a case to make that their exclusion was decided in a cursory manner, that a decision to eliminate them was taken without due diligence? Why was not a single one of them (or any of the three people whose names were handed to Charlie) given the benefit of an interview? And, more immediately, why did Frank Clarke pull out of one process that selected Mary Irvine, but remained part of another, which selected George?

The appointment of Ireland's judges is an unholy mess. The struggle to reform it throughout the last government was relentlessly resisted. Obstacles were placed in my way at every stage. Politicians and judges united in attempts to defeat the Judicial Appointments Commission Bill. Politicians wanted to keep intact the political patronage over appointments to the bench, while judges wished to wrest that power from them and keep it to themselves. Politicians and judges were agreed on one thing: my Judicial Appointments Commission Bill was the work of the devil incarnate. It must be defeated.

As Minister for Justice under Enda Kenny, Frances Fitzgerald was initially given the unenviable task of dealing with Aisling Dunne and me on the reforming bill. Aisling, a lawyer herself, was originally lukewarm on the need for reform, but, as a former barrister, she had priceless insights into the workings of the Law Library. She became a believer and was utterly indispensable in the promotion and understanding of the legal complexities of the bill.

The Department of Justice, the officials in the Attorney General's office and all the major political parties, except Sinn Féin, wanted to retain the status quo. It suited Fianna Fáil, Fine Gael and Labour. In time, each of them had taken their turn to appoint party loyalists as judges. There was a silent understanding that their day would come, as it inevitably did. As power changed hands, so did political patronage. Places on the bench were the spoils of political victory. The Independent Alliance had stood four-square behind an end to the curse of cronyism.

The only chink in our armour occurred one day in the Members' Bar when Boxer Moran, Finian and I were discussing political parties turning loyal supporters into judges. Boxer joked far too loudly, 'Why can't *we* have one of those?' Thankfully, nobody overheard him.

The Independent Alliance's Judicial Appointments Commission Bill was based on two simple principles. The new Commission set up to choose judges would have both an independent lay chair and a lay majority. Judges would play an important role on the new Commission, but lawyers would not be allowed to hold a majority. It was our view that insiders in either politics or in the law should not be able to cram the bench with their cronies and favourites.

As the minister entrusted to deal with Aisling and with me on this issue, Frances Fitzgerald had been asked to tiptoe through a minefield. She was dutiful rather than enthusiastic. She had made it crystal clear during the government formation negotiations that she was less than enamoured with the bill. But she was honourable. She had pledged to implement it. She would stick to the timetable and bite the unpalatable bullet. In truth, hardly anyone in Fine Gael wanted the bill. They had enjoyed their last spell in office, conspicuous for naked political patronage not just in the judiciary, but in political appointments across the board. They were as wedded to political patronage as were Fianna Fáil and Labour. It was buried deep in their DNA.

Yet Frances picked up the ball and ran with it. We had an early discussion with her in her office before the end of May 2016. It was followed by meetings in June and July with her, the Attorney General, Máire Whelan and their officials, as we thrashed out the provisions of the bill. We were moving slowly towards the drafting of a radical measure.

All the while, the background music was deeply hostile. The Law Library, backed by the judges, was mobilising against the bill. The wider legal lobby was weighing in. Those lawyers who double-jobbed as deputies and senators were unanimously opposing it. Labour, as culpable as either of the two big parties at appointing their own followers to plum positions, wanted to retain the current arrangements. Fine Gael backbenchers were briefing the media against the bill. The *Irish Times* hated it, writing countless editorials opposing it.

Over the summer and autumn of 2016, as the opposition to the bill grew louder, we flexed our political muscles and began to block the appointment of all judges. We made it clear to the Fine Gael element in the government that we were not prepared to approve the appointment of any further judges under the present rotten system, unless we saw progress in the promise on judicial reform made in the Programme for Government.

Fianna Fáil boxed clever. In late July an article appeared in the *Sunday Times*, revealing that Jim O'Callaghan, Fianna Fáil Justice spokesperson and senior counsel, was preparing his own Private Members' Bill to reform judicial appointments. Jim's initiative was unexpected, not only in the speed of its appearance, but also in its supposedly noble aspirations. It paid lip service to independent judges, to appointments on merit and to an end to political allegiance influencing judicial appointments. It is, of course, far easier to disdain the perks of office when in opposition. It sounded good. We could even agree with much of the rhetoric in the preamble to Jim's bill. I welcomed parts of it as an acknowledgement of the crying need for change.

In reality, Jim O'Callaghan's bill was an exocet from the Four Courts. It was a pre-emptive strike from the Law Library, designed to torpedo our bill or, at the very least, to muddy the waters. At one cabinet discussion, minister Leo Varadkar rightly dubbed it the 'Law Library Bill'.

Political patronage may well have been targeted in the O'Callaghan bill, but the substitute — dictatorship from the legal eagles — would have been no better. Jim's bill proposed an Appointments Commission of twelve members. Seven of them would be lawyers. Five of those lawyers' positions would be filled by the presidents of each court. The other two legal places would be filled by nominees of the Bar Council and the Law Society. The remaining five members would come from worthy civil society groups, including the Free Legal Advice Centres and the Citizens Information Board. Lawyers would be in a clear majority. The chair would be taken by none other than the Chief Justice. It was a stitch-up. The bill was full of further conditions designed to ensure that even the lay nominees must possess a legal knowledge unattained by most independent laypeople.

It was a cunning manoeuvre and would set the agenda. Political interference was to be replaced by judicial control of the process. Jim O'Callaghan had two masters, Fianna Fáil and the Four Courts. The bill favoured the Four Courts. Jim's bill was introduced on 16 October 2016. Our bill was still not ready. He had stolen a march.

The tension attached to our bill was increasing. I fell into a spat with Chief Justice Susan Denham in early November, after she insisted that the judges were not, as I had suggested, 'fighting change'. She took umbrage, responding publicly that the judiciary had been pushing for reforms. She was right in a sense: they wanted 'change' – but change to take the power of appointment to themselves. Susan seems to have taken it personally. I met her and her husband, Brian, at an international rugby game at the Aviva at a time when the argument was raging. She was seated at a table at half-time, enjoying the corporate hospitality and talking to Dick Spring. I approached the table and spoke to them both for a split second. She simply evaporated into thin air. That was a pity as I had known both her and Brian — on and off — for many years. She was actually a constituent, whom I would bump into occasionally near her home in Sandyford. Somehow, I suspect she didn't vote for me!

Our veto over the appointment of new judges was becoming a running sore. The judiciary was piling on the pressure, claiming that the shortage of judges was making their courts unworkable. Justice, they said, was being denied to people in need.

The Taoiseach, Enda Kenny, was being questioned in the Dáil and by individual judges, but, to his credit, he did not budge an inch on the key matters of a lay chair and a lay majority. He felt obliged, however, to distance himself from remarks I had made to the media about judges 'leading a charmed life' and at times maybe 'forgetting their oath', during my quest to introduce declarations of interest for judges. He later told me that he should have said that it was my 'personal opinion'.

We were deadlocked. The judges were incensed. A crunch meeting was arranged for 17 November in the Attorney General's office. There were hopes of a truce or progress on an agreed bill. Three heavyweight judges arrived in Upper Merrion Street: Supreme Court Judge Donal O'Donnell was accompanied by two Appeal Court Judges, Mary Finlay Geoghegan and George Birmingham. Opposite them sat Frances, Aisling and me, along with some officials, from the Department of Justice and the Attorney General's office, at the far end. In the chair was the Attorney General, Máire Whelan.

The atmosphere was icily polite. Donal O'Donnell outlined the common ground. Like us, he said, the judges wanted independence. Like us, they wanted judges appointed on merit. The judges wanted a public declaration that politics had no part in the way appointments were made. They would even agree to independent lay members.

Frances Fitzgerald seemed distinctly uncomfortable. There she was, a non-believer, pressing a measure against her better instincts. On the opposite side of the table was George Birmingham, a one-time Fine Gael minister. At times during the meeting I felt that Frances yearned to be sitting with the beaks. Nevertheless, she gallantly outlined the main contents of the bill.

George Birmingham was adamant that we couldn't possibly expect the Chief Justice to be an ordinary member of the Appointments Commission. He or she must chair it. George could not have known at that time how eighteen months later he would be appointed to the presidency of the Court of Appeal. The chair on the recommending panel would be a layperson, Jane Williams. Beside her on that occasion would sit none other than his old friend, the Chief Justice Frank Clarke, as a mere *ordinary* member of the committee.

None of the judges sitting opposite us would countenance an independent lay chair. It was outside the blinkered, elitist sphere of their understanding. In relation to the lay members, they rabbited on about 'merit'. It was obvious that 'merit' to their lordships meant something completely different to what it meant to ordinary mortals. They fretted about laypeople with agendas, singling out pro-life supporters or advocates of euthanasia as a particular danger. Could they slip through the net?

Mary Finlay Geoghegan liked what they all approvingly referred to as 'Jim's Bill'. She spoke lyrically about the need for the elusive 'merit' principle. They all worried about who would nominate the nominators, about how they could be sure of quality applications for the lay positions. Their attitude was painfully condescending. The judges wanted the selection process to be independent of politicians. They saw reform as taking away political involvement, by handing the whole process to the judiciary, with a few token laypeople of 'merit' in a minority. They could not tolerate an independent lay chair.

It had to be the Chief Justice. They would not agree to a majority of laypeople on the Commission, despite our willingness to compromise by allowing an input from all five Presidents of each of the courts.

There was little common ground. The Attorney General, who had managed to chair a session devoid of trust, pleasantries and an iota of warmth, adjourned the meeting. No progress had been made. The judges had come along seeking our capitulation and had to leave empty-handed.

The outlook was gloomy. The lack of new judges was becoming a stick with which to beat the bill. We were losing the media war over the courts being clogged up, the truth of which was debatable.

A week later another judge went public. Judge Raymond Groarke, President of the Circuit Court, let fly. He erupted, claiming that he was not going to obey the government's 'legislative strictures' if it was not going to give him enough judges. Was he threatening to break the law? On top of the Chief Justice's comments, it was obvious that a confrontation was looming.

I texted Frances that Friday evening: 'Frances, just consulted with colleagues and legal eagles. We need to hold line on no appointments. Am going to discuss other matter with opposition colleagues shortly.'

It was hardly music to her ears, but I needed to stiffen her resolve ahead of the weekend. We agreed to meet over the coming days to try to break the impasse. On Monday I expected to meet her. She was down at a funeral in Tipperary, but texted to ask if we could meet in the Sycamore Room in Government Buildings at 9 o'clock that evening. I expected a long session on the detail of the bill, especially since she had mentioned that she had 'staff working the issues'.

Two hours later she texted me again: 'Shane, Taoiseach will be at meeting, will call you around 8.30.'

I had another meeting in the constituency. Aisling was unavailable and Fine Gael would outnumber me heavily. I suddenly realised how much I depended on Aisling's agile brain and calm judgement in these high-octane meetings. I texted Frances: 'Can we meet in morning?'

There was a sense of urgency in the Tánaiste's response: 'We really need u to work this out… Can u make 9.30?'

There was more to this meeting than met the eye.

At 9.30 I headed for the Sycamore Room. Frances and Enda were both there surrounded by their officials. They were feeling the heat from the judges, from Jim O'Callaghan's bill and from their own Fine Gael backbenchers. They feared (as I did) that there could be a big backlash if ordinary citizens complained that they were being denied justice because our veto on judicial appointments had clogged up the courts.

They had a point. I suddenly realised that the Blueshirts were not always wrong or untrustworthy! We were all in a jam, but I could not let go of the only leverage I held to get the bill off the ground. They wanted a few judges. I initially said an emphatic no.

There was a sigh. Enda asked me what I needed to let them have their extra judges.

I realised that there was an opportunity. A strict timetable for the bill was essential. Other reforms must be brought forward in the new year. The General Scheme of the bill should be published within days. It should be fast-tracked to the Oireachtas Committee on Justice and Equality and the full bill should be published by the end of January.

Above all, I wanted something done to take the judges' pet project, 'Jim's Bill', off the pitch. It was already ahead of ours, causing confusion and was in danger of being passed by both houses before we were out of the traps. It would be a coup for the Four Courts, disguised as a reform measure.

Enda was helpful, telling me that he would guarantee the end of Jim's bill. Still a Doubting Thomas as far as the Taoiseach was concerned, I asked him how. He mentioned the magic words: 'Money message'. Enda explained that he could refuse to supply a money message to accompany Jim O'Callaghan's bill. That would mean it would fall, because it would not have the necessary government clearance stating that the cost of the bill to the Exchequer was insignificant or that the government approved of the expenditure.

The withholding of the necessary money message became a useful tool for the minority government to block opposition bills, which would have otherwise become law. Over fifty Private Members' Bills were blocked over the lifetime of the government. While I might usually have had concerns about this previously arcane device being used, in this instance I was delighted that Enda was willing to take it out of his armoury.

I gasped in admiration at his brazenness. More importantly, I believed him. Two days later Enda delivered. Jim O'Callaghan's bill was in front of the Oireachtas Committee on Justice and Equality months ahead of ours. It was blocked, dead in the water when it was revealed that the Taoiseach had not sent the necessary money message.

There was, of course, the mother of all rows when this transpired at the committee meeting. Poor Frances, as the Minister for Justice, had to take the abuse from the deputies and senators on the committee.

Among them was an incensed Jim O'Callaghan whose bill died that morning. Relations between O'Callaghan and the minister slumped to a new low, never to recover. A year later Fianna Fáil hounded her out of office. Perhaps the two events were connected.

Enda had gambled. Fianna Fáil huffed and puffed, but did not threaten the 'confidence and supply' agreement. The decks were cleared for our bill. We now had visibility and a timetable for its progress. In exchange, we agreed no longer to veto judicial appointments.

From that day forward, my relationship with Enda improved. It went from bad to good to very good. By the time he left office six months later, we were on excellent terms.

An obstacle had been cleared, but the road ahead was even bumpier. We allowed judges to be appointed, even though the passage of the bill remained tortuously slow. Each judge who was appointed led to a bit of taunting from the media, but it was worth the flak to ensure that the bill advanced, albeit too slowly.

One judicial appointment that caused more than a spot of bother was the decision to send Máire Whelan to the Court of Appeal. It was Enda's last cabinet meeting. He called Frances and me into an office beside the cabinet chamber to break the news. I put my head in my hands. Did the wily Enda have this move in the back of his head six months earlier, when I agreed not to veto any future appointments to the bench provided the bill was making progress? The bill was ready to go, due in the Dáil in two weeks. The Independent Alliance, had agreed to allow judges to be appointed provided the Judicial Appointments Commission Bill was making progress.

In my opinion, Máire Whelan was a highly professional Attorney General, who had been helpful in pushing the bill, whatever her personal feelings about it might be. If I had tried to block her appointment, Fine Gael might have railroaded it through cabinet. Would I have to resign? Would the government fall? Máire Whelan was certainly not a Blueshirt being rewarded by the party in power. Originally, she had been a Labour Party supporter. There had once been a tradition of Attorneys General being promoted to the judiciary. I knew there would be trouble if we let it through, but there might be more difficult consequences if it was blocked. I repeated to the cabinet that I did not like the process used to appoint judges, but Finian McGrath and I let it pass in accordance with our deal not to block judges at the time.

Micheál Martin thundered on in the Dáil about the appointment of the Attorney General to the bench. I reminded him and his troops of his decision to approve the appointment of Bertie Ahern's former partner, Celia Larkin, to the board of the National Consumer Agency in 2005. His spokesperson at the time insisted that she had been picked for her 'ability, experience and skill'. The furore over Máire Whelan's appointment wasn't helped by the fact that the announcement about the reopening the Stepaside Garda Station came on the same day. The Report into Reopening Garda Stations had been so scheduled, partly because Leo wanted it finalised before he took office, but nevertheless the media jumped to conclusions that there had been a quid pro quo. There was none. In reality, it was just the long overdue delivery of a Programme for Government commitment to reopen the six stations!

After Enda Kenny resigned, the atmosphere around the Judicial Appointments Commission Bill changed. Charlie Flanagan made way for Simon Coveney at Foreign Affairs and was moved to Justice. It didn't take me long to yearn for the good old days of Frances Fitzgerald.

Charlie was not the only man new to the job. We had a new Attorney General in Séamus Woulfe. Charlie and Séamus got along famously. Probably too famously. They were both male, both Fine Gael, both lawyers and both of a similar vintage. Quite a different kettle of fish from Frances Fitzgerald and Máire Whelan who preceded them. The new legal duo turned me into a rabid feminist within weeks. At cabinet meetings, I stared longingly at the portrait of Countess Markievicz above me and wondered what she would have made of their sudden dominance over legal decisions.

Charlie's confrontational style could not have been more different from Frances' conciliatory approach. Where she had always sought a meeting of minds, Charlie was a bruiser, a streetfighter, and no lover of independents in government. He and I got off on the wrong foot. The bill arrived in the Dáil within two weeks. I sat alongside Charlie in the Dáil as he proposed it and for the first two days of debate — drawing the ire of the bill's opponents, who likened my presence to that of a baby-sitter or enforcer. When the Taoiseach suggested that the bill might move more speedily in my absence, I agreed. However, in turn, others castigated me for sending Charlie in solo to do my bidding.

On 26 June 2017, the day before the bill came to the Dáil, the judges broke cover. They decided to tackle the new Taoiseach, Leo Varadkar, about the bill. The Presidents of all five courts, including outgoing Chief Justice Susan Denham, took a swipe at the measure, writing to Leo that it had 'serious implications for the administration of justice'. Simultaneously the Association of Judges of Ireland released a statement which described the bill as 'seriously flawed'. Parroting other judicial claims, it declared that the Office of the Chief Justice is 'diminished by the requirement that he or she should be an Ordinary Member of the Commission…'

The sense of entitlement was stunning. They clearly believed that our Chief Justice could not be debased by ordinary member-ship, despite the fact that the Lord Chief Justice of England and Wales sat as an ordinary member of their Judicial Appointments Commission, serving under a lay chair — a renowned surgeon. Apparently that was not to be for our wigged friends.

The Dáil initiated discussion of the bill the following day.

With a truce on appointments, the parliamentary arithmetic and tactics tended to dominate the next few months. The bill passed through the Dáil at second stage by 84 votes to 53 on

5 July 2017. It then took ten months, until May 2018, to reach final stage, passing that by just 55 votes to 49. It had taken an absurdly long time, with over a hundred tabled amendments. It was dogged by delays and contradictory changes that eventually needed correction in the Seanad.

The bill's slow progress exasperated many. Finian and I felt we were being played along by Charlie, whose instincts as a lawyer sometimes seemed to dampen his already tepid enthusiasm for the bill. He did not share my view that cronyism had been rampant in the past. We began to have further dust-ups at cabinet, or beforehand, when judges were due for appointment.

The next exocet came from an unpredictable quarter. The Attorney General, Séamus Woulfe, a clubbable, affable man, was incensed by an amendment passed in the Dáil that removed the Attorney General from membership of the Judicial Appointments Commission. On 23 March 2018, he addressed an Association of European Journalists' lunch in Dublin and famously called the Judicial Appointments Bill a 'dog's dinner'.

I was dumbstruck. The Law Library was euphoric. The government's own Attorney General had dismissed a government bill in derisory terms. He was voicing their views precisely. The *Irish Legal News* led gleefully with the headline: 'Lawyers back Séamus Woulfe over Judicial Appointments Bill criticism'. There was a media frenzy.

Séamus had been pretty expansive. He had told the journalists that the legal system viewed the removal of the Attorney General from the Commission as an 'absolutely crazy thing to do', adding that the Attorney General is 'hopefully a good link person with the bar and knowing the people, knowing the candidates and the judges'. But therein lay the problem.

Personally, I had never approved of the presence of the Attorney General on the Commission, but kept my own counsel because it was part of a government bill. I texted Charlie after

Séamus' statement, saying, 'I am beginning to think that the Attorney should be taken out of the judicial process.' Charlie replied: 'That might now be seen as a petty act of retribution. Let's get on with ensuring the lay chair and lay majority.' And then, in a non sequitur, he texted: 'If the Govt falls in the autumn, we're all damned.' He was standing by his friend.

Leo Varadkar was none too pleased with Séamus Woulfe. I contacted him on the evening of Séamus' address, suggesting that we meet over the weekend. He replied that 'Séamus stuck his foot in it. He seems to be referring to the amendments made which we want reversed, rather than the bill itself, but it's bad.'

The Attorney General's timing could not have been worse. We had already fought a battle over judges in cabinet earlier in the week. Worse still, the high profile appointment of the President of the Court of Appeal was due for approval by the cabinet.

Two days later, on the Sunday morning, I met the Attorney General in his office and cleared the air. Then I did an RTÉ interview and expressed confidence in him. The Taoiseach texted: 'Good interview. Told the lads I am not taking the memo on the President of the Appeal Court until the JAC Bill goes to Report Stage. That should focus the minds over Easter.'

In a later exchange that day I texted the Taoiseach that 'CF seems irritated by RTÉ interview which stuns me'.

The Taoiseach responded with the understatement of the decade. 'Charlie can be irritable. He shouldn't be. Interviewer tried to provoke...'

The next hurdle was the appointment of the President of the Court of Appeal. After a long delay, Charlie had put it on the agenda for 24 April. It was the beginning of nearly two years of guerilla warfare between us. Charlie had told me that George Birmingham was his chosen one.

I texted Leo to ring the alarm bells: 'Just heard it's George Birmingham. This does not make life easy. Can we meet pre-cabinet? Choice of Birmingham explosive.'

Leo agreed to meet me. Finian and I met him with Flanagan and Woulfe before cabinet. It was stormy. We explained that we had had enough. Whatever his merits, George Birmingham was an ex-Fine Gael TD and minister. The Blueshirts were taking us for granted. It was the last such appointment that the Independent Alliance would sanction. A former Fine Gael minister was being appointed. Two out of three (Frank Clarke and Séamus Woulfe) of the advisory committee set up to recommend a name had strong past or present Fine Gael connections. A Fine Gael minister was making the final selection. We received renewed assurances on the passage of the bill from the Taoiseach. He prevented an eruption. He also delivered. The bill passed final stage in the Dáil on 31 May 2018.

George Birmingham was chosen. We withdrew our opposition, but relations with Charlie remained strained. From that day on, each judicial vacancy opened up potential arm to arm combat between Charlie and me. We had heated exchanges on each occasion. Every time Charlie made a selection, he gave it to me before the name went to cabinet. Aisling would attempt to 'Blueshirt-proof' it. He regularly waited till the eleventh hour to provide us with the judges' CVs. The process acted as an effective deterrent against the worst excesses of the crony culture.

We fought battle after battle over the next two years. One of the most difficult was the promotion to the Court of Appeal of Caroline Costello, daughter of former Fine Gael Attorney General Declan Costello and granddaughter of former Taoiseach John A. Costello. I challenged Charlie on her Fine Gael connections.

He replied that 'Caroline Costello was never involved in politics. A judge of the highest standing. And a woman!' In a similar response, apparently justifying his choice of the Fine Gael blue blood, he sent me a note across the cabinet table, writing 'I need a woman. Can't go with 3 men!'

Before cabinet, I had a robust discussion with him and Séamus Woulfe about Caroline Costello. We went into the meeting deadlocked. I strongly suspected that Charlie would hold back her nomination, but couldn't risk it. So I asked Katherine Zappone to pass a note from me to the Taoiseach:

Difficulties with Caroline Costello. Talking to Charlie and Attorney General. Can we postpone if necessary, please? Seems she has a parachute à la Máire Whelan! About 80 people eligible. Following Frank Clarke and Birmingham, it's a bit of a pattern. Shane.

He scribbled his response: 'Sure. Don't know her myself. Can be deferred. LV.'

In a follow-up, Charlie was at his least persuasive when he texted: 'Matters are now critical. Court of Appeal won't function. Chief Justice irate.' He was tempting me.

Eventually we let Costello through. She had good credentials, and a better gender balance on the bench is something I wanted to achieve with the bill — it was high time we had more female judges. I just didn't necessarily want them all to have a perfectly blue-blood pedigree.

Charlie and I regularly played brinkmanship on Tuesday mornings before cabinet. The poor Taoiseach was often called in to adjudicate. It inevitably involved a trade-off between speeding up the progress of the bill (bogged down in a Seanad filibuster) and allowing a few judges to be appointed.

The bill reached the Seanad on 20 June 2018, almost exactly a year since it had begun its life in the Dáil. I was hoping for a constructive debate in a chamber that included seriously independent-minded members, such as Pádraig Ó Céidigh, Lynn Ruane, Alice Mary Higgins, John Dolan, Frances Black, Billy Lawless and Brian Ó Domhnaill.

Unfortunately, an opportunity for improving the bill was squandered. While constructive voices were heard at second stage, the lawyers in the Seanad took over in the later stages. The bill descended into farce.

The Seanad, so nearly abolished in the 2013 referendum, still unreformed, suddenly found a cantankerous role for itself. It was a spoiler. Part-time lawyers in the Seanad had time on their hands. The government was in a minority. A few of the lawyers in the Upper House conspired with others to delay the bill for ever.

In command of the legal squad in the Seanad was undoubtedly senior counsel Michael McDowell. But he was not on his own. Fianna Fáil's Justice spokesperson in the Upper House was Lorraine Clifford-Lee, a qualified solicitor. Their party's Seanad leader, Catherine Ardagh, was a practising solicitor and a vocal opponent of the bill. Labour's loudest voice against it was a barrister, Ivana Bacik, while for Fine Gael, another solicitor and deputy leader in the Seanad, Catherine Noone, backed both horses. She lost no opportunity to voice her hostility to the bill while simultaneously voting with the government. Not a bad trick. Another barrister, independent Rónán Mullen, trotted into the lobbies behind his legal comrades, as required. Every one of them backed the filibuster. The Four Courts whip worked wonders.

McDowell, the Four Courts filibusterer, had a few non-legal followers. Some were lobby fodder. He had the ability to speak for hours and dazzle his audience with legalese. He quickly brought those of lesser stature to his side, like Victor Boyhan, his old disciple from the Progressive Democrats.

The Four Court filibusterer did most of the spadework himself, proposing amendments by the bucketful. His other disciples, like former presidential hopefuls Joan Freeman and Gerard Craughwell, as well as the hapless Boyhan, always fell into line. Another former presidential hopeful, David Norris, was an incurable waffler on the topic, but without peer when it came to the undemanding skill of causing disruption when shouting out single words like 'Vótáil' and 'Quorum' in the chamber. Calls for a time-wasting vote when the result was a foregone conclusion were constant. They were followed by a democratic device, a demand for a 'walkthrough' meaning that the vote had to be repeated, this time by forcing senators to walk through the lobbies to confirm that the numbers on the electronic board were correct. Each such request took anything from ten to twenty minutes from a debate, which may have been scheduled for only ninety minutes. Quorums were regularly demanded, each forcing five-minute delays while the bells were rung, giving time for members to come into the house.

Sinn Féin was rock solid behind the bill, although the party rightly supported many of the more thoughtful amendments. However, understandably, on principle, they and many of the independents resisted all attempts to guillotine the bill. The guillotine was a step too far. It was seen as an undemocratic device, used by governments only, to quell discussion and ram legislation through the house.

There was a stalemate. The bill would go on for as long as McDowell's clique had enough breath in their bodies to talk, or until Sinn Féin and a handful of independents supported a guillotine motion.

We decided to wait until the middle ground had endured enough. The filibuster had delayed other, equally important, legislation. The Seanad itself had become a laughing stock, undermined by lawyers in pursuit of their vested interests.

In early April 2019, we decided to go for the guillotine. Sinn Féin eventually agreed that the time of their senators was too valuable for any more pointless, late-night sittings. Other independents like Donegal's Brian Ó Domhnaill, disability activist John Dolan and independent Dublin University senator Lynn Ruane were thought to be fed up with the time-wasting. The issues had been thrashed out ad nauseam. We were unsure of other independent thinkers, like Frances Black, Pádraig Ó Céidigh and Alice Mary Higgins. We were certain that the entire Fine Gael group of senators and Sinn Féin would be present. We were confident that we would reap the benefit of surprise and would easily carry the closure motion, which was effectively a guillotine and would draw this stage of the bill to a conclusion, regardless of a desire for further debate.

We were wrong. The news of our intentions leaked out the night before. The legal eagles had time to marshal their forces. Senators who were rare attenders in the house turned up. We lacked adequate preparation but we were also unlucky. A fear of our plan being leaked had meant that we had not conferred with the necessary people. The appearance of Nancy Pelosi, speaker of the US House of Representatives, to give a historic address to both deputies and senators in the Dáil chamber attracted absentee senators in large numbers to Leinster House. We had depended on a few missing senators from the opposition parties, but they were forewarned and present.

The vote was close, but we lost marginally, by 24 votes to 26.

Dismayed, we sat back and nursed our wounds. We resolved not do the same again until we were better prepared. There was egg all over my face. Some of the lawyers in the Seanad could not avoid gloating.

Eight months later, we were better prepared. On 11 December 2019, after 125 hours of debate, and meticulous preparation, we broke the filibuster. Later that day, the bill was passed in the Seanad by 25 votes to 23. This time, crucially, independent senators Pádraig Ó Céidigh, Brian Ó Domhnaill and Lynn Ruane voted to end the fiasco. The bill was on its way back to the Dáil, set to be passed within weeks.

On 14 January 2020, Leo Varadkar called a general election. The Judicial Appointments Commission Bill, tantalisingly close to completion after four years, fell at the last hurdle, but can now either be revived in its present form, amended or be allowed to lapse. The Programme for Government promised to revive it, but to amend it to put the Chief Justice in the chair of the Commission. My guess is that the judges will find friendlier faces in Fianna Fáil and the Greens than they did in Fine Gael and the Independent Alliance. The real battle about who picks the judges will now return to an unseemly tussle between political parties and the elite in the Four Courts. If the new government bottles this chance, an opportunity for reform will be lost for another generation.

On 15 July 2020, less than three weeks after the change of government, the last Attorney General Séamus Woulfe was nominated by the Minister for Justice, Fine Gael's Helen McEntee, to be a judge of the Supreme Court. Séamus had applied to be considered after the election was called in January. His appointment was recommended by the Judicial Appointments Advisory Board (JAAB).

As Attorney General, Séamus was an *ex officio* member of JAAB when the board considered his application in March. He, absolutely correctly, absented himself from the meeting.

Among those members of JAAB on the date his application was considered were the Chief Justice, Frank Clarke, and the President of the Court of Appeal, George Birmingham.

Just three years earlier, one of the three people sitting on the committee recommending the appointment of Frank Clarke to the post of Chief Justice was Séamus Woulfe.

Just two years earlier, one of the three people sitting on the committee recommending the appointment of George

Birmingham to be President of the Court of Criminal Appeal was Séamus Woulfe.

Frank was a Fine Gael candidate for the Seanad in the nineteen-eighties. At that time he was George's election agent as a Fine Gael candidate for the Dáil.

George is a former Fine Gael minister.

Séamus was a Fine Gael activist in the same constituency.

Séamus signed off on Frank and George.

Frank and George signed off on Séamus.

Today, all three of them are on the Supreme court.

On Wednesday, 19 August the newly promoted Supreme Court Justice, Séamus Woulfe, was present at an Oireachtas golf outing and gala dinner in the west of Ireland. Eighty others attended. The fallout from the event attracted global media attention and national public outrage as a breach of Covid-19 restrictions.

After the story broke the Minister for Agriculture, Dara Calleary and the Leas-Chathaoirleach (deputy chair) of the Seanad, Jerry Buttimer, almost immediately resigned their positions and apologised for their participation. Six days later an even bigger fish, Ireland's European Commissioner Phil Hogan, fell on his sword.

The only judge in attendance, Supreme Court Justice Séamus Woulfe, did not follow suit. Instead, he merely apologised.

Several politicians who had actually nominated him to one of the highest posts in the land a few weeks earlier suddenly, coyly pleading the 'separation of powers', refused to pass judgement on a member of the Supreme Court behaving in this unacceptable way. Their reluctance was a cop-out, supported by a fig leaf. Where was the 'separation of powers' a few weeks earlier when the same politicians nominated the judge?

Politicians can dismiss judges. Indeed, there is only one way of removing a judge – by a resolution of both houses of Oireachtas, all of whose members are politicians.

Far from there being a real 'separation of powers' between our judges and politicians, they are joined at the hip.

One week after the infamous dinner, while several politicians present had received various forms of penalty, the only Supreme Court Justice in attendance was still in situ, fighting a rearguard action. The logical implication was clear: the required standards for judges are lower than they are for politicians.

Séamus Woulfe's colleague, Chief Justice Frank Clarke, responded to public outrage by cleverly asking none other than Susan Denham, his predecessor as Chief Justice, to review and report on the events to him. Even at this time of crisis, the Chief Justice did not trust an independent outsider to investigate.

Aloof from the fray, the boys on the bench were not going to allow anything as vulgar as popular anger to shatter their cosy customs. They were happy to accept political patronage when convenient, but they were determined to settle any threat to their citadel within their own ranks.

Nothing had changed.

9

Mandarins Rule, OK?

ONE OF THE more amusing stories doing the rounds of Leinster House in late May 2016 concerned the pending appointments of the Ministers of State in Enda Kenny's government. It was widely believed that he phoned up Limerick Fine Gael loyalist Patrick O'Donovan and asked him if he wanted the good news or the bad news. 'Give me the good news,' pleaded the super-eager O'Donovan, who had been tipped for a junior minister's position. 'The good news,' the Taoiseach said, 'is that I am going to make you a minister of state.'

O'Donovan, a youngish Fine Gael Rottweiler, broke into a beam. 'And the bad news?' he asked. 'The bad news,' responded the Taoiseach, 'is the name of your senior minister.'

Patrick knew immediately. In the Members' Bar for over a week, Fine Gael TDs had been drawing short straws for this poisoned prize. The story goes that Enda told Patrick that this was a special assignment to keep Shane Ross in check, to ensure that all the Fine Gael folk were looked after when it came to sports grants and tourism interests. Basically, he was to report to his leader if he found me running amok.

Patrick O'Donovan was to become Minister of State for Tourism and Sport. It was normally a much sought-after portfolio. There was travel galore in the tourism brief and once-in-a-lifetime sporting gigs to attend. The Olympics, the Euros, even the Rugby World Cup beckoned. This time, however, with the notable exception of Michael Ring, the Blueshirts had not been queuing up for the job when they knew I had the cabinet post.

Ours was not a union made in heaven; it was an arranged marriage. Both Patrick and I turned out to be equally uncongenial colleagues. After ten tumultuous months of our partnership, Enda sent me a text: 'I need to talk to you tomorrow re. Min O'Donovan. He is really pissed off at the way he is being treated and would be your best advocate. We need to sort it. Thanks E.'

I responded: 'Happy to talk about Patrick tomorrow. What's bugging him?' And then in a reference to another matter, a pending report on Stepaside Garda Station: 'I will be lynched if decision delayed.'

The Taoiseach, agitated by the spat between Patrick and me, hit back: 'I will be lynched if we don't sort out your Min State. He will do as you ask but give him his head. Will talk re this when I get chance.'

The row rumbled beneath the surface for a fortnight until O'Donovan made a bold move. He was billed to be allowed to address the cabinet on a matter specifically within my remit — Ireland's Rugby World Cup bid. When I heard the news, I sent a text to the Taoiseach:

Taoiseach, I hear Mark Kennelly [Enda's chief of staff] wants Minister of State O'Donovan at cabinet meeting for RWC [Rugby World Cup] item tomorrow. This is inappropriate as it has always been exclusive part of senior minister's portfolio… It has been my responsibility since last May and specifically remains there in the 'shared office' notice. I only heard this on the grapevine tonight and ask you please to leave this item as originally billed. I have spent most of today preparing for this underwriting issue. Shane.

Patrick and I must have been driving Enda mad with this turf war. Enda replied:

I mentioned this to you before, your Min of State is seriously pissed off in that he is not allowed to work to you with any of the responsibilities that Govt assigned to him but for which he has not been given imprimatur by you!! It makes for poor working relationship. He would be your best advocate for anything you want done with yourself to take whatever limelight you wanted.

Limelight? Me? Enda knew what buttons to press. And then the Taoiseach dramatically upped the ante:

We need to sort out what Patrick's responsibilities are or he will walk. You should both work together with you as the Snr man at all times. Can I see you both at 9 [am] for 10 mins to sort it? We have jnr Mins in every week or so to back up their Snrs. David Stanton, Helen McEntee, Michael Ring (tomorrow also), Damien English, Seán Kyne, Catherine Byrne etc. I need the best from both of you and he wants to help you in all these matters. Bring the shared notice with you as I never saw that. Thanks. E.

Patrick threatening to walk was not a prospect I dreaded. It might have been a bit harder for Enda, under pressure from Fine Gael deputies at that moment, just three months before his departure.

It had been a rocky baptism in the department. I hardly knew Patrick, except as a top-class heckler. Enda had never consulted me on who would be a compatible colleague. A few weeks before Patrick's appointment and ahead of the government's formation, I had been waiting for my turn to speak in the Dáil. Danny Healy-Rae was rabbiting on when the Ceann Comhairle, Seán Ó Fearghaíl, intervened to curtail him: 'You are cutting into Deputy Ross' time.'

Quick as a flash from the Fine Gael backbenches Patrick O'Donovan TD roared out, 'Keep going!'

Even I laughed. He was good value.

But we never settled down together properly in the department. We co-operated well over the Olympic Games crisis, the solution provided by the Judge Moran report and the downfall of Pat Hickey. We both heartily agreed about the merit of reappointing John Treacy as boss of Sport Ireland but mistrust grew, because Patrick thought I was stealing some of the better gigs and not giving him his head. He felt that Michael Ring, as a junior minister for sport under Paschal Donohoe, had undoubtedly been allowed to play a more prominent role in the sporting world than he was doing, but Patrick did most of the tourism stuff and seemed to enjoy it.

I was probably less than generous in the amount I allowed him to do, although our civil servants drew up a 'staff (or shared) notice' document identical to the allocation of duties agreed between Paschal and Michael Ring before us. Our relationship gradually deteriorated and we were seldom in contact.

I was not the only one having difficulties with Patrick. Civil servants found him to be unpredictable. His 'prima donna' nature earned him the uncomplimentary nickname around the department of 'The Princess'.

He was not enamoured with my staff either. He would refer to Aisling in very unflattering terms, presuming she was the Lady Macbeth of the operation. It was not all sweetness and harmony in the department of trains and boats and planes.

Our relationship reached its lowest point early one morning in December 2016. Aisling and I were driving up to a North-South ministerial meeting in Armagh. We turned on RTÉ's *Morning Ireland*. A familiar voice suddenly bounced on to the airwaves announcing a completely new policy departure on gender quotas for sporting bodies. Not only were gender quotas suddenly now government policy, any National Governing Body (NGB) that did not comply with Patrick's sudden diktat would be punished and would see their funding cut.

He had correctly identified a problem, but had flagrantly overstepped the mark in announcing a solution. I did not even favour gender quotas as the answer. Patrick followed up this solo run with further prearranged publicity. Not only was I unaware of his exploits, neither was any department official.

I rang Enda. He too knew nothing about Patrick's stunt. He left me to deal with it.

I called a meeting of all the NGBs of sport for the end of the week and invited Patrick to that meeting. He asked me if I was going to 'throw him under a bus'. I told him I was. He declined the invitation. Nearly every NGB showed up. The mood was curious, but most bodies were very wary of gender quotas and firmly against financial penalties. I reassured them. Patrick's initiative was dead and our relationship was permanently sundered.

That was the background to Enda's intervention. Bad blood, mistrust and public disagreements.

At that cabinet meeting when Patrick did not, in the end, appear, I received a scribbled note from Enda: 'Shane. After the meeting, across the hall. You, me, Minister of State, Sec Gen of your department. 5 mins and get everything working. Min of State will not attend @ cabinet meeting. E.'

We all met. I expected a mild dressing-down from Enda, to keep his party loyalist happy. Instead, he told Patrick that he had seen the staff notice and that Patrick had, after all, a lot of responsibilities. He asked for future co-operation from both of us, and we agreed to mend fences.

It didn't happen. I had very little contact with Patrick O'Donovan from that day until the time Enda left office in June 2017. My efforts to text or ring him usually met with no replies. My last text to him as my minister of state on 19 May was meant to be humorous:

> Patrick. Sorry you could not meet as arranged, at 12.15 yesterday. My office received message from yours that you had to go to Limerick. Especially disappointing as you were in Members' Bar at the time. Equally disappointed that you have not yet phoned as promised when we unexpectedly met there at 12.35. Wanted to tell you that I was sending the letter to NGBs and that Greenways [funding for various greenways' projects around the country] are on the move. Will update you on other matters next week, if you have time. Shane.

A totally dysfunctional relationship between a minister and a minister of state was coming to an end.

When Leo Varadkar took over from Enda, he asked me, without prompting, if I wanted a change of minister of state. I sent him a text: 'On reflection I think an amicable separation for POD might be in all our interests.'

Subsequently Leo 'promoted' Patrick to Minister of State at the Department of Public Expenditure and Reform with special responsibility for Public Procurement, Open Government and eGovernment. Patrick disappeared without a trace under that pile. His subsequent senior minister, Paschal Donohoe, was obviously a more compatible colleague than I had been.

In late November 2019, more than two years after Patrick and I had parted company on bad terms, my private secretary Chris Smith most unusually interrupted a meeting in my office. Chris looked as though he had seen a ghost. And he had. He said that Minister O'Donovan had arrived unexpectedly and wondered if I was free now. I shuddered, anticipating trouble. I couldn't talk to him but rang him later.

Patrick was in funny form. He wanted to mend fences. He sounded a bit like someone on his deathbed, befriending his enemies. It was a really pleasant gesture. He didn't know how we actually 'fell out' but life was too short … He thought it might have been because of the perception that Kenny had given him the job as a special mission to monitor the senior minister. It was a very engaging olive branch.

We agreed to have lunch. A few days later we met in the Members' restaurant and enjoyed a meal and a good number of laughs. We parted very best friends, at least temporarily.

Patrick was replaced as minister of state by Brendan Griffin. I smelled trouble. Brendan had been chairman of the Oireachtas Committee on Transport, Tourism and Sport for the previous year. He had summoned me, as the relevant minister, regularly down to the Leinster House dungeons to answer questions. The truth is that ministers hate appearing at these committees. They invariably begin their opening addresses with the utterly insincere mantra: 'I am delighted to be here today to…' In truth, they would far rather be anywhere else in the world.

I usually opened a session by delivering those words to Brendan, followed by an equally anodyne script. Then he would release the dogs of war for a couple of hours.

Traditionally a government deputy in the chair of a committee gave a minister an element of protection. Brendan, unfortunately, had turned out to be an annoyingly impartial chairman. He gave me no quarter. One of my most difficult tasks at the committee was when I took the Road Traffic Bill, dealing with drink-driving, to one meeting for preliminary legislative scrutiny. Brendan, a former publican, was obviously not a fan of the measure. He had probably been strongly lobbied by those opposing it. In my view at the time, he had allowed Fianna Fáil's Robert Troy and Kevin O'Keeffe far too much leeway to oppose and delay the bill.

Brendan and I were chalk and cheese. He was in his mid-thirties and was impatient and ambitious. He was rural, from faraway Kerry. I was a Dublin TD, in the Oireachtas for over thirty years. Nevertheless, I was curious about him. For his first five years in the Dáil he had done something laudable, possibly unique. He had accepted only half his TD's pay, donating the other half to a local Kerry national school to fund a teacher's salary.

I was apprehensive. If we didn't hit it off, my reputation, already low in the Fine Gael party, would hit rock bottom and their fifty deputies would all agree that I was an impossible colleague. I guessed that Brendan was not overjoyed about his senior minister, though he was assuredly the envy of colleagues for winning the sports and tourism portfolio.

Working with Brendan turned out to be a revelation. It was one of the most agreeable experiences of my tenure as a minister. We disagreed about almost everything, whether it was greyhounds or drink or sports capital grants. Our backgrounds were worlds apart. We represented directly opposing interests on nearly every issue, but unlike Patrick O'Donovan, Brendan was no Rottweiler. He was a problem-solver. Where we differed, we often struggled, but we always found a solution. Voices were never raised. On issues like the FAI, he was invaluable, resourceful, but never undermining. We appeared in the Dáil for oral questions side by side, often defending the indefensible. He was a bright, articulate and loyal colleague.

Greyhounds divided us. I was a loner on this issue both inside and outside the cabinet, emphatically on the side of the poor greyhound. I embarrassed Brendan by preventing Fáilte Ireland from using greyhound racing as a marketing tool for tourism. Brendan and I sorted it in a grown-up way by making it plain that we openly disagreed. It was no big deal. He travelled abroad in the line of duty far more often than a young father with a family would want to do, but it gave him a mastery of the sport and tourism sector that I would never match. His natural diplomacy will make him a superb Minister for Foreign Affairs one day.

Patrick and Brendan were only one, albeit very important, introduction to the life of a minister and his department. In May 2016, I had to adjust from being a chaotic, independent freewheeler into a life of ministers of state, civil service structures, state-sponsored bodies, handlers galore, drivers, private secretaries and advisers on a multitude of matters.

Civil servants are probably the most conservative group of people on the planet. They are unfailingly polite, good, decent, God-fearing citizens, but I wondered on my first day as I entered the offices in Dublin's Leeson Lane, if everything that was said about them was true? Civil servants are no bundle of laughs. They love formality. I asked them not to call me 'minister'. It sounded awkward. My name was Shane. Paschal Donohoe had rightly told me that if his senior officials needed to give him a title to show him respect, he felt he had not earned it. Some adjusted, but about 50 per cent refused to drop the formalities. They preferred there to be a distance in the relationship.

The most abiding memory of my first day in the office was Chris Smith, my private secretary, telling me about the bizarre existence of the ministerial private lavatory. I asked who used it, only to be told that it was exclusively for me. That was an embarrassing moment. There can be few more ridiculous wastes of space and money than a private loo for a person who is rarely in the building. I never entered it, nor do I, to this day, know where it is. From time to time I would bump into staff in the department's lavatory and they would helpfully point me in the direction of the minister's private facilities. I hope it is still in the same impeccable condition that it must have been on my first day in office in 2016.

Somebody told me on the day before I ever went into the office that the minister's private secretary was the Secretary General's spy. I am sure that was not true in Chris' case, but he originally felt it was his job to satisfy a suffocating duty to know where I was at every minute of the day. Chris' offices, in both Leinster House and Leeson Lane, were right outside mine. His desk faced straight into the corridor. The door never closed, so that I could not enter or exit without him knowing.

On one of my first days in the department, the senior mandarins enquired if I would share my diary with them. I innocently said yes but later I regretted it. Not only did they all know exactly what you were up to every minute of the day, they seemed to feel that any blank slots needed to be filled with a countless number of briefing sessions from them.

Before my first cabinet meeting my Secretary General, Graham Doyle, suggested that it was normal practice for the minister to brief him following cabinet meetings. After the first few episodes of this, I let it lapse. Not because I did not trust Graham, but I was aware of a strong civil servant mafia that had a life of its own, a power base for senior mandarins who swapped information to control their ministers. No career mandarins are allowed into the cabinet room except the Secretary General to the Department of the Taoiseach, Martin Fraser.

On my first trip abroad, to Luxembourg for a European Transport Council meeting, Chris asked me how many civil servants I wanted to take with me. He looked stunned when I said none. Apparently, it caused consternation among some of the mandarins, accustomed to travelling everywhere with the minister of the day. When I arrived at these continental destinations, the hotel, the airport and the meeting rooms were packed with Irish civil servants permanently stationed at EU locations so, even without my coterie of domestic mandarins, I was well handled and monitored by them.

In Europe, the Irish civil servants were particularly controlling. They would give you scripts for what they called 'interventions' (speeches) in the proceedings. You were discouraged from drifting one iota from the script. They would arrange 'one-to-ones' with key European transport ministers, inevitably trying to make them turn into 'two-to-ones' to include themselves. If they caught you talking to another transport minister off-piste, they would often join you, uninvited, or stand a few feet away, their backs turned, listening in. They would have struck up alliances with other EU member states of which I would know nothing. They seemed fearful that sometimes an understanding might be jeopardised by allowing a minister to meet counterparts, without being monitored.

At my final meeting in Brussels in December 2019, there was the usual private lunch for ministers, alone. It was a mandarin-free zone. The civil servants quickly suggested other options, which I declined. I enjoyed my lunch that day, but was interrupted before it finished by one of the Irish team who had spotted me talking for far too long with a highly heretical, but very amusing, transport minister from an eastern European country.

Yes, there were a lot of control freaks in the civil service. Back home they were not as intense as their European counterparts, but if they thought any of their favourite projects were going to be torpedoed, they instantly forgot their faux humility and moved into protection mode.

Their most protected species were the twenty-three state-sponsored bodies under the department. I came into the ministry rattling my sabre at these quangos. I quickly realised that the mandarins were worried by this threatened assault on their protectorate. My journalist son-in-law, Nick Webb, and I had written a book about these bodies, unflatteringly called

Wasters. A lot of our criticism centred on the appalling appointments made to their boards. At one point the directors' names had read like an honours list for the walking wounded from past political party battles. CIÉ, the Shannon Group, Dublin Port, the Dublin Airport Authority, the National Transport Authority and Transport Infrastructure Ireland had all been in our sights. We had exposed wanton waste and corruption at CIÉ and malpractices at FÁS that resulted in the dismantling of the state's employment and training authority.

Graham Doyle was anxious for me to meet the chairs and chief executives of the state-sponsored sector at an early date. I wanted to devise a new way of appointing their directors, as had been promised in the Independent Alliance manifesto, removing all ministers' ability to put their cronies on state boards. The boards seemed too big and should be slimmed down, preferably by removing as many of the present band of party-political appointments as possible.

The department officials did not want change. The present system suited them. Political nominees rarely rock the boat. They do what they are told, in the hope of reappointment and an annual stipend.

One morning, I asked Aisling why on earth the mandarins were so besotted with their agencies? Why did they want to protect them so fiercely? She hit the nail on the head. 'Don't you understand,' she replied, 'they are their babies?' She was right; there was a parent-child relationship. The department did not want any interference with their almost total control of their obedient creations.

There was a problem. I had previous form with many of their babies. I had crossed swords with the chairs of DAA, CIÉ and the Shannon Group in the past. In my other book with Nick, *The Untouchables*, we had called the appointment of Pádraig Ó Ríordáin as chair of DAA 'an extraordinarily arrogant appointment by Transport Minister, Leo Varadkar'. Now, since I was Leo's successor as minister, I had inherited Pádraig.

Pádraig, as at that time, the recently retired managing partner of well-connected solicitors Arthur Cox, had been forced to answer questions at the Oireachtas committee about possible conflicts of interest in the allocation of state work. Arthur Cox had acted for the DAA in cases against Ryanair and others. The firm was one of DAA's bevy of legal advisers, as well as being a legal adviser to Aer Lingus.

Back in 2012, in private conversation, Leo had actually asked me — quietly — what I thought of the idea of appointing Ó Ríordáin to the chair of the DAA. I was not enthusiastic, because I had an aversion to the magic circle who receive so much state patronage. But Leo appointed him anyway. Four years later, I had the task of working with Pádraig, who was due for reappointment soon.

The mandarins wanted Ó Ríordáin to receive, at least, a further three-year term. He was their sort of guy, no boat rocker, establishment to his fingertips. They said it was imperative that he remain as chairman because we were in the middle of negotiations to complete the second runway at Dublin airport. There was always a good reason. Since I had been in the department only a month and had made the development of the runway a high priority, I accepted that Ó Ríordáin should stay, but only for a further eighteen months, until the end of 2017. It was all he wanted then. However, by the end of that period, he had changed his mind — he wanted to do a full term. A tussle ensued, but after a few exchanges, he was prepared to go. His graceful exit was publicly presented as a willing departure.

CIÉ was more embarrassing. Their chairperson, Vivienne Jupp, was another of Leo's appointees. She would be eligible for a further three- or four-year term in July 2017. Unfortunately, when writing in the *Sunday Independent*, I had been one of her harshest critics. I had worried about her 'underperforming' and had actually called on her 'to resign for presiding over a shambles'. As a journalist I had, very disrespectfully, called her a 'quango queen' because she held so many state board appointments, dubbing her tenure in the CIÉ chair as 'a disaster, marked by falling passenger numbers and financial crises'. The mandarins wanted me to meet her and bury the hatchet. We met on a couple of occasions. She found it hard to smile. So did I. Eventually when the time came to decide on her reappointment, I rang her and thanked her for her services and said goodbye. She accepted my decision gracefully.

The third appointment that promised to be an awkward encounter was Rose Hynes' position as chair of the Shannon Group. She had originally been appointed as chair of the Shannon Airport Authority — again by Leo — in 2013 and been promoted to the chair of the Shannon Group on its incorporation in 2014. She was long past her sell-by date as a non-executive director.

Rose Hynes had been a director of the Bank of Ireland during the crash and chaired its remuneration committee when it was handing out outrageous salaries to top executives. She was appointed to the board of Aer Lingus by another Fine Gael leader, Alan Dukes, in 1997. Rose had a good line to the Blueshirts. I had savaged her in the *Sunday Independent* for being a serial director and for her stewardship at the Bank of Ireland remuneration committee.

My meetings with all three of the chairpersons were difficult. Even though they had all been appointed by Leo at one stage or another, he never contacted me when I failed to reappoint Pádraig and Vivienne. I thought I had shaken off the Blueshirts.

Rose came up for reappointment as chair of the Shannon Group in August 2019. My aviation mandarins wanted her to stay on. They pleaded her case, maintaining that the Shannon Group needed her because it was facing a crisis. Their dreaded safety valve 'continuity' was again invoked. I was determined not to give her this extension and told my officials so. They strongly resisted, but in the end threw in the towel and suggested that I tell Rose myself.

I had a few terse conversations with her. She was not impressed. Rose was a street fighter, not giving up without a battle. She wanted to stay, giving a host of reasons why she should, including the recent setbacks at Shannon airport following several blows, not of her making. These included the grounding of the Boeing 737 Max aircrafts, which had a disproportionate effect on Shannon airport, with Norwegian airlines and Air Canada cancelling services as a result. I was firm, but, out of courtesy, told her that I would think about it for a few days. We talked about giving her an extra year, and presumably she was hoping that I would be out of office before that year was over. She was a shrewd judge.

After one of my conversations with Rose, I hadn't put the telephone down five minutes before I received a text from the Taoiseach. 'Hi Shane, Can you take a call re the Shannon airport chair?'

Rose is some mover.

I replied 'OMG! Of course.'

Rose had been on the blower to Leo. And she had got through.

He did what Leo does best. He said it was not important, he was not doing anything to pressurise me, but... was there a case to keep her in place because Shannon was in difficult straits? The Taoiseach left it with me. It was not a *casus belli* but, all other things being equal, and if I had no one else in mind...

A few days later I texted Leo to update him. This was realpolitik. 'Taoiseach, I propose to reappoint Rose Hynes for another year. Hope that fits the bill. It was definitely not the original intention.'

'How did Rose react?' he texted back.

'I met her on Thursday and told her I would reconsider in the light of what you and she had said. Just texted her now so no reply yet. Will let you know when she responds.'

No one was more delighted than my mandarins. Another of their beloved babies had been protected. I still wonder whether the mandarin mafia had been beavering away behind the scenes.

It was not that the babies did not cause their parents trouble. At no times were the mandarins more agitated than when there were threats of industrial action from their transport companies. And they had plenty of opportunities to show it during my first year in office. First it was the Luas, next Dublin Bus, followed by Bus Éireann and finally Iarnród Éireann. All of them took it in turn to declare industrial warfare. Understandably, each workforce fed off the others' pay demands.

At the first sign of industrial trouble on the Luas, the mandarins sat me down to tell me the score. Industrial relations were a special skill. I need not bother doing anything about them but should leave the problem to the institutions of the state. Ministers should never get involved in such disputes. They would keep me informed of developments.

I couldn't help recalling Bertie Ahern, when Minister for Labour in the late 1980s, arriving late at industrial relations disputes with an eleventh-hour solution. It usually involved dispensing exchequer funds, but the optics reflected very well on him. That was the last thing the officials wanted. I was tempted, but never yielded.

They assured me that I would learn that their approach was a tried and tested process. Dermot O'Leary, the *enfant terrible* of the trade union movement, had to play a part. He would shout and roar; he would bait the minister; he would bring the staff to the brink of a strike; the management would resist; he would call them out onto the picket lines for a few days; the families of the staff would feel the pinch; the Workplace Relations Commission or the Labour Court would call in all parties; there would be a late-night proposal from the state's mediation services; the management would reluctantly accept the deal; the trades unions would recommend it to their members and ballot them; they would vote for it; both sides would claim victory. It worked like clockwork.

According to the mandarins, every move was a matter of timing. The union leaders understood the ritual just as well as the management. It was a game, but they were smug. They prided themselves on their expertise. They were exceptionally well practised at it. By implication, both the Services Industrial Professional and Technical Union (SIPTU) and the National Bus and Rail Union (NBRU) played by the same rules. The rights and wrongs of the wage claim rarely entered the equation. I would be better off leaving it all to them.

By and large the mandarins were right. They kept a seriously tight hold on the reins of the disputes, making sure that I was updated. But a minister should feel deeply uncomfortable about such a one-sided stance. All my information was coming from the management side.

The department assumed a phoney, supposedly neutral, stance in the disputes. The mandarins hauled the chairpersons of the transport companies in to brief me as each dispute developed. I was privy to a great deal of confidential information, but this inevitably compromised my neutrality.

Perhaps as minister, and therefore the company's main shareholder, I had a primary duty to the profit and loss account and to the balance sheet, but, as a minister, I also had an obligation to the general travelling public, as well as a social role to the workforce.

So one day, while in conclave with one of the mandarins, I had a brave suggestion. I thought we should bring Dermot O'Leary of the NBRU, as well as a representative of SIPTU, into the department for a chat. The floorboards in Leeson Lane began to shudder. I thought the mandarin was going to self-destruct. A normally genial, gentle public servant hammered the table and appeared to be bursting several blood vessels. His whole body seemed to implode on the spot. He had spent his entire career in the civil service devoted to promoting the interests of transport and now he was being offered this insane suggestion. It took him twenty minutes to calm down.

The problem with this mandarin's visceral reaction was that it confirmed the fears that O'Leary and his squad so often expressed: that the department and the transport company chiefs were as thick as thieves. It gave the workforce the hate figures they needed and gave O'Leary a target for his wilder rhetoric.

I rather liked O'Leary personally. He was a pussycat who knew how to use a megaphone, but there was little malice in his industrial relations guerilla warfare. He did a lot of good for people with disabilities. However, he caused two of my Independent Alliance colleagues, Finian McGrath and John Halligan, a lot of grief during those turbulent times. O'Leary was astute enough to know that it would not be easy for two old lefties, like Finian and John, to back a minister who was refusing to talk to workers in industrial disputes. Both were embedded in the trade union tradition. O'Leary and his counterparts in SIPTU publicly called on them both to use their political clout to make me produce the nation's cheque book.

Finian, John and I were close friends, which helps in this sort of political difficulty. Both of them were adept at dodging such bullets. Finian had an ingenious solution. He was a compulsive leaflet dropper. During one of the transport disputes, he somehow — by coincidence — happened to pick an area for his weekly drop that was adjacent to the Dublin Bus depot in Clontarf. Also — again by coincidence — he happened to be passing by when a large group of staff in dispute were outside the depot. As luck would have it, they invited him in to talk to them. Finian told them that he was 100 per cent behind their industrial action and pay claim. He wanted to listen to them. They gave him a piece of their mind and he promised to relay it to me the next day. I cannot be certain that Finian spoke of me in glowing terms on that occasion, but by the end of his utterly chance encounter with the Dublin Bus staff, he was the minister inside the cabinet batting for the busmen.

John Halligan was equally adept. An old Workers' Party warhorse, John might have been expected to buckle under O'Leary's pressure, but he doesn't do buckling. A few of the brethren arrived one morning to picket his Waterford office. John hijacked the delegation before their arrival, brought them in for coffee, tea and scones and told them that 'Shane Ross is doing his best and is under pressure from his department not to back a strike.' John could talk his way out of a paper bag.

The department operated a disciplined plan during industrial disputes, but there was no thinking beyond the end of the next strike. They became aware that I was involved in back channel talks to try and redress longer-term running sores. They did not like it, but there was nothing they could do. As a result of these talks, I promised one of the union chiefs that I would hold a transport stakeholders' forum once the dispute was over. I soon made that promise public, despite knowing that it would receive a cold reception in Leeson Lane. The status quo, the age-old path of orderly confrontation, was the civil servants' comfort zone. The certainties of industrial warfare suited them far better than the unknown dangers of industrial peace.

In the middle of one of the strikes, I had suggested to a couple of mandarins that we should consider share options for the staff at all our state-owned companies. There was a flicker of disbelief on their faces. There was no explosion, as there had been at the heresy of actually supping with the enemy, but simply a frosty response to the entire idea: it had been looked at already, there were real problems, all the companies were subsidised, so there was no meaningful profit. Had I thought through what I was proposing?

And then the solution: 'We'll ask NewEra to look at the idea for you.' NewEra, the New Economy and Recovery Authority, is a state body set up to provide financial and commercial advice to government ministers. They are not exactly the state's undertakers, but they have been known to bury a few unwelcome projects in their time. Nor are they one of the Department of Transport's babies, but the mandarins at the Department of Finance were first cousins of our own. They have a common culture and a deep understanding of how state bodies work, and a similar vision of how they ought to work. The idea of state companies issuing shares to employees had ceased after Eircom and Aer Lingus.

I lost the will to live. The mandarins from both Finance and Transport were formidable opposition. There was talk of the need for further 'reports'. I had other fish to fry, not least the need to deliver the promised transport stakeholders' forum. Share options would have to wait.

The forum was an event we were determined to hold. There was no enthusiasm for it among my officials, but once I irrevocably decided to hold it, they implemented it in full. They were good people, who regarded it as their duty to give the best advice. If it was ignored, they would still do what the minister wanted. Their bona fides was never in doubt.

After dozens of delays, we finally set a date for the forum. On 21 May 2018 we took the Round Room in the Mansion House. Trade unions, management, staff, politicians, customers, regulators, economists, cycling activists, disability advocates, mandarins and others assembled to shoot the breeze about the state of Irish transport. My officials wanted it to be a once-off event, never to be repeated. They wished to run it with military precision, and they didn't want it to last too long. Dermot O'Leary saw it as something permanent, a platform where he and his trade union associates would enjoy a voice in the decision-making process.

The forum was arranged with a mandarin-like grip on proceedings. There were to be speeches and panels of well-balanced voices. The nervous civil servants had briefed me on the agenda and I had cleared the programme. It was looking good. We did not expect peace and harmony, but at the least we anticipated a robust debate, maybe even some, slightly patronisingly permitted, venting of frustrations.

When we arrived in the Round Room at around 8.30 a.m., the stage was superbly set, the places ready, with a seat for every participant. They turned up in their droves. We met the independent chairman, Professor Alan Barrett, Director of the Economic and Social Research Institute and went through the running order.

I asked the mandarin one question only. Where will the media be sitting? I might as well have been asking if there was a seat for Attila the Hun. I was rapidly informed that the media would not be attending; this was a closed meeting.

I froze. A stand-up row erupted, on the floor of the Mansion House, with less than an hour to go until the start of proceedings. Nothing later that day came near it for passion and anger. Noise levels were kept low, but tensions rose to a high point. I was adamant, but so was the civil servant arguing with me. For the first time in my ministerial career, I witnessed open anger from the mandarins: I was obviously ruining all the meticulous preparation that had been put into the occasion; I was told that some of the participants would be grandstanding for the cameras. Was this a veiled dig at the minister or at Dermot O'Leary?

The mandarins contacted Aisling, on her way to the meeting, hoping to persuade her of the merits of their case and warn her that I had erupted when I learnt of the exclusion of the media. She was always the wise young head whom they relied on to curtail my excesses. She didn't even try, but she managed to calm the atmosphere. One of the top civil servants suspected that I had done a deal about media coverage with O'Leary and offered to accommodate it. Nothing of the sort had happened.

The idea of excluding the media from an event of such public interest was out of the question. We would have been rightly eviscerated by the trade unions and by the press.

Eventually I had to issue an undignified direction that the media must be admitted. They had clearly already expected to be in attendance, arrived in large numbers and covered the proceedings fairly.

The meeting went off exactly as planned. There was some fiery stuff from Dermot O'Leary who described the forum — which he had long demanded — as 'a PR gig' and proceeded to squeeze as much public relations out of it as possible for himself! SIPTU's Greg Ennis warned of the dangers of the 'ticking time bomb', CIÉ's pension fund. The general secretary of the Irish Congress of Trade Unions (ICTU), Patricia King, gave me a bit of a lash. We all did our own share of harmless grandstanding.

Summing up, in a somewhat childish reminder to the mandarins that it was not their gig, I discarded nearly all their supplied script and held out an olive branch to the transport companies' staff. It was time to test them and their union leaders on the subject of share options or profit-sharing. Here was a rare opportunity for a discussion on a new initiative. In my closing speech I promised to consult NewEra and see if they could offer a way forward.

I contacted NewEra by phone one week later. This was followed up by discussions with department officials and a face-to-face meeting with NewEra in my office in August. They produced a predictable, but coherent, presentation of why share options were unlikely to work well in this case.

Most dispiriting was the reality that the idea never received a positive response from the mandarins, or more importantly, from the unions.

The transport stakeholders forum was the stormiest day in my, often difficult, relationship with the department. It was one of the rare occasions where I saw a civil servant lose their cool.

Over the four years we had several other differences. They were appalled at my ambition to build a third terminal at Dublin airport in anticipation of greater travelling numbers, to provide competition to the monopolistic ways of the DAA. In the light of the catastrophic effect of Covid-19 on the aviation industry, their caution has been proved correct.

Secretly, the department's senior figures probably believed that issues like Brexit, capital spending, industrial relations, tourism and sport, should never be allowed near a politician. They are trained at biting their tongues until their teeth are worn thin. They implemented measures with which they profoundly disagreed on several occasions, including the appointment of a National Cycling Officer. Once a decision was made that we should extract a special dividend out of one of their favourite babies, the Irish Aviation Authority, they were unapologetic and effective, pointing out that the IAA was sitting on a cash pile of €200 million. They needed no public applause. Politicians' thinking is shorter term. We crave publicity; we need the media, apparently the nemesis of the public service.

The civil servants' contempt for the media can be two-faced. A few, usually those at the higher levels, do leak to the media. On one occasion, it was surprising to see a blatant contradiction between the ethos and the practice. The *Irish Times'* political editor, Pat Leahy, wrote a piece in March 2018 about the Independent Alliance, of which he was no fan. The civil service had apparently been leaking to the *Irish Times* about my ministerial modus operandi. Leahy wrote that, 'If half the things his civil servants and his ministerial colleagues say are true, it [his experience of government] has been a very unhappy one.' He went on to quote one senior civil servant as saying about me as a minister: 'He's not a Minister in the conventional sense of the word. He doesn't sit at his desk, read briefs, make decisions.' And another: 'He has no interest in his brief at all.'

Such anonymous comments are regular pieces of treachery from one minister about another. It is almost unique for civil servants to speak of senior ministers in these terms. Some people in my department were shocked. The Secretary General, Graham Doyle, rang to reassure me that no one on the staff had been talking indiscreetly.

As it happens, I know who it was. A civil servant in my department spoke to another highly placed civil servant, who was not averse to talking out of turn to the media.

I have rarely met a more talented group of people than those in the top posts at the Department of Transport, Tourism and Sport. They are without peer in their knowledge of their specialist subjects. Their generosity with their insights in the public interest is impressive, a generosity not reciprocated by politicians, who tend to reserve, for their own self-interest, information they have acquired.

It was the civil servants who prepared our memos for government and briefed us for every meeting with chiefs of state-sponsored bodies, overseas visitors and vested interests. They prepared us for Brexit issues and for every dogfight we attended. They accompanied me to Oireachtas committee meetings, the Dáil, the Seanad and to cabinet subcommittees where I was capable of putting my foot straight into the manure. They would often patiently draft a clarifying statement to help me out of a hole I had energetically dug for myself.

Sometimes they missed a trick, but Aisling was always there to rescue me from the inevitable knowledge gap or public stumble. Once, at a supercharged cabinet subcommittee about the very sensitive issue of introducing graduated speeding penalties in an upcoming bill, the Taoiseach Leo Varadkar turned to me and asked if there was anything else of any significance in the bill?

I had mugged up the graduated speeding briefing to the last comma, because of its political sensitivities on the Fine Gael backbenches.

'No,' I volunteered confidently, in the presence of most members of the cabinet and a host of top mandarins. The meeting moved on.

A few minutes later, I received a note from Aisling, who was sitting nearby:

Shane, the Taoiseach just asked you if there was anything else in the Road Traffic (Miscellaneous Provisions) Bill apart from the issue of graduated speeding. You said NO.

The answer is YES.

You never mentioned variable speed limits for the M50 and some changes to the medical fitness to drive requirements. You should clarify that before the meeting ends.

There was none of the deference of the mandarin in that admonishing note.

I am going to miss them.

10

Irish Football Pulls Back from the Brink

'I DON'T HEAR people giving out. I hear it in the press all right. There's a lot of criticism of John Delaney. My own experience is that when I go to these local games in the constituency... I see John Delaney and representatives of the FAI there all the time. They're always on the ground doing things, relating to those really important things that young people are doing.'

Back in 2018, that is what I said about John Delaney, chief executive of the Football Association of Ireland, in reply to a question on Newstalk.

As a TD and later as Minister for Sport, I spent many weekends attending local sports events, especially football and GAA games. It was the most enjoyable part of the job. The atmosphere was unbeatable. In every case, the community was at its best; volunteers were working like beavers for the benefit of the young boys and girls of the neighbourhood. Parents and teachers were giving of their free time for the mental and physical health of the next generation.

Football at grass roots level was, and is, probably the most popular sport in Ireland. It constantly needed help, grants and encouragement from government, Sport Ireland and leading sporting figures. The occasional appearance of soccer stars at local games was a huge boost to a club's morale. Niall Quinn, Liam Brady, John Giles and other heroes of the young dreamers made regular guest appearances to stimulate the ambitions of Ireland's schoolchildren. What surprised me was that possibly the most consistent of these prominent visitors was John Delaney.

In my constituency alone, I saw Delaney at numerous football gigs during my time as Minister for Sport. I remember him turning up on separate occasions at Leicester Celtic in Ballinteer, at Dundrum Football Club, at Wayside Celtic in Kilternan at least twice, at Ballyogan Celtic Football Club and lots of others too. He was invariably given a warm reception. Delaney seemed to know the local club officers by their first names and gave them plenty of his time, often presenting medals at ceremonies that lasted for hours. He sometimes ended the gig by promising to give everybody in the audience a ticket to the next international match at the Aviva Stadium, which he always delivered on. He was a good mixer.

These clubs often felt well served by the FAI. They received the benefits of the Association's development officers, a troop of faithful football fanatics, coaches and mentors, passionate about promoting the game. Many of them worked a sixty-hour week for the FAI and topped it up with voluntary hours, coaching the coaches.

Football numbers on the ground were swelling, thanks to the volunteers, the development officers and the unpaid community activists in the local clubs. Members held fundraisers to keep the clubs' heads above water. The government could never give enough money to grassroots sport. The department ran a life-saving sports capital grants programme, from which football benefited.

John Delaney sometimes satisfied that hunger for funds. Stories from FAI headquarters at Abbotstown have emerged about him arriving to work on a Monday morning with the news that he had given away tens of thousands of euros' worth of tickets the previous day to a small club. Sometimes it was a direct grant to a club in need. Insiders say that there was rarely any money in the FAI coffers to accommodate Delaney's largesse.

On the surface, Delaney was doing what he did best. He was gregarious. He related really well to the grassroots. He had an attractive, if cavalier, personality. He was a politician masking as a chief executive. His generosity to the clubs had two effects. It helped struggling football teams to survive, but it also consolidated Delaney's grip on the FAI. All the time he was being generous to clubs over a weekend, he was building up his power base. He needed the rank and file to re-elect him and for his clique to control the FAI through the board and the FAI council. (The FAI council was a powerful group of members, which sat alongside the board. It elected the president and vice-president, nominated some committee members and voted on major decisions.) And every time Delaney threw money at a small club in a weekend splurge, he left an already financially fragile FAI in a weaker position. On one occasion when I was at a local club that Delaney was visiting, he gave away tickets to the competitors 'at the request of the minister'. I had made no such request, but undoubtedly he felt it would do our relationship no harm to credit me with such generosity.

He was sport's answer to Charles J. Haughey. Where Haughey was said to have paid for the turkeys of Raheny supermarket shoppers at Christmas, Delaney would distribute tickets to young fans at medal ceremonies. Both had the same effect.

While it should be acknowledged that celebrity visits tended to boost the morale of neglected local clubs, Irish football was dysfunctional. At the bottom it flourished on a shoestring. At the top it rotted in the grip of an unseen malaise of greed and inefficiency.

When I became a minister, I had been a long-time football fan, most recently courtesy of my grandchildren. I took them to nearly all Ireland's home matches, we went abroad to the European Championship in Poland in 2012, and to Premier League games in Britain. We had seen Chelsea play at Stamford Bridge, Manchester United at Old Trafford, Arsenal at the Emirates and — to be a bit different — League Two's Scunthorpe United at Glanford Park. I was a member of the Oireachtas Republic of Ireland Supporters Club. We rang the FAI for tickets for international matches but always paid for them.

During those days, I would sometimes meet Delaney. He would come to Leinster House to lobby TDs. Oireachtas members were entertained, along with dozens of others, in modest pre-match hospitality at Ireland's games at the Aviva. Sandwiches were on the house, but you bought your own drinks.

During that period, Ireland began paying its managers whopping sums. In 2008, Giovanni Trapattoni landed a two-year contract as Ireland team manager at an annual salary of €1.7 million. Billionaire Denis O'Brien promised to pay half this amount, topping it up to €2.02m to subsidise 50 per cent of the backroom staff's pay. Trap's predecessor, Steve Staunton, had been paid about a quarter of the Italian's salary, at €450,000 a year.

O'Brien and Delaney built up a strong relationship; so strong that, despite only moderate results on the field of play, O'Brien again agreed to pay half of Trapattoni's salary of €1.5 million as part of his renewed contract in 2011. Trap's days were numbered in 2013 when Ireland failed to qualify for the World Cup in Brazil. Denis O'Brien again stepped into the breach when Delaney signed up Martin O'Neill and Roy Keane ('the dream team') to share the mantle. O'Neill was given €1.2 million a year, with an €800,000 bonus if Ireland qualified for the 2016 European Championship. Keane, merely the assistant manager, had to settle for €700,000.

In 2014, Delaney celebrated ten years at the helm of the FAI. He was deeply embedded. All this monopoly money for the managers enabled him to justify his own salary of €360,000 a year. A gulf existed in the Irish soccer world between the astronomical remuneration at the top and the volunteerism at the bottom. Reality on the ground was a world apart from the runaway funny money being spent on the elite. The prize money for winning first place in the League of Ireland in 2014 was €110,000, less than a third of Delaney's salary.

In 2015, Martin O'Neill started achieving results when, owing to a memorable goal from Shane Long, Ireland beat world champions Germany and subsequently qualified for Euro 2016. We were off to France for the Championship!

There, Ireland progressed through its group with a dramatic 1-0 victory over Italy, thanks to another equally sensational late goal, this time a header from Robbie Brady. We were knocked out in the next round by France, but it was a good overall performance. It was also the high point for O'Neill. According to a study conducted by Portuguese football finance experts, Finance Football, he was the ninth highest paid manager in a table of twenty-four European rivals in 2016. His pay (before any possible bonuses) at €1 million dwarfed the annual salary of his Northern Ireland counterpart, Michael O'Neill, at €320,000.

Martin's moment of glory was short-lived. In 2017 Ireland failed to qualify for the 2018 World Cup. A disastrous 5-1 home defeat to Denmark in the Aviva marked the beginning of the end for the O'Neill-Keane duo. O'Neill limped on until November 2018, but then parted company with Ireland 'by mutual agreement'. Delaney signed up Mick McCarthy and Stephen Kenny as manager and manager designate. McCarthy was to remain with Ireland on €1.2 million a year until the European Championship in 2020, but Covid-19 put off the competition for a year. So Stephen Kenny, manager of Ireland's under-21 team, took over, at a modest salary of €540,000, only about 20 per cent more than Steve Staunton was earning way back in 2006/07.

The football results had been mixed in Delaney's time. Over twelve years, Ireland had failed to reach a World Cup, though they had qualified for two European Championships. The players and fans had captured the wider public imagination. There was enormous popular goodwill for the team, partly because of its plucky performances but also because the fans were widely regarded as boosting 'Brand Ireland' by their good humour and impeccable behaviour when overseas.

Football had become a national passion during the Jack Charlton years. Unfortunately, in 2019 we were to discover that simultaneously the great game's guardian, the FAI, had become a basket case. All the mad spending had landed the Association in dire debt. The FAI had been teetering on the verge of bankruptcy for several years.

It took a journalist, Mark Tighe of the *Sunday Times*, to blow the lid off all the hype surrounding Irish football. On 17 March 2019, he revealed that Delaney had lent the FAI €100,000 in April 2017. The nation's mind boggled. How come an individual employee, admittedly with a hefty €360,000 salary, had lent €100,000 to one of our largest sporting bodies with a turnover of €50 million? Delaney had fought in court against Tighe's right to publish this information, and he had lost.

All hell broke loose. There was a media frenzy around the sensational news. The FAI issued a statement saying that it was 'a once-off bridging loan to the Association to aid a very short-term cash flow issue'. They hoped that would put it to bed. It didn't.

That evening, by coincidence, I was due to attend the FAI International Awards Ceremony at RTÉ's Montrose. It was billed as a historic occasion, not least because ex-Ireland international footballer Emma Byrne was going to be the first female player ever inducted into the FAI 'Hall of Fame'. It was meant to be the night that the FAI embraced gender equality. It was the FAI's way of detaching itself from the public relations disaster of two years earlier, when, with its indefensible stance over pay and conditions, it had taken on the women's team. Byrne had been among those who stood firm. The women's team's rightful demands were met when the FAI backed down. The awards that evening were due to be a silent recognition — in front of the television cameras — that the row had been patched up. The male-dominated FAI was due to pay silent homage.

There was plenty of media interest in the awards that night. Unfortunately, their interest was in Delaney, not in Emma Byrne.

When I arrived at RTÉ, the atmosphere was tense. I was greeted by John Delaney himself and treated as politely as ever, but the man looked drained and there was little of his usual bravado. He was nervous. In conversation he immediately addressed the €100,000 loan to the FAI and explained it precisely in line with the press release — that it was a short-term loan. The storm would blow over, he said.

The narrative Delaney gave was surprising. It was time for him to switch to another job in the FAI. He had served his term as chief executive. The FAI had already commissioned an independent report, which had recommended a shake-up. In future, he would be dealing with overseas matters, liaising with Union of European Football Associations (UEFA) and the Fédération Internationale de Football Association (FIFA). He told me all this as a heads-up.

At the awards ceremony I was seated beside FAI president, Donal Conway. He was on message, giving me exactly the same yarn, *sotto voce*, about how 'John' would be moving on, describing the new job and its *raison d'être* in identical terms to Delaney's explanation. Conway was testing my reaction. I was non-committal.

No one at the ceremony could have been in any doubt. Mark Tighe had broken a mega story. Both Delaney and Conway were rattled that night, but seemed determined to weather the storm. Shifting Delaney to a higher role within the FAI would do the trick. The FAI felt that a fresh face at the helm, with executive vice president Delaney doing the hard graft on the international circuit, would work. After all, he had been comfortably elected to the executive committee of UEFA two years earlier; the change he was planning would reflect his new role.

But it was about ten years too late. The discovery of the €100,000 loan had opened the way to an avalanche of revelations, leading to nothing less than the demise of the old FAI. It took a while for many of the old guard to realise that it was the end of the road for them.

Two days later, Sport Ireland's John Treacy led the response. Treacy is a thoughtful, measured man; he does not rush to judgement. He was concerned that Sport Ireland, which funded the FAI, 'had not been notified in 2017 about any material deterioration' in the FAI's financial position, as was its entitlement. A reasonable question, when the FAI was in such severe straits as to need a loan of a hundred grand from its boss.

The following Saturday, 23 March, I received a courtesy call from John Delaney, telling me formally that he was moving from his post as chief executive to the new role of executive vice president, as he had outlined to me the previous Sunday. It was a brief call from faraway Gibraltar, where Ireland had just beaten the home side 1-0 in a dismal match. It was the last contact I ever had with Delaney.

The next day, the *Sunday Times* carried a story that the FAI had been paying Delaney's €3,000 a month rent on his house over and above his €360,000 a year salary. On 14 April, the same newspaper covered Delaney's credit card spending for 2016, suggesting that it had been used for duty-free drink and other inappropriate purposes.

As various stories of debt and disasters broke, investigations popped up in response. The Oireachtas Joint Committee on Transport, Tourism and Sport was intent on holding hearings. In late March, the FAI directors arranged for Mazars Ireland, a leading professional services firm, to investigate internal concerns and report back. Sport Ireland and the FAI established a Governance Review Group which was to report by mid-June, in time to make recommendations on corporate governance failures in advance of the FAI's July AGM. Even more ominously, the Office of the Director of Corporate Enforcement (ODCE) was posing questions. Sport Ireland announced on 10 May that it had asked the KOSI Corporation to carry out a thorough audit of the FAI's accounts.

On 3 April, John Treacy appeared before the Oireachtas committee and refused to express confidence in the board of the FAI. It was a telling moment. The next day Sport Ireland released a statement confirming the suspension of state funding to the FAI.

A week later, Delaney, Conway and other members of the FAI board appeared before the same committee. There, they lost any scintilla of goodwill there might have remained for them. Delaney refused to answer questions about his time in the FAI, apparently on legal advice. Conway was less obstructive, but was economical with information.

On 15 April, five days after his disastrous appearance before the committee, Delaney went on 'gardening leave' from the FAI. One day later, company auditors Deloitte stated that the FAI did not keep proper accounting records.

It was my turn for the Oireachtas committee on 16 April. They wanted to know what the minister was going to do to sort out the financial quagmire. Although it was not in my power to arrange it, I had already decided that there was only one solution: a complete clearout of the FAI directors, without exception. We had seen enough at the Oireachtas committee the week before to know that all the directors shared various degrees of responsibility for the unfolding revelations about the lapses of corporate governance. The board's failure to ask the questions that would have exposed the wrongdoings much earlier was unpardonable.

Some of my department officials were not as convinced as I was of the merits of a full-scale purge. Civil servants, more prudent than I, love concepts like 'continuity', or at least a little of it. It seemed to me that the last thing we needed now was continuity. They felt that not everyone on the FAI board was equally culpable. In particular, they believed that Niamh O'Donoghue, appointed only in 2017, had been embroiled in a situation that was not of her making. It was probably no coincidence because Niamh was a former Secretary General in the Department of Social Protection, but she had also been a member of the FAI council long before becoming the first female member of the FAI board. (I had met her in 2017 when she arrived in my office with John Delaney for a meeting with Brendan Griffin and me in search of money for women's football.)

Niamh was amiable and competent, but I was sure that if we started to pick and choose who should remain, we would run into trouble on several fronts. Others felt, not least himself, that perhaps president Donal Conway should stay on as president for the transition period. That was a fiercer battle, destined to be fought with intensity, but later on.

While the internal tussle between officials and me was still going on the morning of my appearance before the Oireachtas committee, a letter came in from Donal Conway. He wanted the committee to know that the entire board would resign at the AGM in July. Problem solved. Or so we thought. It would be a clean sweep. I read out the letter to the committee.

It was a mere gambit. It seems that Donal Conway was soon contemplating Plan B.

Unfortunately, Conway himself was not the only one who wanted him to stay on. The Governance Review Group, set up in April, was an amalgam of two FAI nominees (acting chief executive Rea Walshe and Niamh O'Donoghue) and three nominees from Sport Ireland. The two from the FAI would have been regarded as long-time Delaney loyalists and, by extension, probable allies of Conway. The five-person committee, including the Sport Ireland nominees, was leaning in the direction of some 'continuity'.

The Conway faction was fighting a rearguard action. Before Delaney had taken gardening leave in mid-April, there had been signs of sporadic grassroots support for him. At the end of March, the four provincial associations of Ulster, Munster, Leinster and Connacht, as well as the FAI Junior Council, issued a joint statement in support of Delaney. They mentioned that he had visited 'almost 2,000 grassroots clubs all over the country from Wexford to Donegal and Kerry to Louth'. They listed all his achievements and they wanted him to stay on. Some smaller clubs rallied around. Lee Power of Waterford FC and Pat O'Sullivan of Limerick FC supported the beleaguered FAI boss.

Somebody was trying, at worst, to orchestrate a comeback or, at best, to slow the pace of reform. The diehards were calling in their chips, trying to create a momentum. At board level, they were resisting change. If there were Trojan horses paying lip service to reform, but still sitting on the new board, biding their time, the veterans would be far from finished.

There was trouble on another front. The FAI insiders were well connected in high places. As a member of the powerful executive committee of UEFA, Delaney himself was a rising star in European football's ruling body. On a personal note, in 2017 the Slovenian UEFA president, Aleksander Čeferin, had travelled to Dublin for Delaney's lavish fiftieth birthday party in Mount Juliet, County Kilkenny. In 2016, Delaney had delivered the FAI's support for Čeferin's election as president. UEFA was funding the FAI on life support.

According to FAI board members, clear signals had come from UEFA and FIFA, warning Ireland that governments should not be interfering in sport. There were hints of sanctions or possibly even of the establishment of a 'normalisation committee' to take over the running of the FAI. UEFA and FIFA representatives came to Ireland to meet the FAI and Sport Ireland on 7 May, expressing concern at the perceived government interference. By 15 May, on a visit to Ireland, Bjorn Vassallo from Malta, FIFA's Director of Member Associations in Europe, stated, 'FIFA's objective is to safeguard the autonomy of the FAI.' Brendan Griffin and I got the distinct feeling that somebody was stirring up trouble in the background. The threat that Ireland could be banned from international football and that the government would be blamed was not a prospect we relished.

We might have been talking tough at Oireachtas committee meetings, but UEFA had us over a bit of a barrel. In early April, Conway's FAI board went directly to UEFA in search of an interim chief executive to replace Delaney. Lo and behold, who came out of the mix but an old Delaney loyalist working in UEFA headquarters in Nyon, Switzerland. The FAI had specifically asked UEFA for the loan of a man called Noel Mooney. UEFA said yes. I had a canary.

Mooney was an old ally of Delaney from his five years working in the FAI's headquarters. His appointment, 'temporary' until the end of November at a minimum, was a challenge. We could either accept it or set out on a collision course. Brendan Griffin, who had courage to burn, agreed that we should not take the prospect lying down. I therefore objected to the appointment, asking Conway, in a tense meeting in Leinster House, to think again. He and his board refused. Mooney was installed on 3 June. Conway claimed that UEFA was insisting on the appointment, given the extent of its investment in the FAI. We were on the back foot.

Despite Delaney's decades of nurturing the grassroots, we sensed that the old FAI, while influential, did not have the loyalty of the mass of volunteers, coaches, fans, officials and small clubs. We decided to hold a football forum in the Round Room of Dublin's Mansion House to take the temperature at community level. We would invite the FAI, of course, members of UEFA and all stakeholders, but the emphasis would be on the local volunteers, players, staff, fans, the guys who tog out at the weekends. This would be their day to voice their concerns. It would also give us a chance to send out a message that we were not prepared to see Irish football controlled by a cabal.

Over two hundred football fans, coaches, volunteers and officials gathered in the Mansion House on Friday, 31 May. It was an occasion without precedent. We asked the FAI to contribute to two panels during the sessions. They declined, but sent along Rea Walshe and Niamh O'Donoghue as delegates. We broke the two hundred delegates into twenty-one round tables of about ten people each and placed a member of the Sports department's staff at each table to minute the discussions.

Two panel sessions were held on the future of Irish football. RTÉ's Darragh Maloney chaired them both. Among the guests on the panel were Niall Quinn, footballer Stephanie Roche, Ciarán Kane (South Dublin Football League), Pat Fenlon of the League of Ireland and the Professional Footballers Association of Ireland's Stephen McGuinness, while the second panel included Sarah Keane of the Olympic Federation of Ireland, former FAI boss Brendan Menton, Tony Considine of the You Boys in Green (YBIG) supporters group and economist and strong soccer supporter Colm McCarthy. Each panel session was followed by a discussion at the tables. The civil servant seated with each group took a note of all the proposals and conclusions. They in turn were fed into the Governance Review Group, preparing the report on corporate governance reform ahead of the FAI's crucial July AGM.

The forum was a worthwhile exercise. There were probably a few shadowy figures from the past lurking in the room, but none put their head above the parapet. The level of discontent and disconnect from the FAI was palpable, almost unanimous. The ideas from the stakeholders were multiple, but not yet connected. Our job was to weave them into a coherence that would benefit the sport. The fightback — to wrestle Irish football from the clutches of a cabal — was on the way.

As I left the Mansion House that day, I had a word with Aidan Horan, chairman of the Governance Review Group that was looking at the possible make-up of the new FAI board following a mass exodus in July. He mentioned the need for the dreaded 'continuity', namely his desire for at least two of the old guard to stay on. He was not for turning. I knew that if the Group issued its report with this recommendation, Donal Conway would seize on it as a lifeline for himself and others. It would be presented as a Sport Ireland initiative. Didn't Sport Ireland (and by proxy the government) have a majority on the Governance Review Group? Not for the first time, the minister's agency was slightly out of line with the minister.

We were still fighting against combative forces at home and overseas. The forum had given us an unscientific, but obvious, mandate to pursue reform. The diehards were plotting a revival, but were unable to stand over the activities or culture of the old regime.

UEFA was the key to further reform. Sadly, it provided Delaney's chosen refuge (he was still on the executive board). The FAI had the ear of UEFA. It was funded by them. And Noel Mooney, a UEFA man, was back in charge at the Abbotstown headquarters. Conway and fellow FAI director Eamon Naughton remained as members of two of UEFA's permanent committees.

We needed to do a lot of work with UEFA. They had not attended our forum, an indication of the prevailing cool relations. A telecon meeting with president Čeferin on 28 May had been impossible because of a bad line from Baku. It was rescheduled for the Bank Holiday Monday, 3 June, in Government Buildings. Assistant Secretary General Ken Spratt, Aisling Dunne and I made the call. Čeferin was courteous. We assured him that we fully subscribed to the independence of sport from government. We respected the autonomy of the FAI and of UEFA. We explained to him the difficulties of accepting Noel Mooney's nomination because he was a reminder of a bygone time, one that was currently a running sore. We made it clear that there were numerous serious inquiries being held to investigate the activities of the FAI. These included the Governance Review Group, the Mazars Report, the KOSI report sponsored by Sport Ireland, the ODCE inquiry and another audit by Grant Thornton, commissioned by the FAI. The FAI's accounts were under the closest scrutiny. We did not want to leave UEFA unprepared for the dramatic implications of adverse findings.

Čeferin responded that Noel Mooney was not a UEFA nominee to the chief executive's post; the FAI had specifically requested him. He seemed up to date and well briefed about the gravity of the situation, and, though he yielded no ground, the ice had been broken. He gave me the distinct impression of being accustomed to talking down to governments as the senior partner in the dialogue. We hoped we had given him enough food for thought.

All eyes were now fixed on the report of the Governance Review Group, due on 21 June. It was important that the recommendations were released in time to be included among the proposals at the FAI's crunch AGM in Trim, County Meath, on 27 July.

The proposals offered limited progress, but did not live up to the hopes of those of us who were advocating serious reform. They included a board of twelve, of whom four should be independent, and within two years, four of the twelve would be female. Its chair would be drawn from one of the four new independent directors. The six football representatives on the board were to be elected by the FAI council, which was to be enlarged to redress the representative imbalance.

Some good suggestions were included, but the key recommendation betrayed the considerable influence of the old FAI board on the Governance Review Group. Aidan Horan and his fellow Sport Ireland nominees had agreed to recommend that up to two members of the old regime should be on the new board. Add them to the six members to be elected by the council and an old regime majority was possible.

The old regime was safe. Donal Conway had won approval from a Sport Ireland-sponsored review to continue as president for another year.

Not surprisingly, in the weeks leading up to the AGM, Conway campaigned energetically among the voting FAI members for the reforms that would leave him in situ. He was a reassuring figure to those resisting change. On 15 July, he was nominated unopposed to continue in office for a period of one year. Back in April he had written to me insisting that the entire board, including himself, would step down at the AGM. They were backsliding.

One day after he was nominated, I wrote to Conway asking him to withdraw his bid to stay on as president, reminding him of his promise to me that he would not go forward 'to allow for new leadership with credible reform credentials, in the best interests of football'. To no avail.

Three days later, on 19 July, as general manager of the FAI, Noel Mooney received a letter from his UEFA and FIFA colleagues saying they were 'seriously concerned'. They claimed that my comments in the letter to Conway might have constituted government interference. According to the FAI press release, both governing bodies mentioned 'sanctions' and a 'possible suspension' for the FAI and the Republic of Ireland international teams if 'undue influence from a third party' was present and proven. This was a moment of great peril for the whole reform programme.

As luck would have it, both FIFA and UEFA were in Ireland the following week to attend the FAI's AGM. A meeting between them and us was hastily arranged to defuse a dangerous situation.

Aisling, Ken Spratt and I met UEFA's Thierry Favre and Yann Hafner and FIFA's Sara Solemale on Friday evening, 26 July, in my office in Leeson Lane, along with Niamh O'Donoghue for the FAI, although she remained very quiet throughout. The UEFA and FIFA delegates reassured me that they were not doing the bidding of either John Delaney or of the remaining old regime in the FAI. They truly wished to avoid state interference. However, they also conceded that there were serious allegations of financial misconduct and corporate governance failings in the FAI, which government could not overlook, particularly since the FAI was in receipt of state funds. There were no fireworks, but it seemed the risk of a UEFA/FIFA intervention receded as a result of this meeting.

The next day, at the long-awaited AGM, the recommendations of the Governance Review Group were passed by an overwhelming majority. Donal Conway called a triumphant press conference, holding out an 'olive branch' to the minister.

Eight board members had been elected, including Conway himself and a long-time Delaney opponent, Paul Cooke, as vice president. Six others, including a few depressingly familiar figures, had been returned from various FAI constituencies, including John Earley, another former board member. There had been a short-lived attempt to stretch the bounds of reality when a third sitting board member, Noel Fitzroy, stood for re-election. However, thankfully, under significant pressure from the media and the department, he withdrew his candidacy at a late hour to 'avoid a further crisis'.

Welcoming his newly elected fellow board members, Conway claimed that there was now 'much more stability than there was at the outset' of this crisis. In the first flush of victory he rashly promised: 'We'll get to work very quickly — beginning with a meeting on Tuesday — on getting the final four members of the full board.'

That is what he promised on 27 July 2019. The 'final four' independent directors had still not been appointed by the beginning of 2020.

Conway's was a hollow victory. Alongside his election at the AGM was the dark news that the FAI, over which he had presided, could not produce audited accounts for 2018. The investigations were continuing and the real state of the FAI's books would be spelled out shortly. They were to provide a more chilling yardstick for judging Conway's stewardship since he had first joined the board in 2005. We were dreading news of the accounts, while wondering how Conway could survive their release. The independent KOSI Corporation report, with its promise of an account of what really went on behind closed doors at the FAI, was due in October. There would be nowhere to hide when the unvarnished truth emerged.

It was clear that the FAI's tactics now were to brazen it out. They had managed to keep UEFA on board, while still making early drawdowns from the funding UEFA provided. They had parachuted in Mooney as general manager and kept Conway as president. The Minister of Sport might be taking a hard line, but they still had the ear of others in the cabinet and the Dáil who were unhappy with our uncompromising stance. But the FAI's finances, worsened by the number of costly reports being prepared, were now in a perilous situation.

Brendan Griffin and I decided to wait for the inevitable deluge. We refused to meet Mooney or Conway, declining their invitations to be their guests at the Aviva at both Ireland's September match against Switzerland and the game against Denmark in November. We asked our cabinet colleagues to decline any blandishments or invitation to enjoy FAI hospitality. The Taoiseach and the rest of the cabinet agreed. There was a single exception. One member of the cabinet, Michael Ring, made a point of going to the Denmark game despite my requests to him not to give the FAI any comfort.

Ring had been a friend of the FAI in his days as Minister for Sport when nothing was known of the present shenanigans. Recently, he was among others whom the FAI had courted. He brushed aside my efforts to dissuade him to boycott the games and went one step worse, bringing Fine Gael Minister of State Pat Breen with him to the Denmark game. It was a small chink in our armour and I heard that the two ministers were greeted like kings on arrival . There were numerous empty VIP seats on that day. Brendan and I had a great evening at the Swiss game. He was sitting in the stands with a friend while I was there with two of my grandchildren. The game against Denmark was equally enjoyable. We did not miss the hospitality of the FAI.

We were determined to put the slow squeeze on the FAI and to play a longer game. We publicly repeated that there was no question of the restoration of funding until the new independent directors were in place. Nor would the FAI be given any access to government. We were waiting for the publication of the revised accounts for 2018 and for the findings of the deepest of the diggers, the KOSI report, being prepared for Sport Ireland.

While there had been a short summer lull, the omens for further tranquillity in the autumn were dispiriting. Every month, a flimsy excuse was offered for the delay in the appointment of the independent directors, promised 'within weeks' of Conway's triumph at the July AGM.

July passed. August passed. September passed. October passed. Even November passed. There was no sign of the independent directors, just lame excuses for the delay.

During the autumn months, minor bouts of guerilla warfare broke out.

One Monday in early October the *Irish Sun* newspaper ran a story that the FAI had paid for my accommodation while I was on a private visit to a Denmark match in Copenhagen in 2017. They presented it as an exclusive. The truth was that when I went to the hotel reception to settle my bill, I had, to my surprise, found that it had been paid by the FAI. I had immediately reimbursed the FAI on my return to Dublin. Someone had leaked the story to the *Irish Sun* without saying that I had instantly repaid the hotel bill. Luckily, I could produce the receipt, after the FAI had claimed that they could not find any record of the reimbursement. To its credit, the newspaper printed my rebuttal.

The dirty tricks brigade was out in force. The same story also tried to compromise Minister of State Brendan Griffin, who attended the game in an official capacity, for travelling home from Denmark that night on the FAI plane. In truth, there was an empty seat and it would have cost the state overnight accommodation if he had stayed in Copenhagen.

Such diversions demonstrated the low level to which some were stooping. Meanwhile, there was still not a whisper about the independent directors, only excuses for the postponement of their appointment. We felt that we might have been suckered.

On 26 November, the KOSI report was sent to Sport Ireland and forwarded to me. It was dynamite. We referred it to the Garda Síochána. That itself sent a message to the FAI and in particular to UEFA. The most immediate significant finding of KOSI was that the FAI was unfit to receive public funds.

In the background preparations were being made for Noel Mooney's departure, ending his stint as the FAI's unwelcome general manager on 30 November. No advertising for his successor had appeared. It emerged that Conway and company had teed up yet another former FAI man to take over in an 'interim' capacity. John Foley, a decent man but with too many past links to the FAI, had been hand-picked by the board to step into the breach. Brendan and I had made it perfectly clear that we felt that Mooney's successor as chief executive, whether interim or permanent, should have no previous association with the FAI. To my relief, Foley withdrew at the last minute, but it left the Association rudderless, on life support.

Vice president Paul Cooke took up the position. This time the job description was as 'executive lead'.

On 4 December, telecommunications provider Three Ireland pulled out of its sponsorship deal with the FAI. The FAI was now reeling from a series of killer blows. KOSI alone was lethal, but followed by the Foley fiasco and now the desertion of Three Ireland, its position looked hopeless. Conway's position was back in the balance.

The knockout blow was not long in coming. On 6 December, the long-awaited 2018 accounts were published. The FAI had net current liabilities of €55 million. The announcement was devastating, far worse than the most pessimistic forecast. And, adding salt to the wound, the accounts revealed that a settlement of €462,000 had been made to John Delaney. The board justified this extraordinary payment because the directors in 2014 had signed off on a mind-blowing contract extension, entitling Delaney to a payment of €3 million upon expiration of that contract in 2021.

In a deadly article in the *Irish Times*, the country's leading corporate governance guru, Professor Niamh Brennan of UCD, was damning, describing the FAI as 'broke'. She said the directors were 'in denial', and even raised the possibility of prosecutions under the Companies Act. She finished her article: 'The organisation is at death's door. As I see it, only government intervention can save Irish soccer.'

Donal Conway announced that he would resign on 25 January at an extraordinary general meeting. I welcomed it. He had hung on until this day, when the auditors stated that they could not even say whether the FAI was a going concern. At the same time, bizarrely, Paul Cooke denied that the Association was insolvent.

The survival of the FAI was now in the balance. The possibilities of examinership and receivership were in the air. Suddenly events began to move with speed. The accounts had been so shocking that alarm must have been felt in the boardrooms of the main creditors at the Bank of Ireland, at UEFA and FIFA, but most crucially among the FAI staff, whose livelihoods were now at stake. As minister, I had refused to meet the FAI until the independent directors were appointed. Eventually, as the crisis deepened, we decided it was time to move. We did not want to see Irish football, the staff, the volunteers or the grass-roots in the communities damaged, but we were determined not to reward wrongdoing.

We had a settlement in mind. We might be able to restore funding if we saw the back of Conway, and the installation of the independent directors, but only if UEFA and the Bank of Ireland shared the pain. We were all on the hook: the taxpayer, the fans, the staff, the government, UEFA, the League of Ireland, the creditors and the Bank of Ireland.

Messages were coming in from everywhere: would we meet the FAI? There were alarmist signals being sent that the staff payroll could not be met at the end of December. The FAI was definitely trying to bounce us into bringing our cheque book to the table.

I would have held out against talks for a while longer, but I had been having regular meetings with football heavyweights to receive feedback. I had met objective commentators like former FAI boss Brendan Menton, former Ireland manager Brian Kerr and even, at one stage, the universally respected former Irish goalie Packie Bonner, all people who loved football. At this moment they were anxious that the FAI might soon be beyond the point of no return.

I had also held back-channel meetings with a senior figure in the FAI hierarchy for several weeks. We had met the previous Saturday in The Dropping Well pub in Milltown. He relayed how he was having sleepless nights worrying that the FAI was now trading recklessly and how the whole pack of cards could come tumbling down at any moment.

Eventually Brendan Griffin and I agreed to meet Paul Cooke and five other directors in Leinster House on 16 December. They brought along their new accountants, Grant Thornton. They told a tale of woe. Their presentation was grim. At the end of it, they summed up their position by saying that they needed €18 million cash immediately.

The meeting ended without agreement. It was perfectly obvious that the FAI had no real plan, other than to make over forty junior members of staff redundant and expect the taxpayers to bail them out. They were headless chickens in need of help. Paul Cooke went out and told the media that the talks had been 'constructive'. They had not been, but we now had a clear view of the situation. It was dire. We believed the FAI, but reckoned there was little they could now do for themselves, bar finally stop blocking the appointment of independent directors.

We had to take the initiative. While making hardline noises, we were preparing to meet Bank of Ireland and UEFA in pursuit of a four-way deal. We were meeting the Oireachtas committee on 18 December for another public session and resolved to be upfront on all matters, spelling out the gravity of the situation.

Our initiative backfired. While we were positioning ourselves for a final settlement, we needed to pitch our narrative to the Bank of Ireland, the FAI and UEFA. We held the line that there was no bailout money available, while deliberately revealing the extent of the FAI's problem by publicising the €18 million figure. I told the committee that the KOSI report specifically stated that the FAI was unfit for public money, so how could there be funds available? We needed to see the whites of the eyes of the new independent directors and reforms on the way before restoration of funding could be considered.

We had already arranged a meeting with UEFA in Dublin for 14 January and the department had been reliably informed that the FAI would survive until then. Behind the scenes there was, suddenly, encouraging movement on the appointment of the four independent directors.

The questions at the joint committee tended to focus on the League of Ireland, where I was rightly exposed by Sinn Féin's Jonathan O'Brien as having kept myself inadequately informed. We rapidly arranged for a meeting with the League on 3 January, one of the most productive of all our encounters.

Unfortunately, the tough line we had taken at the Oireachtas committee spooked my cabinet colleagues and annoyed Cooke. The FAI's 'executive lead' issued a statement criticising the fact that I had divulged the €18 million figure to the committee and the public. He quietly wrote a letter to the Taoiseach seeking a meeting. Leo correctly referred it to his officials.

The reverberations from the meeting with the Oireachtas committee spread wider than I'd expected. Before the cabinet meeting the following day, I received an anxious call from Paschal Donohoe. It was unlike him to be spooked, but Paschal had been speaking to someone who had warned him that stakeholders were anxious about my attitude in the committee the day before. He obviously feared that the bank might pull the plug. Paschal did not want to see football threatened in Ireland. My guess was that his Secretary General, Robert Watt, who had a genuine interest in the game, had been whispering in his ear.

Paschal's was only one of many cabinet ministers' sudden signs of anxiety about FAI funding on that morning. His call came before the cabinet meeting, but unusually — since it was not on the agenda — Leo himself raised the matter of the FAI at the end of the proceedings.

All ministers have a tedious, self-assessed expertise when it comes to football. After Simon Coveney spoke, I formed the distinct impression that there had been a Fine Gael powwow about the rhetoric I had used at the committee the day before. A general election was looming, and they were all obviously worried about their local football clubs. I told the cabinet little detail of our plans, because collectively they could not be trusted not to have the news in the public arena within minutes. Simon kindly suggested that maybe I should use the services of NewEra to examine the FAI books. The services of the state were at my disposal. I have always liked Simon, but that morning I would have cheerfully strangled him.

Meanwhile, later that day, powerful civil servants seemed to lose the run of themselves on the FAI issue. They were quietly arranging a meeting with the FAI behind my back. Three Secretaries General were involved, including my own. I alerted Leo about the meeting at midnight, on 19 December, the night before it was to take place. The next morning he responded: 'Hi Shane, some of this is news to me too. Knew FAI were coming in to meet some of my officials on foot of letter they wrote to me. Assumed you were in the loop. Didn't know 3 Sec Gens involved. Let me find out more and call you later. Nothing will be done on FAI without you.'

I responded, 'Thank you. I think meeting should probably be cancelled. I was not consulted. Shane.' A few minutes later he replied, 'That meeting is off. In something now, but will call you.'

We spoke later that day and it was sorted. Leo never undermined his ministers. He would sometimes pinch your best gigs, but that was a Taoiseach's prerogative. He would not publicly let you down.

Public servants, just like politicians, have an unusual passion for football. Cabinet Secretary Martin Fraser is a Liverpool fan. Robert Watt coaches in Drumcondra. Others are regular attenders at international games.

Robert Watt's interest had not yet surfaced. He had seriously surprised me three months earlier. He had made contact with me as far back as 10 September, alerting me to his wish to be a director of the FAI. He said he had been approached, but would not accept the nomination without my clearance. It was a highly unorthodox move for a top civil servant.

Initially, after he had come to my office to discuss the subject, I asked him to let me think about it. Following considerable thought, I told him that I believed it was not appropriate. I envisaged that once the path was clear at the FAI and true reform was under way, I, on behalf of the FAI would, in due course, be seeking funds from his department for football. Robert would be both the principal public servant heading up DPER, the department dishing out the money, and at the same time a director of the beneficiary. He would be hopelessly compromised. He was not pleased and said that Paschal had no objection to the idea. We left it at that. He accepted my view.

I was under the clear understanding that Robert had withdrawn from consideration. Indeed I sent him a message at Christmas, after I had met the FAI and they had requested the €18 million from the state, presumably from Robert's department. My text included a pointed reference to his prior interest in the FAI directorship: 'Meeting with FAI went better. In the middle of it I thanked my lucky stars that you declined to pursue a place on the board. Imagine if you had been asking yourself for €18m!'

He did not respond to the comment.

Funnily enough, two days earlier the Taoiseach had sent me a text message about whether he himself would attend the proposed meeting with the FAI about the funding crisis. He was unable to come: 'You can meet them though! Would be good to have Martin F there if he's free. Or Robert W. You may need money.'

Precisely. Watt was the key to money for the FAI.

I replied: 'Will probably do Monday with Watt, Fraser (or whoever you nominate), Graham, Ken Spratt and their number cruncher from Grant Thornton…'

Indeed Watt declined an invitation to meet the FAI in my office on Monday, 23 December without giving any explanation. However, two weeks later, three new independent directors were appointed. Mysteriously, one place was held vacant.

The vacant place was being secretly kept for Robert Watt. In the end it was held for six months. Indeed, it was being held specifically until I left office. Only two days after the 2020 general election, after I had lost my seat — yet was still Minister for Sport — but in the departure lounge, I received word that Robert was about to be announced as the fourth director. I immediately made it absolutely clear to chairman Roy Barrett that I would publicly oppose the appointment, since I believed Watt would be hopelessly conflicted whenever the FAI was seeking state funds. As a result, the announcement was not made.

I left office on 27 June. Robert Watt was announced as the fourth independent director after the July board meeting less than one month later. I wonder how the GAA and the IRFU feel about Robert's decision to sit on a board competing with them for state funds. More nervously, I wonder how UEFA and FIFA feel about the Secretary General of the Irish government's spending department sitting as a supposedly independent director on the FAI board. They have strong views on government interference in football after all.

On 19 June my department negotiated a large €70 million Covid-19 payment from DPER, explicitly for sport. A substantial chunk of that money is destined to go to the FAI.

The FAI is likely to be beating down the door for more money from Robert's department in the near future. This was a bad decision on Robert's part and on the part of the FAI board.

But prior to all those shenanigans, the meeting that Paul Cooke and his cohorts had hoped would be with the Taoiseach was referred back to my office on 23 December. The mood music was not good. In a sense, they were out of the equation since they had little to bring to the party except the begging bowl and bad news, which they produced in torrents. They thought they might possibly reach the mid-January payroll date without a collapse. We wished them a Merry Christmas and had to leave it at that for the time being.

While the crisis was being hyped before Christmas, in the background progress was being made. The FAI nomination committee, headed by Conway, had finally got the message that the key to unlocking the door was the nomination of the independent chair and other independent directors. Names were beginning to surface about a possible board chair.

At one point I thought the nominations committee must have gone off the reservation when I heard of the cavalier way they treated David Hall's application. David was chairman of the Irish Mortgage Holders Organisation and had not even been given an interview. Elsewhere, I doubted their sanity when the rumour mill threw up the name of Maurice Pratt as a live runner for the chair. It was unbelievable that either Amrop — the FAI's recruiting agency — or its nomination committee was resorting to tired old shipwrecks from the Celtic Tiger. Pratt was famous for being chair of the Bank of Scotland that had collapsed in the property boom, for presiding over a disastrous period at the C&C Group, which produces cider, and for his past presidency of IBEC, which produces nothing. What hidden talents had this man to lead a company out of near-bankruptcy?

Happily, Pratt's name disappeared as fast as it had been floated. But one name in the frame was Roy Barrett, the boss of Goodbody Stockbrokers. Over Christmas, I had heard that Amrop had sounded him out. He had not applied, but he was interested. He was low profile, had no skeletons, a genuine interest in football and was still enjoying a successful career in the corporate sector with Goodbodys. First, he wanted to speak to all the stakeholders involved, including Sport Ireland, UEFA, the Bank of Ireland, the FAI, the staff and the minister. Roy was a dealmaker.

A meeting was arranged with him on 30 December. It was not meant to be an interview. Within a few minutes, he was interviewing me in my office! Roy was concerned that all parties were genuinely interested in a solution. Otherwise, it was, for him, a non-runner. The meeting went well. He was understated, strong, no lover of the limelight, but a lover of football.

Roy was also a fast mover. A few minutes after I had bid him goodbye at the corner of Lower Leeson Street, I walked up to the Conrad Hotel for a quiet coffee. There he was, already meeting with Sport Ireland chief John Treacy!

We were shifting into solution mode. The megaphone was back in the cupboard.

Both meetings seem to have reassured Roy that we were anxious to act swiftly. We still needed the independent directors on board before we could engage in serious talks. It was essential that there was enough goodwill from all parties to salvage the FAI. Roy made it his business to take the temperature from all the major stakeholders.

One week later, on 8 January, after a series of meetings and contacts, Roy Barrett accepted the appointment as independent chairperson of the FAI. The same day two women, lawyer Catherine Guy, chief executive of Autolease Fleet Management, and Liz Joyce, director of Human Resources at the Central Bank of Ireland, filled two of the three remaining vacant seats on the board.

This was the breakthrough we needed. The next day Brendan Griffin, Aisling, Ken and I met all three in the department. It was a boon to meet fresh, friendly, FAI faces, an encounter without confrontation. They needed funds. We needed reform. We were anxious to restore funding, they were instinctive reformers. Goodwill was evident, but there were only five days until UEFA came to town.

That afternoon Aisling and I headed to another meeting. Senator Pádraig Ó Céidigh had asked us to meet Irish football legend Packie Bonner and Brendan Menton as soon as possible. I had met Brendan several times already, but not Packie.

These guys were not seeking glory, reward or recognition. In the basement of the Merrion Hotel, we heard of their experiences and of the passion they felt for Irish football. They were fearful that this was the last chance in a generation to reform the FAI, but that it might be wasted. They made further suggestions about ensuring that there was no backsliding, requests that carried the convictions of those who still bore the wounds of past battles. Our encounters with people like Packie, Brendan and Brian Kerr gave us the confidence to press on, deep into unexplored terrain, where many members of the cabinet and top civil servants had feared to tread.

On 14 January, the four-person UEFA delegation, including general secretary Theodore Theodoridis and financial director Josef Koller, arrived in Leinster House to meet Brendan Griffin, Aisling, Ken Spratt, Peter Hogan (Ken's right-hand man) and me. Roy Barrett was there for the FAI. My most recent contact with Theodoridis had not been a warm one. It was he who had written to me six months earlier to warn me of the dangers of political interference in the independence of football after I had called for Donal Conway to bow out of the contest for the FAI chair.

Theodoridis was a heavy hitter. He had either come to read the Riot Act or to offer support. Initially, he was obviously on his guard. I guessed he may have been briefed on this volatile, difficult Irish Sports Minister, and been warily bracing himself for a repeat performance. But that time had now passed. Three of the four independent directors had been appointed; the release of the dour state of the FAI finances had exposed the shortcomings of the previous regime; the KOSI report had found the withholding of funding to have been justified.

It was time for Brendan and me to recognise that there was a new dawn. We stated our anxiety to restore funding and to join with UEFA, the new FAI and the Bank of Ireland in finding a solution. Both of us expressed full respect for the independence of the FAI, an important principle for UEFA.

Theodoridis looked relieved. He smiled. His demeanour was friendly, not confrontational. He was ready for a settlement.

He never mentioned the old wound of our alleged disrespect for the independence of the FAI. He bought into the model of three-legged support for the FAI. UEFA was already keeping it alive. They would stay in touch with Roy Barrett and were prepared to return to Dublin, if needed to approve any further progress. We were beginning to dare to hope.

The next day we met Tom Hayes and Fergus McDonald from the fourth piece in the jigsaw, the biggest creditor of the FAI, the Bank of Ireland. Roy was again present, obviously testing the temperature for any potential deal.

The Bank of Ireland could easily pull the plug at a day's notice and put the Association into liquidation or examinership. I was convinced that they had been spooked by some of the recent events, in particular the talk of doomsday at the Oireachtas committee. I was suspicious that it was the top brass at the bank who had given senior civil servants and even Paschal Donohoe the jitters just before Christmas. The FAI owed them a cool €30 million. They had probably suffered more sleepless nights than Donal Conway.

We should have met the bank weeks earlier. We explained to them that the atmosphere had now changed with Roy and the new directors on board and volunteered that the government would be prepared to share the pain in certain circumstances. The bank officials responded that writing off debt was usually unthinkable, but that there were other ways of the Bank of Ireland giving support to the FAI. We knew what they meant. We left the meeting feeling upbeat.

Roy stayed on after the bankers had left. He felt we were edging forward. He had already held a useful one-to-one meeting with the Bank of Ireland and Grant Thornton. UEFA wanted to be constructive. Relationships had improved dramatically in a matter of days. There was an element of trust creeping into the negotiations.

Aisling and I headed for our second meeting with the FAI staff within a month. They needed reassurance that jobs would be protected, that any redundancies would be voluntary and would include people at the top. We could not give cast-iron assurances about a non-government body, but we ensured that the final settlement reflected their concerns. Roy Barrett, stockbroker as he is, was particularly sympathetic to this requirement.

We were still working against the clock. The FAI had no chief executive, although Paul Cooke was standing in as 'executive lead'. However, on 20 January, the board announced the appointments of Gary Owens as interim chief executive and, three days later, Niall Quinn as his deputy.

Roy Barrett, Niall and Gary had all been members of the 'visionary group' that had published a blueprint for the future of Irish football. Their previous links with one another attracted some criticism, but Owens' and Quinn's appointments were interim. The posts were due to be publicly advertised within six months.

Owens was the first of four chief executives since Delaney not to be tainted by close ties with the FAI. He came straight from Down Syndrome Ireland. His business acumen combined with a long-term interest in football. Quinn, widely respected in the football world, was the key to winning back public trust. A reforming team without old regime baggage was at last in place to steer the FAI through the next turbulent months. Brendan and I, with our officials, met Owens the day after his appointment.

We now had a new look FAI board and executive, but we still needed a settlement to give the new team an Association to manage. The ball was now in chairman Roy Barrett's court. All the necessary meetings had been held. Despite the outpouring of goodwill from all quarters, the consummate dealmaker would be challenged to rescue such a fragile operation hovering on the brink of bankruptcy.

On 23 January 2020, we met the new chairman in the Marker Hotel on the Liffey's north quays. Roy was gloomy. There had been an issue with a delayed $500,000 payment from FIFA that had just been resolved. He needed Sport Ireland not only to restore the annual €2.9 million but to double it to €5.8 million, for at least the next three years. On top of that, he wanted between €7.5 and €8 million over three years, to be linked to the Aviva Stadium licence fee. He was working on UEFA to write down existing loans. And he needed the Bank of Ireland to restructure the existing term loan of approximately €30 million. He was also looking for the bank to become the FAI's financial partner for the next four years. These arrangements were what he called 'interdependencies', meaning that no one would deliver unless the others did.

Ken, Aisling and I gulped in unison.

In turn, we spelled out what we needed from the FAI. We remembered what Packie and Brendan Menton had said a fortnight earlier. This was the last chance for real reform. Go for it.

We did. We told Roy that we needed cast-iron assurances of reform. We required that all the changes suggested in the KOSI report would be implemented by the end of 2020; that all FAI low-to middle-income earners should be protected from compulsory redundancies for eighteen months; that half of the twelve-person board, including the chair, must be independents; that limits would be placed on the chief executive's pay in line with higher civil service levels.

Roy swallowed. He repeated that we were all on a precipice.

We parted on good terms, both our positions crystal clear. The makings of a deal were in place. As politicians, I expected Brendan and I would be scalped either way. With a general election only two weeks away, we would be accused of seeking cheap publicity for electoral success if we delivered. If we provided funding, it would be a sell-out to the FAI. If we didn't, our efforts would be deemed to be a failure. Yet the unseemly haste in recent weeks had been prompted by the disastrous state of the FAI's finances, not by political interests.

Over the next week, the FAI agreed to deliver on our reform demands. In return, we agreed to double the funding to €5.8 million per annum, for grassroots football only, and to provide the extra €7.6 million, but as a loan, not a grant. It was to be used specifically for the licence fee on the Aviva Stadium. It could not be used to pay back creditors. The terms agreed by the Bank of Ireland and UEFA are commercially sensitive, but it has been widely reported that the Bank of Ireland restructured the loans and that UEFA wrote off a substantial amount of debt. The state contributed its fair share, no more.

A Memorandum of Understanding was drawn up, to be signed by Roy and me in the presence of the other two stake-holders, UEFA and the Bank of Ireland.

Nevertheless the deal, and its impending announcement, did not go without an eleventh-hour hiccup. A late torpedo came hurtling towards us from an unexpected quarter. At 10 p.m. on 30 January, the night before the press event to announce that the FAI had been saved, Aisling received an extraordinary email from the Secretary General of our department, Graham Doyle. It read:

Minister,

The approach to the crisis in the FAI that you're taking to Government tomorrow is obviously one of significant urgency that Government has had to deal with despite the pending election. I fully understand the need to explain your approach to the public in the circumstances that have surrounded this issue and the public's interest in it.

I believe you are planning quite a bit of media engagement to this end tomorrow after the agreement of the Cabinet is reached, though I don't know the full extent of your plans. Given the advice issued by the Secretary to the Government around announcements and other activities during a General Election, I would ask that you bear this advice in mind and that Department officials are not in a position where they may be judged to be engaging in anything beyond what is necessary to inform the public or that could be considered as being political.

Regards

Graham

That letter was deliberately subject to Freedom of Information access. The message could far more easily have been conveyed by telephone.

Aisling replied an hour later:

Many thanks Graham for your email.

We are acutely aware of the need for caution during the election period. However, given the clear and urgent need for approval of a restoration of state funding and agreement to a financial pathway for the FAI, to ensure its future, approval by the Ministers of the plan is unavoidable at this time.

As for press, the media has been consistently interested in the future of the FAI and any failure to present the plan or be transparent could be detrimental to them [the FAI] and their recovery. It is also essential that the public understand that this plan involves all parties — not just the Irish taxpayers. For that reason, I think tomorrow's event is essential.

I have included you on an email, moments ago, which outlines the plans for tomorrow. The expectation is that the Ministers and one FAI rep (Roy or Gary or Niall, still TBC but they are all apparently happy to do it) would provide the media with a factual briefing outside the Dept after the MOU [Memorandum of Understanding] has been signed. There is no expectation that any civil servants would take part in that briefing. At most, there might be a visual shot of Ken and/or Peter [Hogan] at the meeting, however if you would prefer to avoid that, we can arrange for them not to be in the shot.

I totally understand the need for caution during this period. The intention is tomorrow to provide a factual update to the public on the decision of government to ensure the future of Irish football — a decision which clearly falls into the urgent and pressing category.

Please let me know if you have any further thoughts on the plans for tomorrow.

Many thanks

Aisling

Special Advisor to
Minister Shane Ross

It was a polite, but firm, way of telling a mandarin to go and jump in a lake.

Graham's intervention was extraordinary. Assistant Secretary General Ken Spratt and Principal Officer Peter Hogan had played a major part in the entire FAI saga. Admittedly Graham and other mandarins had tried to stick their oar into the process from time to time, but we had managed to keep them at bay. Secretaries General who want to be players in big stories are dangerous animals. Graham has now been promoted to the Department of Housing.

The following morning the measures were passed by the cabinet at an incorporeal meeting. After the cabinet meeting,

Roy Barrett and I signed the Memorandum of Understanding on behalf of the government and the FAI. The two civil servants were highly visible in the camera shot. A short press event went ahead as planned. Niall Quinn and Gary Owens spoke briefly in response to Brendan Griffin and me. The public was entitled to no less, because football was close to the heart of hundreds of thousands of Irish families. The event was attended by both UEFA and the Bank of Ireland. Their presence was of high importance, as was their contribution to the outcome.

In truth, each of the four parties had a gun pointed at its head. The future of Irish football, not the fate of the FAI, was at stake. No one wanted the ignominy of having destroyed a sport that is responsible for healthy minds and bodies throughout Ireland.

The FAI story is far from over. While the Memorandum has been agreed, its contents will have to be passed with a 75 per cent positive vote at an FAI extraordinary general meeting in the near future.

As usual, old guard resistance to reform is attempting to regroup its forces. On 6 July, the president of the FAI, Gerry McAnaney, made a move without informing the chair, Roy Barrett. He contacted UEFA about the January deal that had been struck between the four parties. It appears that some directors, including McAnaney, will lose out under the Memorandum because it weighs the balance of power further in the direction of the independent board members. Under its terms, McAnaney will, unfortunately, be one of those who will have to stand down.

In these circumstances it is understandable that McAnaney wants to change the terms of the deal, but his present stance contrasts markedly with his statement in January that the deal 'will ensure the future of Irish football'.

That statement was a ringing endorsement of the deal: 'As President of the FAI, I wish to offer my sincere congratulations to our Independent Chairperson and his team on reaching an agreement with the Government and other important stakeholders.'

After McAnaney had made contact with UEFA, the senior minister and then junior minister in the newly formed Department of Media, Tourism, Arts, Culture, Sport and the Gaeltacht, Catherine Martin and Dara Calleary, wrote to the board of the FAI to notify them that the Memorandum of Understanding, signed in January, would not be changed.

There are always many bumps on the road to reform.

11

The Covid Cabinet: A Big Win for Leo

THE BLUESHIRTS BLOSSOMED under the cloud of the deadly coronavirus. Landed in political limbo by the 2020 general election, they seized the hour of the catastrophe to rise miraculously from the ashes. The five-month caretaker regime that followed was the weirdest government in Ireland's history.

The general election result had perverse consequences. The winners were without doubt Sinn Féin, who ended with the largest popular vote and 37 seats. The big losers were Fine Gael and Fianna Fáil. The Independent Alliance was, of course, wiped out. Yet the spoils of war fell into the hands of the losers of the election, along with a few Greens. The biggest winner was locked out in the cold.

After the results, Leo was quick out of the traps. He accepted defeat and declared that he would be leading Fine Gael into opposition. Mary Lou McDonald strode majestically around, like the uncrowned Queen of Ireland, for a few short weeks. When it became clear that neither Fianna Fáil nor Fine Gael would enter the same room as her, she was isolated, reduced to meaningless talks with the Greens, the hard left and various independent groupings. Ostracised or not, it had been a magnificent election for the leader of Sinn Féin.

The Shinners' success had horrified the chattering middle classes. Their beloved Greens initially wanted a national government, or a government of the left, or even a government of the right with a climate change agenda as a fig leaf. It rapidly became evident that Eamon Ryan, a veteran of the disastrous Fianna Fáil-Green coalition of 2007 to 2011, would jump into bed with anyone. Eventually he did. After the election, the first were last and the last were first.

Fine Gael lost 12 seats, more than any other party. Fianna Fáil lost 8 to end up with 37 seats plus the Ceann Comhairle, Seán Ó Fearghaíl, who was automatically returned. For the second general election in a row, a Fine Gael Taoiseach had called it at the wrong time. Fine Gael's tally of a miserable 35 deputies was a far cry from Enda's glory days of 2011, when they had won 76 seats, tantalisingly close to an overall majority in Dáil Éireann.

Perhaps the bad timing of the election was not Leo's fault. He was pushed. At Christmas 2019, those of us in government knew that we would be facing a vote of no confidence in Health Minister Simon Harris immediately after the recess. The motion would have passed, highlighting the weakness of our minority government. Leo, faced with a reality of no longer having the power to pick his own cabinet, would then have been forced to call an election. It seemed better for him to dissolve the Dáil and take his chances.

Fine Gael suffered a rout, the worst defeat in its history, with just 21 per cent of the popular vote. There seemed to be nowhere else but the opposition benches for the party. On the night of the count there were even calls from former Fine Gael Minister for Health James Reilly and others in the party for the Taoiseach to 'reflect long and hard' on his continued leadership.

And then the slow mating dance began. Little happened initially. Twelve days after the election, on 20 February, the new Dáil sat. No one was elected Taoiseach. The Dáil adjourned for three long weeks. Leo and the rest of us carried on in a caretaker cabinet. On 26 February, the Taoiseach and Micheál Martin met. Leo declined to open talks on government formation with Fianna Fáil. After the meeting, he reaffirmed that Fine Gael was continuing to prepare for opposition. The stand-off remained. Micheál, desperately wanting to be Taoiseach, was prepared to make positive purring noises in Leo's direction, as he faced the possible ignominy of being the first Fianna Fáil leader never to hold the top job.

Leo had no such obvious fears. He seemed in no hurry. Indeed, he gave the impression of moderate indifference to Micheál's problem. It was almost as though he was waiting, in the words of Charles Dickens' Wilkins Micawber in *David Copperfield*, in the hope that 'something will turn up'.

It did. Away from politics, while Ireland was moving towards forming a new government at a snail's pace, a monster was stalking the world. Covid-19, originally dismissed as an overseas disease, had taken root in Europe. By mid-February, it had started to cause death and panic in Italy. The contagion was moving closer to Ireland.

An immediate threat loomed. Ireland was due to play a Six Nations rugby game against Italy on 7 March at the Aviva Stadium. Thousands of Italian fans had booked to travel. Suddenly the government was faced with a dilemma. Should we insist that the match be cancelled?

Simon Harris, still Minister for Health, in whom the opposition had shown no confidence before the election, was still in the hot seat. It is normally harder for a caretaker minister to take big decisions, but Harris moved fast, so fast that the Irish Rugby Football Union (IRFU) didn't even know what was going to happen. On 25 February, Harris announced on RTÉ's *Six One News* that the government wanted the Italian match to be called off. Ireland's National Public Health Emergency

Team was of the 'very clear view' that the game should not go ahead. The IRFU were not happy campers. Harris met them the next morning and tried to soothe their understandably ruffled feathers.

As Minister for Sport, I was asked if I approved of the decision. I gave the same answer as we were all going to repeat in the next months: that I would take the advice of the experts in the health service, because we were determined to save lives and contain the virus.

Harris' decision, while tactlessly delivered, was on the money. It was the first of many from him. Northern Italy was a blackspot for the virus and it would have been reckless to welcome as visitors to Ireland thousands of Italian fans from the worst-affected region in Europe.

As the danger grew, further actions followed. A ban on such mass gatherings was rapidly to become the norm in Ireland. Caretaker government ministers found themselves in the middle of a pandemic that they had never anticipated. The normal protocol of inactivity from an interim regime did not apply in this crisis. Thousands of Irish citizens' lives were endangered. It was no time to stay aloof and refuse to intervene because the cabinet had no democratic mandate.

The decision to cancel the Italy game was a minor one compared with the next big event under government scrutiny. St Patrick's Day beckoned on 17 March. There would be approximately 500,000 people lining the streets of Dublin for the annual parade, with more out in force in cities and towns around the country. The day always marked the start of the tourist season. A blanket ban on the bank holiday festivities was far more serious than stopping a single game of rugby. It would be taken around the world as a message that Ireland was closed for business. In the weeks leading up to it, as Minister for Tourism, I met regularly with the St Patrick's Festival chief executive, Susan Kirby, and tourism stakeholders to consider the options.

As we pondered our decision, the background noises were worsening by the day. On 29 February, Ireland's first case of coronavirus, a teenager who had travelled back to Ireland from Italy, was confirmed. On 1 March, his school closed down. On 2 March, the mighty multinational Google told its headquarters staff in Dublin to work from home. On 3 March, a second coronavirus case was reported in the east of Ireland. By 7 March, the count of confirmed cases had risen to nineteen. The *Sunday Business Post* carried an alarmist story that the number of coronavirus cases in Ireland could reach 1.9 million; the head of the Health and Safety Executive, Paul Reid, responded ominously by admitting that he could not dispute that figure.

We had no choice. St Patrick's Day festivals all round Ireland were cancelled. The government strongly advised against non-essential travel to parts of Spain and Italy. On 10 March, the Irish stock market dropped by 6.4 per cent, bringing its losses over eleven days to €22.7 billion. Ryanair and Aer Lingus suspended all flights to and from Italy following a lockdown by the Italian government.

On 11 March, the inevitable tragedy happened. Ireland suffered its first death from coronavirus. An elderly woman with an underlying condition died in Naas General Hospital, County Kildare. On the same day the World Health Organization pronounced Covid-19 to be a pandemic. Both were sobering moments.

The health crisis was immediately dogged by an economic emergency. Ireland was looking over two cliffs, not one. And we had a government without a mandate. Three full cabinet ministers with significant responsibilities in the worst-hit sectors were unelected, but still in office. Regina Doherty in Social Protection was in the middle of the storm now breaking out. Katherine Zappone had headaches in the childcare space. Mine was possibly the most blighted portfolio: tourism was collapsing; sport was closing for probably many months; aviation was down by over 99 per cent, and public transport was essential, but hugely expensive to operate, under the growing restrictions.

A complete change of mindset was necessary from the cabinet. The determination of Fine Gael to go into opposition was first shelved and then seamlessly abandoned. Cabinet ministers who had lost their seats (and were anticipating a quiet life!) found themselves in the thick of combating the ravages of a killer disease and helping to save the economy.

The talks to form a government took a back seat. The public mind was more fixed on survival than on political gamesmanship. Micheál Martin's ambitions to be Taoiseach were not at the forefront of citizens' thoughts. The Fianna Fáil Taoiseach-in-waiting was compelled to join in the effort for national survival, but essentially as a spectator. The Greens went hot and cold on government formation.

Paschal Donohoe must have been broken-hearted. He had spent years reducing the deficit, looking after the Rainy Day Fund and resisting his cabinet colleagues' demands for latitude and generosity. Nobody had consistently pleaded that the cupboard was empty better than Paschal. Now, suddenly, it really was. On 9 March, the government agreed an aid package of €3 billion to soften the economic pain and the impact of the virus on public health.

Paschal, normally as chirpy as a sparrow in the spring, occasionally showed his disappointment. At one meeting with my department when we were seeking a rescue package for the tourism sector, while turning us down he showed an uncharacteristic frustration. Although he put his brightest spin on the disaster that had struck the economy, he could not resist claiming that we would come through because the state of the national finances had improved so much in recent years that the international lending banks had regained their confidence 'in Ireland, in the economy and in me'. Modesty was not Paschal's strongest suit that day. He sounded unappreciated. He was right. Yet his bête noire — borrowing — was back in spades. His sole consolation was that interest rates seemed low and lenders would be queuing up to accommodate us.

The political quicksands were moving fast. The caretaker cabinet was thinking longer-term.

Leo was the first to spot a political gap. While all the St Patrick's Day celebrations were cancelled at home, the Taoiseach was still determined to fulfil his annual visit to Washington. Cynics dismissed it as another photo op, but he has always been an unrelenting advocate of nurturing good relations with the US, Trump or no Trump. Besides, it made him look not just like a national leader in a time of crisis, but like a statesman, being greeted by the most powerful man in the world.

Not only did Leo keep his links with the US, he managed a little bi-location. After curtailing his trip by a couple of days, he decided to broadcast to the Irish nation from faraway Washington on the morning of 12 March. A bold move for a Taoiseach on the way out, but three years earlier Enda too had used the St Patrick's Day gig in the White House as a lap of honour.

An even bigger surprise happened when Leo decided to appear on the steps of Blair House, the US president's guest quarters adjacent to the White House, to announce new measures to the Irish people. Standing beside the Irish flag, he began: 'I need to speak to you about coronavirus and Covid-19.' The 'You' was the Irish people, not the assembled media corps standing in front of him. At the end of the speech he took no questions. This was epic Leo. He was the statesman abroad, addressing his flock back home. This was no run-of-the-mill media scrap.

Someone had persuaded RTÉ to broadcast the Taoiseach's speech to the Irish people live from Washington. It was a rallying cry, ending with a rhetorical flourish: 'Ireland is a great nation. And we are a great people. We have experienced hardship and struggle before. We have overcome many trials in the past with our determination and our spirit. We will prevail.'

Back in Dublin, Simon Coveney, Simon Harris, Heather Humphreys and the Chief Medical Officer, Dr Tony Holohan, waited dutifully for the Taoiseach's speech to end before playing second fiddle and holding their own press conference in Government Buildings. They put flesh on the bones, so dramatically revealed by the Taoiseach just a few minutes earlier. The two events were superbly synchronised. A cabinet meeting followed soon afterwards to endorse the new measures Leo had announced in Washington, but which Dr Tony Holohan had recommended the night before.

It was a military-style operation. The coronavirus message was being delivered with precision and authority by Fine Gael and particularly by Leo Varadkar. He had suddenly retaken centre stage, a leader of a nation, no longer a defeated Taoiseach. Forgotten was his ambition to be the leader of the opposition.

What had happened?

Fine Gael had grabbed the high ground. The man who had lost the election, the party that had received a bloody nose at the polls, was emphatically back in charge. Varadkar, Coveney, Harris and Humphreys stood shoulder to shoulder with the increasingly popular media star, Dr Tony Holohan.

Observers pointed out that this too was the week that John Concannon, the Taoiseach's former communications guru, had quietly returned to the Fine Gael fold. Concannon, a master spin doctor, had led the Special Communications Unit in the early days of Leo's leadership, but it had been disbanded in 2018 under a cloud, after the opposition parties in the Dáil successfully passed a motion demanding its closure.

Two years earlier, Concannon had been Leo's disciple, promoting the Varadkar cult. His fingerprints were now evident all over the sudden energy behind the coronavirus message: Leo was the man to lead us out of the crisis; Fine Gael was the party to steady the ship. The killer virus was suddenly a platform for a political resurrection. The nation was in good, safe hands. Leo was the Defender of the Faith.

On 16 March, a key cabinet subcommittee on Covid-19 met. Inside the imposing Sycamore Room in Government Buildings, the subcommittee was like a council of war. Top civil servants including Robert Watt, and Leo's chief of staff, Brian Murphy, joined the Taoiseach, Simon Coveney, Paschal Donohoe, Heather Humphreys, Simon Harris and other key ministers in absorbing the grim messages from Chief Medical Officer Dr Tony Holohan and HSE chief executive officer Paul Reid.

Item number one on the agenda: Dr Tony Holohan, confirming that we were on a war footing, painted an alarming picture of the impending perils from Covid-19 in the weeks to come.

Other items included imminent emergency legislation on mass gatherings and dire warnings of the economic developments on the way.

Item number four on the agenda: all communications now needed to be centrally approved, taking a step into a new, far more politically controlled world. I sensed Concannon's fingerprints.

It was a seminal moment. I shuddered as a new, rigid communications regime was spelled out. A daily meeting was to be held, chaired by the font of all government messages, the Government Information Services (GIS). The language in the memo was positively Sovietesque: 9.30 a.m. meetings were ordered for every morning; tighter messaging was needed across all departments, each with a dedicated representative; attendance was mandatory; all information was to flow to the GIS, located in the Department of the Taoiseach; updates were to be provided to the GIS by 3 p.m. every day; failure to do so would prompt urgent escalation. All roads led to the secretariat. The flow of information was being 'centralised', a familiar phrase.

The Department of Finance paper on the economic and budgetary implications of Covid-19, presented to the same meeting, spelled out the prospect of a gloomy budget deficit. The pre-Covid-19 prediction of a small surplus was now Paschal's distant pipedream. Measures of over €3 billion, announced only the week before, would not be nearly enough. The Department of Finance, the offspring of Scrooge, was being forced to open up. Additional supports were on the way. Ominously, the document stated the obvious, that 'the resources available to the state are not unlimited'.

A day later, on St Patrick's Day, the Taoiseach surprised the nation (and many of his cabinet colleagues) by taking to the airwaves once again. This time, he was in the seat of power in Government Buildings, flanked by the Irish and European Union flags.

This time, he warned of the surge to come.

This time, he spoke of his own family. He spoke of his partner, his two sisters and their husbands, all healthcare workers, and how proud he was of all of them. He paid tribute to the health workers. He mentioned the army cadets, librarians and civil servants, all united in the national effort. The teachers, the hauliers, even the journalists and those who had lost their jobs were not forgotten. It was a tour de force, full of soundbites. He even closely paraphrased Winston Churchill when he said that 'Never will so many ask so much of so few'.

This time, the Taoiseach delayed RTÉ's *Nine O'Clock News* for his broadcast. He gained the largest RTÉ television audience of the year. The public's response was almost universally positive. The nation loved it. He was reassuring, compassionate and human. He, and he alone, was emphatically in charge of the fight against Covid-19. He was the personification of the citizens' hopes and fears on St Patrick's Day. It was, in another phrase from Churchill, Leo's 'finest hour'.

And he knew it. So did his spinners. No one else was in sight that day. No Simon Coveney, no Simon Harris, no Paschal Donohoe. Micheál Martin, Ireland's probable Taoiseach-in-waiting, had been sidelined.

Leo was on a roll. On 27 March, he addressed the nation yet again. This time he invoked the Terminator as he announced the lockdown measures. 'There is no fate, but what we make for ourselves,' he declared, quoting word for word a line from *Terminator 2: Judgment Day*.

The formula of Leo addressing the nation was working. Next, he took advantage of the Good Friday break on 10 April to stand outside Government Buildings and quote Seamus Heaney at the beginning and end of another of his orations. He invoked the Good Friday Agreement to draw an analogy between the Northern Ireland troubles and Covid-19, quoting Ireland's most recent Nobel laureate: 'If we winter this one out, we can summer anywhere.' Strangely, poetic as it sounds, it was taken, not from a poem, but from an interview Heaney had given in 1972 in reference to the Northern crisis.

Two days later, on 12 April, Leo delivered an appropriate Easter Sunday sermon, this time from his humble Twitter account: 'Whether we have faith or not, people should remember the Easter message of suffering and sacrifice followed by rebirth and renewal and, above all, a message of hope as winter turns to spring.' Leo was promising an end to suffering.

He stopped short of quoting from the Bible, but the message was clearly delivered with a Christian spin. Suffering was worthwhile.

On 15 May, Leo began to announce the turn of the tide. From Government Buildings, he confirmed that Phase 1 of the 'Roadmap for Reopening Society and Business' was going ahead. Leo, and no one else, was beginning to reopen Ireland.

On 5 June, he was back again. There he was, in Government Buildings, announcing that Ireland was ready to launch Phase 2 of the Roadmap. This time he quoted Samwise Gamgee in the final film of Tolkien's *The Lord of the Rings*. 'In the end, it's only a passing thing, this shadow, even darkness must pass. A new day will come, and when the sun shines, it will shine out the clearer.'

Earlier in the same speech, he had called in no less an ally than Cicero, the great Roman statesman whose powers of oratory were unparalleled: 'the safety of the people shall be our highest law'.

The quotations were all a bit over the top, but he carried it off. By this stage, the Irish people were eating out of the palm of his hand. He relaxed the restrictions way beyond everyone's expectations. As RTÉ's Paul Cunningham concluded afterwards: 'However, Leo Varadkar, the man who closed down the Irish economy due to Covid-19, effectively announced its reopening today.'

Leo could not have wished for a better endorsement. He had stood behind the Irish people, their guardian in the dark days and nights. And now he was leading them back into the sunlight.

In the background, while people were dying from coronavirus, a bitter political battle was being fought. Coalition talks were being conducted, sometimes deliberately, in slow motion. The battle to save lives and the battle to win power became inextricably intertwined. At the same time, the interim government was in the hands of a small number of Fine Gael ministers, advised by senior civil servants, mostly from the health service. Leo was miles ahead in both contests. And he was rationing the limelight, keeping most of it to himself.

The desperate pickle in which Leo had landed post-election a few weeks earlier was forgotten, never exposed or properly analysed. Apart from having led the Blueshirts to the worst result in the party's history, his own personal vote in the Dublin West constituency had tanked. He had been trounced into second place with 8,478 votes against 12,456 for Sinn Féin's Paul Donnelly. It was the first time ever that an outgoing Taoiseach had failed to top the poll. Worse still, it took him five counts to be elected. His early response to the humiliation was to claim the opposition benches. His party had trailed in third, so there was no hope of him staying on as Taoiseach. More worrying still was the Fine Gael rule that the party leader must face re-election after defeat in a general election, unless the party was on the way back into power.

Leo Varadkar would not have been human if he was not looking over his shoulder during those immediate, woeful post-mortems. Tánaiste Simon Coveney, though unflinchingly loyal after his defeat at Leo's hands in the 2017 contest, was waiting in the wings. Coveney had been the 2019 cabinet superstar because of his mature performance on Brexit. Furthermore, he had proved in the leadership contest that he was more popular than his leader among the Fine Gael grassroots. Leo had sewn up the parliamentary party before the contest, but Coveney had held the hearts of the ordinary members.

After the general election debacle, expressions of loyalty to Leo started flowing in fast. Paschal Donohoe and Richard Bruton were joined by Simon Coveney himself in public expressions of support, usually a danger signal.

And then Covid-19 rode to the Taoiseach's rescue. He grabbed the ball and ran with it.

At some unknown point, the Taoiseach changed his mind about heading into opposition. It was probably around the end of February, just after he had met Micheál Martin and reaffirmed his intention to take the opposition road. After that, he began to shift position: he would stay in power if possible. As the soundly defeated loser — in third place — he knew he could not be re-elected Taoiseach. It is far more likely that he silently set his eyes on the Tánaiste's job, and acted accordingly.

Micheál Martin languished in a weaker position than Varadkar. Martin was in the last chance saloon. Even more desperately, he needed to be Taoiseach, or he was toast. Both men, politically weakened by the election, had something they could offer each other: a spell as Taoiseach. Micheál had marginally more seats (38 versus 35 for Fine Gael), but Leo was in situ, fiercely fighting the coronavirus.

On 30 March, Red C, one of the most reputable of Ireland's opinion pollsters, published its first post-election poll on the political parties' standing. It was sensational. Since the February general election Fine Gael had shot up by 13% to a lofty 34%. Sinn Féin had gained another 3% to 28% and Fianna Fáil had lost 4% to a miserable 18%. The Greens had fallen 2% to 5%. Fine Gael was winning nearly twice as many votes as Fianna Fáil.

Whatever Leo was doing, it had restored him to prime position in the people's affections. It had relegated Micheál Martin to a humiliating level. Was Leo now going to sit back and give a party which had the support of less than one in five people a free pass? He must have ruminated on the success of his great strategy, his dramatic, live appearances on RTÉ from Washington DC and from Government Buildings. All that palaver with the tricolour, the stars and stripes and the European flag had worked. Was he going to hand over the top job to a wounded spectator? He had now positioned himself well for a general election, if one was forced, or at the very least as Tánaiste and Taoiseach-in-waiting.

But the success was not all down to Leo and his spinner, John Concannon. While he was busy making himself impregnable within the party, he had allowed some trusted colleagues a slice of airtime too. Practically every day, GIS would organise a press conference in Government Buildings where one of the favoured Fine Gael ministers was wheeled out to announce available bits of good news, emphasising the great work the caretaker government was doing for Ireland at a time of crisis. Finian and I were rarely, if ever, invited to those gigs. Independent Katherine Zappone managed to squeeze in a few guest appearances, but most prominent on these occasions were Simon Harris, Paschal Donohoe and of course, as the most senior female Fine Gael minister, Heather Humphreys.

Nations inevitably rally to sitting governments in times of emergency. Even to sitting caretakers. This emergency was being milked for all it was worth.

So Leo set about forming a virtual Fine Gael government. As a party that had garnered only 21 per cent of the vote, it hardly had a democratic mandate to introduce dramatic changes. Yet the caretakers took over, under the cover of the emergency. Although there is a long-established protocol that outgoing governments must refrain from policy changes or controversial appointments during the interregnum, Leo, Paschal and Simon Harris embarked upon a programme of economic measures unprecedented in Irish history.

The opposition, including Fianna Fáil, the Greens, Sinn Féin and Labour, were briefed on key decisions, necessary because of the emergency. No party had yet won a new democratic mandate, so a consensus was required for major expenditure.

Huge commitments were made to protect citizens' health, businesses and employment, to save both lives and the economy. The cost of preserving employment, of medical equipment, of supplementing incomes, of business supports and of subsidising transport all rocketed. Billions were spent on the Temporary Wage Subsidy Scheme and the Pandemic Unemployment Payments to keep jobs and provide for those who had lost theirs.

While the Dáil continued to meet, it had no sense of normality. It went through the motions, no more. Micheál Martin pulled his punches because he did not want to upset Leo. Ditto Eamon Ryan. Mary Lou led the opposition, but the severe social distancing restrictions on numbers in the chamber made for toothless tussles.

I was among the defeated deputies, but still caretaker ministers, who were rightly called into the chamber to answer questions about our portfolios. The sessions were the tamest ever seen in Leinster House. Fianna Fáil usually availed of the entire time allotted for their questions to make statements, frequently designed for local constituency consumption. They often, purposely, left no time for ministers to answer. The sessions were limited to two hours among all the parties because of the health restrictions. On each occasion in which I was called in, I spent the best part of two full days preparing, in anticipation of the normal mauling. It was all unnecessary. I had never felt less accountable. Democracy took a rest for four months.

The Dáil was rendered dysfunctional not only because of the pandemic, but also because normal political combat was paralysed by the negotiations going on offstage. More worrying was evidence that shortcuts were being taken in the decision-making process. Apart from the centralisation of communications to control the Covid-19 message, other bad habits were undermining procedures.

Cabinet meetings changed utterly. Physical distancing required two or three rooms to be used, with video-link connections between them. The Taoiseach and Tánaiste often sat in separate rooms to prevent both of them catching the virus at the same time. Since I was cocooning, I attended many of the cabinet sessions by video link from home, at a distinct disadvantage, particularly because the beautiful oak-panelled rooms in Government Buildings have brutal acoustics.

Others who sometimes took the video-link option from home included Michael Ring, Michael Creed, Joe McHugh and Mary Mitchell O'Connor. Away from the tough talking about Covid-19, in moments of light relief, pre-cabinet, we exchanged banter about the visible interior of each other's houses, which we could spot on their screens. I suspected that many of them had specially altered their rooms for the prying eyes of their colleagues and for the cameras. Michael Ring sat in front of a magnificent framed extract from the *Mayo News* headed 'Ring Wins the West', recording the day he won the Mayo by-election in 1994; Joe McHugh surprisingly revealed his strong Democratic Party feelings with a poster of Barack Obama and Joe Biden in the background, marking his presence at the Democratic Convention in Denver in 2008; Katherine Zappone settled for a more tranquil message with a beautiful large watercolour of mountains and the sea. Charlie Flanagan displayed a cartoon of his late father, Oliver J., to prove his Blueshirt credentials — in case anyone in the room doubted them. Mary Mitchell O'Connor revealed a library of beautifully bound books, the sort of décor you would expect from a teacher from the Dún Laoghaire constituency. In my own small study at home, I cleared the decks behind me to mask my chaotic filing system.

But the cabinet under the coronavirus, seen through a screen, was a different place from the cabinet in the cabinet room. Bad connections, three separate rooms, video links, less body language and the two-hour time limit all contributed to a far less potent atmosphere.

The process was different too. The balance of power had changed. The political insiders were few, namely the Taoiseach, Finance Minister Paschal Donohoe and Minister for Health Simon Harris. Because this triumvirate brought most of the crisis memos to cabinet, they were the harbingers of the bulk of the information. The two-hour restriction — because of the dangers of Covid-19 — ensured an indecently hasty passage of measures that had often been introduced without giving ministers time to consider them. Routine cabinet measures tended to go through on the nod as they made room for the deadly Covid-19 business. It was government by guillotine.

At cabinet meetings, it became apparent that decisions were being made elsewhere. Everyone respected the supremacy in health matters of the top public servants in that field, but several ministers deeply resented the lack of consultation with themselves. The nation's hero, the man who starred on the television screens every night, Chief Medical Officer Dr Tony Holohan, was not the same popular figure with cabinet members as he was with the people. Some of my colleagues saw him as a usurper who had taken power away from them and was becoming a national icon, a reassuring father figure.

As if to compensate, Leo arranged ministerial meetings with Holohan so that those ministers outside the inner circle of three could question the man some perceived as the new czar about decisions with which they disagreed. A discontented group of ministers, including Michael Creed and Michael Ring, who favoured speedier reopening of the economy, got a chance to discover whether Holohan was god or guru.

In reality it was Leo's way of letting mere mortals in the cabinet feel they had a part to play. It was notable that few of the inner circle were present, because obviously they had already been well briefed. This was only to bring the 'children' at the table up to speed.

After appearing at a relatively calm, but solemn, cabinet subcommittee with HSE chief executive Paul Reid on 3 April, Holohan turned up to brief us again at a strictly private meeting on 30 April. By this time hopes were high that the contagion might have peaked.

The ministers were bullish but respectful, many querying the value of face masks. Charlie Flanagan politely asked if children were vectors? Michael Creed upped the tempo when he requested that Holohan give the over-seventies a break from their isolation in their homes. Suddenly Michael Ring let fly, bemoaning not only the treatment of the over-seventies, but at one point using the emotive words 'police state'. He demanded that the people be given hope or 'they'll be on the streets'.

Holohan was as calm as ever. He retorted that masks were not always used properly and they were not 'magic', despite what people might think. He said it was still unclear whether children were vectors, but he thought they *could* carry the virus. He warned that there was no certainty of a vaccine in the near future or guarantee of immunity. The Chief Medical Officer said that he was 'sensitive' to the over-seventies and would think about their position 'early'.

After Holohan had spoken, the secretary of the cabinet, Martin Fraser, entered the fray. He flashed a red light to some of the politicians surrounding him. Reinforcing Dr Holohan's message, he went even further. Fraser warned impatient ministers, gung-ho for an early reopening programme, that the disease could easily restart. There was 'no treatment, no vaccine'. It was not over, he insisted, and there was still potential for disaster. 'It could go out of control,' he asserted. Fraser went on to spell out the next day's cabinet timetable, insisting that it 'will start with the safe stuff'.

The mandarin was setting the agenda.

Ring and Creed were not accustomed to being addressed in this way by a mandarin, albeit the most powerful in the land. Fraser's words were perceived to be his absent master's voice. They were beginning to realise where the power really lay in this emergency. It was certainly not being exercised by the two Michaels.

On 27 May, Holohan turned up to give ministers another, strictly behind closed doors, confidential briefing. This time the trend in the number of infections had, thankfully, been reversed. Once again, neither the Taoiseach, Paschal Donohoe nor Simon Harris were there with the rest of us. Why would they be? They were in the loop. The *éminence grise* Fraser was present again, joined, as observers, by Brian Murphy, the Taoiseach's chief of staff, and Clare Mungovan, one of the Taoiseach's advisers.

The issues were different. Holohan set a better tone by saying that the infection numbers were lower across the board. This time, the questions concentrated on the relative merits of social distancing at one or two metres. Holohan was unyielding. He convincingly asserted that the great majority of 'droplets' did not travel more than two metres while 60 per cent travelled for one metre. Medically, he insisted, there was a significant gulf between one metre and two. It would have been wrong of him, he said, to advise differently, other countries notwithstanding. Paul Kehoe, a consistent advocate for caution, weighed in four-square behind Holohan.

Finian McGrath wanted to compromise at 1.5 metres, but Holohan wouldn't bite. Heather Humphreys dwelled on mental health, restaurants and hairdressers. Charlie Flanagan echoed Michael Ring's dismissive response to the move from two kilometres to five for the maximum distance people could walk from their homes. 'I'm rural,' he declared triumphantly. 'That's urbancentric. Why aren't doctors looking at quarantine from the constitutional and security point of view?' The dig was not lost on Dr Holohan. Eoghan Murphy joined the hawks seeking shorter social distancing.

Nor did the good doctor yield to demands that we stop requiring people to quarantine on arrival in Ireland.

On that day, Ring was vintage Ring. His home town, Westport, depended on tourism. He took a swipe at me about the Tourism Recovery Task Force, asking why big business group IBEC and small business organisations were not represented on it. Nor did he have much sympathy for the dire state of the Irish Rugby Football Union, for whom I had made a plea. Ring asserted that he was a GAA man and there should be 'no special deal for rugby'. And then in typical, but magnificent, Ring style, he thundered to Holohan that '15,000 people elected me in Mayo'. He might as well have been on the back of a lorry in the West instead of the elegant surroundings of the Department of the Taoiseach.

Ring was still in full flight when the chairman, the ever-patient Simon Coveney, tried to hurry him up. Simon should have known better. Ring was having none of it. Referring to the ignominy of being called last to speak, he raised his voice: 'We're always last from rural Ireland. Same at cabinet meetings.' He was allowed to finish. Everyone was very fond of Michael, although he could drive the urban Blueshirts mad when he repeated his rural Ireland single transferable victim speech *ad nauseam*.

Despite the views of cabinet ministers, the opinions of the public servants, Holohan and Fraser, prevailed. The exercise was successful. Those outside the loop, a dozen members of a cabinet of fifteen, were given a chance to let off steam and pontificate in front of Holohan.

It was a worrying time for lovers of process. Cabinet ministers may have been bellyaching at the cavalier attitude to the conduct of business, but the opinion polls were giving Fine Gael continued comfort. Red C took two more opinion polls, at the beginning and at the end of May. Both showed Fine Gael on 35%, with Fianna Fáil at 14% in one poll and at 15% in the other. An election could leave Fianna Fáil with fewer than twenty seats. Sinn Féin was holding firm on 27%.

Leo was beginning to look like the nation's messiah. In one conversation with him, he told me that several of his people wanted him to dissolve the Dáil, but he felt that would be wrong. The people could punish Fine Gael for opportunism. He was obviously content to become Tánaiste, breathing down poor Micheál Martin's neck, and with an eventual sharing of the spoils. The alternative was a general election, not unattractive on the current poll results. Micheál was snookered. If he had moved against the caretaker regime, he risked being punished by a nervous public in no mood for destabilising a government coping with a pandemic.

Government by guillotine continued unchecked. It was popular with the people, but the opinion polls were not reflected at cabinet meetings. As the shape of the next government became more apparent, those less likely to survive the inevitable purge of Fine Gael ministers in a Fine Gael-Fianna Fáil-Green coalition began to bare their teeth. Grumblings about a politburo of three could be heard. Elder statesmen of Fine Gael, calculating that theirs would be among the seven Fine Gael cabinet seats lost in a new government, already felt the axe falling. Questions were even being asked about whether Tánaiste Simon Coveney was in the small loop of key politicians and top civil servants?

The discontent surfaced at several cabinet meetings. There were many mutterings about why complex proposals for cabinet were arriving at the last moment. On 21 April, a highly significant nine-page memo, a controversial and important update on Covid-19, arrived at 11.15 a.m. for a meeting that had begun at 11.00 a.m. No cabinet member, bar those few already privy to it, had been given a chance to examine the memo in advance. It was only one part of a full cabinet agenda, needing to be completed within two hours because of Covid-19 health rules.

An intervention from Michael Creed early on signalled the simmering discontent. Noting that he was 'not on the cabinet subcommittee' — so was not in the loop — Creed suggested that the cabinet should meet more often, adding that, in his view, 'it is almost treachery to question public health advice'. The gloves were coming off. Creed was obviously — and realistically — giving up hope of being in the next cabinet. The thought of yielding his Agriculture portfolio to a Green must have made the man from the Cork Fine Gael farming family bristle.

Ten days later, on 1 May, the 'Roadmap for Reopening Society and Business' was launched. It was an effort to appease the cabinet critics, as well as an impatient population. Creed again protested about how we needed more time, that the over-seventies were still being badly treated and that we shouldn't have to sign off on the plan within such a short window of two hours.

On the following day, a Saturday, the cabinet sat again. This time we were presented with a package of economic measures costing billions. Paschal's presentation was, as usual, superb but the proposal flew through with little scrutiny.

On 8 May, when the Minister for Education, Joe McHugh, presented his proposal to cancel the Leaving Certificate, our contributions were limited to two minutes per minister. It was a controversial measure, but apparently needed to be rushed. Creed was again annoyed. 'Why in the name of God can't we hold an exam?' he asked. 'Everything else will be open.' Charlie Flanagan too was uneasy but insisted 'everyone must back Joe'.

The Attorney General, Séamus Woulfe, was confident he could see off any legal challenge to the move.

Coveney, ever the conciliator, sympathised with Joe's difficult decision. He shared Creed's frustrations, but he concluded: 'We have to get over them.'

Most cabinet ministers who spoke had reservations. The Taoiseach supported Joe McHugh. The proposal was passed and the exams were cancelled.

There may have been only a few minutes to make the big government decisions, but at the next cabinet meeting on 15 May, there was time for an unusual outburst. Katherine Zappone had a conniption.

The meeting started cheerfully enough at 11 a.m. Leo warned that time was, as ever, limited because 'I have to take a call from Boris at 1.15'.

Finian McGrath, a football fan missing the buzz, quipped that he should 'ask him about the Premiership!'

Katherine Zappone did not join in the frivolity, but instantly asked for the floor. She got it. The Minister for Children launched a no-holds-barred attack on anonymous cabinet colleagues. Her anger arose over an article by journalist Philip Ryan in that morning's *Irish Independent*. Katherine had annoyed cabinet colleagues a few weeks earlier with a hasty childcare scheme for front-line workers. Fine Gael ministers had resisted it as too hurried and not properly thought through. Still, she had ploughed ahead. She was later forced to cancel the venture in a humiliating climbdown.

Philip Ryan collected a few prize quotes from cabinet colleagues about Katherine and her political volte-face. I was not among them, so must presume that they were nearly all Blueshirts.

One contemptuously said that Katherine had 'been causing unbelievable grief and still didn't manage to get it over the line'. Another was damning: 'she has been asked to do just one thing and it ends up a mess'. Yet another insisted that 'Leo should have sacked her ages ago, but he hates confrontation'.

Katherine lashed out angrily at her colleagues. Their remarks were 'disrespectful, lacking in courage and demeaning of cabinet'. She was badly stung by the article and the words of some of those sitting beside her. And then, in a defiant gesture to us all, she declared that she was staying in the room afterwards so that those who had such criticisms of her could come and tell her to her face what they were whispering in the ears of journalists. And for those on video link, she read out her telephone number.

Katherine had earned the nickname 'Nana Mouskouri' in Leinster House because of her political and physical likeness to the famous Greek singer and politician. Both entered politics late in life; both showed equal passion for children's issues. Mouskouri had been a spokesperson for the children's charity UNICEF before she became a Member of the European Parliament in 1994. At an earlier cabinet meeting Katherine, Minister for Children, had read out a long poem she had written to honour the memory of the dead Tuam babies. Mouskouri had deep pacifist convictions. On that day in the cabinet Katherine showed no signs of pacifism. She was gagging for a fight.

I am no saint in any of these matters, but I was not guilty in this instance. Because I was not among those who spoke to Philip Ryan, I never accepted Katherine's offer. I do not believe anyone else did either.

Finian and I were accustomed to Blueshirts briefing against us. I had been targeted on and off for four years. Perhaps this was Katherine's first time, for she had been more of a protected creature in the media. The criticisms I received were often perfectly legitimate, sometimes a bit extreme, but the skin thickens after a short while. Cabinet colleagues frequently slander one another and then enjoy a drink together afterwards.

Leo muttered about the need for us all to stick together and to avoid 'that kind of shite in the papers'.

The rest of that meeting featured a discussion on Covid-19 restrictions for people coming into the country. Charlie Flanagan was particularly animated, insisting that we were not a 'police state' and rubbished the idea of 'self-isolation' in a centre for those without suitable locations to stay. 'Who,' asked the Minister for Justice, 'will guard that centre? It will make Direct Provision look like a tea party.'

In robust mood, maybe encouraged by Katherine's earlier outburst, Charlie declared that golfers needed the distance they were allowed to travel to a course to be extended. Otherwise Gardaí would be 'arresting former colleagues' — presumably breaking the limits by travelling to their distant golf clubs.

Later cabinet meetings of Leo's regime were dominated by discussions about the more pleasant matters of when restrictions would be lifted. Memos remained painfully late, especially for key decisions, such as on the public-private hospital deal. Time for discussion was nearly always still confined to two hours. On one occasion there was a long debate on leaks from cabinet. It was unreal, because most ministers knew who was leaking which pieces of information. No one was ever directly accused of leaking, but you only had to identify who benefited from the leak to name the culprit. Or, in an expression often used by Leo's hero, Cicero, 'Cui bono?'

The trouble was, as the Taoiseach so rightly pointed out, cabinet members were now reluctant to voice their views. Sometimes, RTÉ might as well have had a microphone in the room. Perhaps that is why so many of the preliminary discourses were taken away from prying cabinet eyes and ears? Perhaps that is why so many cabinet memos arrived too late for meaningful discussions? Perhaps the matters under discussion were too serious to be left to politicians? And maybe that is why so many incorporeal meetings were suddenly being held on important items?

Between 1 April, as the coronavirus crisis began to reach a peak, and 19 June, when it was declining, there were eighteen cabinet meetings, of which seven were incorporeals. Some of these dealt with run-of-the-mill technicalities, but others included important decisions, such as the approval of a special Covid-19 allocation to the Arts of €25 million and providing indemnities for teachers undertaking the new Leaving Certificate assessment process.

On 9 June at 7.38 p.m. I received a typical text from my private secretary, Chris Smith:

Shane,

Just got word from Cabinet Secretariat that there is an Incorporeal Govt meeting this evening at 8.45pm. Ministers are asked to approve a funding model for phased reopening of childcare services for an 8 week period wef [with effect from] 29/06/2020. Memo from D/Children. I sent the email with the memo.

Chris

This measure didn't take effect for nearly three weeks. What was the rush? Why was it not held over until the next cabinet meeting three days later? Was it too contentious after Katherine Zappone's outburst, so would be best dealt with without any discussion?

I was telephoned for approval of the measure by a civil servant from the Taoiseach's office at 8.50 p.m. I approved it without advice and without any ministerial exchanges or presentation. I read through the five-page memorandum in ten minutes. It was all the time I was given. The measure was to cost the state €75 million. The civil servant did a ring-around, made fifteen identical calls and received fifteen similar responses. The rubber stamp was in full swing.

That was typical of government by guillotine. The cabinet handbook was now being regularly bypassed. Given that there was a health emergency, there could sometimes be legitimate reasons for such a helter-skelter, but it seems to have been used as a means for shortcutting cabinet discussion and controversy. Other well-established safeguards and scrutinies at civil service level were also being circumvented.

Government by guillotine was certainly working for Leo and for Fine Gael. On 16 June, yet another opinion poll was published, this time by the *Irish Times*. Leo Varadkar's ratings were through the roof. His approval had soared by 45 points to 75%, nearly as high as Bertie Ahern at his peak. Satisfaction with the government stood at 72%. Fine Gael at 37% had gone up 16% since the general election, Sinn Féin were unchanged at 25% and Fianna Fáil down 9% at an embarrassing 14%.

The poll appeared one day after Fine Gael, Fianna Fáil and the Greens had signed the deal to go into government. All three parliamentary parties had approved it. Fine Gael had already decided to hold a Friday cabinet meeting to signal a further relief of the Covid-19 restrictions. There was no way Leo was leaving any good news in the can for Micheál to deliver.

On that Friday evening, 19 June, Minister of State Brendan Griffin and I were due to make a major announcement that the cabinet had given the go-ahead for €70 million funding for Irish sport. We had booked the Press Centre in Government Buildings and were expecting to be joined by the Taoiseach. After the cabinet meeting that afternoon, I bumped into Leo in the corridor and mentioned that we were looking forward to him joining us for the €70 million good news gig. He looked non-plussed and muttered that Paschal was doing it.

A few minutes later I glanced down at the doors of Government Buildings. A single lectern had been placed in a familiar place. The Irish and European flags were positioned on either side of it. The media were assembling. There was a red carpet. There was room for only one person between the flags.

RTÉ was preparing to cover the Taoiseach, whenever he was ready, to broadcast to the nation, solo, about how he had released the Irish people from the bondage of Covid-19.

While giving the nation hope that society could re-emerge from these dark times, he also managed to work into his speech one of his more obscure quotes. Leo assured the people the 'limit does not exist', thus fulfilling a bet waged weeks earlier by *Lord of the Rings* actor Sean Astin that Leo would not be able to quote from teen comedy film *Mean Girls*. While some believed his pop-culture references were a sign of immaturity in the middle of a global pandemic, others argued that he was making his speech relevant and was speaking to those who needed to hear him. Whatever his motivation, his star has continued to rise. Like all his other addresses to the nation, this one worked a dream.

There were still a few days to go before the government formation deal was sealed. Our outgoing coalition had unfinished business. Two urgent matters needed to be resolved.

As luck would have it, the two most urgent matters fell to my department. First, international travel restrictions were boiling over into a major controversy, while, secondly, Bus Éireann was facing liquidation within a few days.

Licensed commercial operators, including Bus Éireann, needed a state subsidy. Otherwise, many commercial outfits operating important routes under social distancing rules would collapse. These were routes that usually would wash their own face and were not supported by the state, but times had changed. Social distancing needed to be relaxed to allow more passengers, but compulsory face coverings had to be introduced as a balancing measure for health protection. A cabinet subcommittee was called for 24 June to assess the merits of the proposals. Like many other discussions in public life, the outcome was a piece of cake.

For the first time in four years, just as I was departing office, I saw nakedly, at first hand, how power is wielded in Ireland when the chips are down.

Three rooms were necessary for the cabinet subcommittee meeting because of the requirements of social distancing. There were only six ministers present, all together in the Sycamore Room. The Taoiseach was in the chair. As Minister for Transport, I was needed, as were the others attending, because Tánaiste Simon Coveney, ministers Paschal Donohoe, Heather Humphreys and Simon Harris all had a legitimate interest in both topics.

Far more intriguing was the immediate realisation that the cream of Ireland's civil service was there in full force. The politicians certainly voiced their opinions, but they were outnumbered by mandarins from many of the powerful departments of state. There were more bodies present than at a full cabinet meeting.

The Secretary of the Department of the Taoiseach, Martin Fraser, was there, as was the Second Secretary of his Department, John Callinan. Liz Canavan, another powerful mandarin from the Taoiseach's Department sat sphinx-like throughout the proceedings. Paschal's Secretary General from Public Expenditure, the loquacious Robert Watt, was in attendance, as were Simon Harris' and Heather Humphreys' top officials. The Secretary General from Foreign Affairs, Niall Burgess, was there to back up Simon Coveney. My own Secretary General, Graham Doyle, attended the session by video link. Several advisers, including the Taoiseach's chief of staff, Brian Murphy and his head of policy, John Carroll, all gathered, as did Aisling Dunne to back me up. And, most importantly, Deputy Chief Medical Officer, Dr Ronan Glynn, was needed to advise on the crucial health implications of the measures.

Surprisingly, the proceedings were led by the mandarins, not the ministers. John Callinan reported from a meeting of Secretaries General and their deputies known as the Senior Officials Group (SOG) about travel restrictions. The SOG recommended that Ireland should implement a limited lifting of restrictions for countries with similar or better Covid levels. At the same time, non-essential travel from countries that did not satisfy the comparability criteria would continue to be advised against. Caution was the order of the day. Several decisions were postponed for a short time on the mandarins' recommendation. They were hardly challenged.

The fundamental divisions within the cabinet again surfaced. Simon Harris remained wedded to the supremacy of the health arguments above the economic pressures to open up. Naturally enough, Paschal bemoaned the injustice of a nation that had been relatively successful in fighting the disease now paying a higher economic price, continuing the shutdown of its economy and closing itself off from the rest of Europe. Simon Coveney remained in the middle, advocating clearer guidance, but, as always, acutely aware of the diplomatic consequences of offending our biggest trading partners, the UK and the US, by excluding them from the green list.

On the public transport proposal, the wearing of compulsory face coverings was accepted, as was the move to 50 per cent passenger capacity to replace two-metre social distancing.

There was a full discussion. It was reassuring to realise that the quality of our public servants matched their generous quantity on that afternoon. Their knowledge, wisdom and evidence-based advice was a great comfort in the crisis.

Callinan and Fraser were particularly impressive in their thorough and calm approach. Their heavyweight intelligence is an asset to the nation of which the electorate is totally unaware.

Nevertheless, I left the meeting with a nagging feeling that the influence of the senior public servants was greater than the politicians', that, although we had desperately needed their expertise and professionalism in a crisis, they might not only be setting the agenda, but also controlling it.

The next day was the government's last cabinet meeting. The mandarins' measures from the previous day's cabinet subcommittee came up for approval. The cabinet did what was expected of them. The measures flew through, provoking plenty of predictable, strictly off-topic discussion, but no opposition. Lots of ministers let off steam, but there was a sense of unreality since so many decisions were being left over for the incoming government, but, crucially, for exactly the same civil servants. Besides, acrimony was unlikely because many of us were gathering for a final time.

Leo said farewell with a few words. He was complimentary about the partnership government. He omitted to say that there had been plenty of rough and tumble in the first four years but that everything had run smoothly for him and for Fine Gael in the final four months. The coronavirus had revived his political fortunes. Fine Gael had taken advantage of it. Most notably and with feeling, he confided that 'history will be kinder to this government than the electorate was'.

Epilogue

SENATOR JAMES REILLY had just failed to regain his Dáil seat in the 2020 general election. The former Fine Gael deputy leader was being interviewed by RTÉ and claimed, manfully and bravely, that at least his wife would be delighted.

She should be in trauma. James was calling a halt to a long career in politics. The sight of a TD or senator arriving home after losing his or her seat must put the fear of God into their spouses. In the weeks following an election, defeated TDs return to their houses with sacks of books, suitcases of files, surplus pieces of furniture, cups, saucers, cutlery, the works; unbelievable clutter to drive the rest of their family mad.

They try to talk up their new situation. There's life after politics, they say, courageously. More time with the family…

I wonder. Did anyone ever ask the family?

The TD will eulogise the prospects of spending time at home, doing a bit of cooking, watching the box with the children, free evenings, regular meals. No more residents' association meetings, clinics, community events, funerals or legislation to study. Freedom beckons.

The trouble will be that the family has long ago found a way to manage without them. And they manage pretty well. This foreign body hanging around all day will be an obstacle to the normal routine of family life.

After a couple of weeks, the long-suffering spouse will inevitably crack. Once the sympathy has worn off, the most frequent phrase heard by any losing TD will be 'When in the name of God are you going to get a job?'

The late Minister for Posts and Telegraphs, Conor Cruise O'Brien, used to start many a conversation with the words, 'I shall always be eternally grateful to the good people of Dublin North-East who decided, in their wisdom, not to re-elect me.' As a minister, he was not very good at installing telephone lines for constituents, but he had a habit of straying into important parts of other ministers' portfolios. Sounds familiar? He went on to be Editor-in-Chief of the *Observer* newspaper and to get up the noses of entire nations.

Few are blessed with Conor's provocative talents. He wouldn't have been happy hanging around the kitchen sink back in 1977 when he lost his Dáil seat. Conor survived four years in bed with the Blueshirts from 1973 to 1977. I used to meet him for lunch on many occasions after that. It was surprising what a fondness he developed for the Liam Cosgraves, the Paddy Cooneys of the world in that time. Even as Blueshirts go, they were deeply conservative – which he was not – but he felt a tangible affinity with the gritty integrity of their stand against terrorism.

I was given my P45 by the people of Dublin Rathdown after four years in office with the Blueshirts. So thankfully there are plenty of noble precedents.

The Blueshirts have many admirable qualities. They are mostly honest, polite, prudent and reliable. They also have a degree of condescension, a sense of a divine right to rule that would embarrass the House of Windsor. They are joined at the hip to Ireland's middle classes and large farmers. Compared with Fianna Fáil, they can be incredibly boring.

They would also cut your throat for a few lines of favourable media coverage. They are savages in a savage business. And they would have a good laugh with you afterwards.

So saying goodbye to them was a less than sentimental

occasion. Even before Covid-19, they didn't do hugs, kisses, backslapping and embraces. There was no send-off, no party, no formal goodbyes. After the last cabinet meeting in Dublin Castle, I had a few words with Leo, Simon Coveney and Paschal Donohoe. Off we went in our cars. Job done.

On that day, I observed to the Taoiseach that one of the odd things about politics is how few of the cabinet ministers, if any, are personal friends. Political friendships are something different. They are binding only in that they are alliances of convenience. They die when you leave politics.

Several other ministers have confirmed since, that nearly all their real friends are outside politics.

Fine Gael are not a club, they do not visit each other's houses with their spouses. They remain a tribe. They are bound together by an endless battle against a common political enemy. They might occasionally have a drink with one another in the Dáil Members' Bar, but the talk will be business.

We in the Independent Alliance were not members of their tribe. We had formed a partnership with them on conditions that were not wilfully dishonoured but were never completed.

This book has given me time to reflect on whether jumping into bed with the Blueshirts was a suicide mission or a worthwhile experiment, allowing responsible independents to play a meaningful role in the government of the country.

As it happens, we had little option; we could have walked away from any deal. But then, what would have been the point of being in politics? We had fortunately found ourselves holding the balance of power, given the numbers in the Dáil. We were in the perfect position for a small group.

We could have walked. Instead, we dealt.

The inevitable cries of 'sell-out' descended on us all. While John Halligan, Finian McGrath, Boxer Moran and I cannot claim to have saved the nation from the ravages of Covid-19, we do feel that in government we achieved many, if not all, of our objectives. We lost a few battles, of course.

I hope that lives have been saved as a result of the stricter drink-driving legislation. It was hard fought in the face of much opposition from most parties, including our partners, the Blueshirts.

We can claim many successes in the four budgets under the last government, particularly where the old and the sick were concerned.

We hope we have ended the curse of crony culture. A new system of giving the minister minimal discretion over appointments in my department infuriated other politicians and their friends, but it worked to improve the quality of board members throughout all the semi-states. After one row at the beginning of the term, no further attempts were made to pull political strokes over juicy, financially rewarding jobs being doled out by the cabinet.

The appointment of judges continues to be a closed shop, dictated by the ruling party, although we were only a tantalising few weeks away from the most radical ever shake-up of Ireland's rotten system for appointing judges.

The Football Association of Ireland (FAI) and the Olympic Federation of Ireland (OFI) are organisations reformed beyond all recognition since we shared power.

Did the experiment work? Well, none of us are any longer in the Dáil.

John Halligan and Finian McGrath stood down voluntarily. Boxer Moran and I lost our seats.

So, we bid farewell to the Blueshirts.

No hard feelings. No regrets. Few friendships.

But God help our unfortunate families!

Acknowledgments

THOSE WHO MAKE the greatest sacrifices often receive the least thanks. My most treasured memory of the last four years will not be the bigwigs, but the volunteers. Those who turned up at night, at election time in deepest winter, willing to pound the pavements and knock on doors of strangers, are my political heroes.

Their task is thankless. Their efforts at democratic persuasion are often met by abuse rather than welcome, but our political team kept the faith in good times and in bad. We had both. And in a new departure for Irish politics, not one of them found themselves rewarded with a soft seat on a state board. Nevertheless, after more than four years of being kicked around for supporting a controversial minister they turned up again in 2020. Thank you.

I had a brilliant permanent constituency squad led by Caroline Greene. She is multi-talented and highly motivated. I loved her attitude: she was deeply competitive, yet great with people. Her efficiency landed her with the unenviable task of 'managing the minister's constituency accounts', a task that no doubt caused her nightmares. Caroline discovered that although I had spent part of my earlier life as Business Editor of the *Sunday Independent* preaching to punters, my own bookkeeping discipline was chaotic.

Caroline lived in one of the Ballinteer estates with her delightful parents, Seamus and Ann. Her young life had all been spent in the area, so her familiarity with the constituency was a big plus. She was fearless, not only in confronting officialdom, but also in challenging her boss when he had taken off on a wild tangent. Sometimes I would only need to look at her approaching me before reaching for the white flag.

Samira Nicolo joined Caroline on the constituency team. She often staffed the office in Main Street Dundrum. She was calm. She needed to be, so when I was in high doh about a minor matter – as happened far too often – Samira would be unfazed and produce a considered solution. She had been at school at Wesley, an item on her CV that sent mixed messages! She was a wonderful team leader on a canvass and would keep her head when others were losing the plot.

Yet another Ballinteer woman, Sheila O'Neill, worked three mornings a week in the constituency office. Sheila, a lawyer, was overqualified for the job, but was a big hit with constituents; a sympathetic ear, knowledgeable and enthusiastic. Sheila was immensely likeable and a person of great moral calibre.

In addition, in an attempt to reduce the gaffe-count we hired a young social-media-savvy woman, Sine Finn, in the months before the 2020 election. She had the thankless task of instructing a reluctant minister on the merits of social-media clips. Sine has now gone over to the dark side and joined Fine Gael TD, Colm Brophy. He is a lucky deputy.

Finally, my daughter, Rebecca, volunteered to join the team in the pre-election months. Politicians often employ family members against all the advice. Rebecca was not on the payroll, so she needed to be fed and watered when I was in the constituency. That was great therapy for me. She grounded the local TD when he lost the run of himself. She is an ego basher without rival. That alone was a full-time job. But she, like the others, excelled in the role of meeting people and solving problems. Despite all her commitment, as she lives in an adjoining constituency, I am deeply suspicious that she voted for either the Greens or the Social Democrats.

As a minister it was not possible to operate a totally celebrity-free zone. One of the highlights of the term was a delightful encounter in February 2019 with Arlene Foster, currently First Minister of Northern Ireland. No one would ever have expected the reputedly dour Arlene to provide one of the more memorable moments of the entire period in office. We had just jointly opened a cross-border greenway linking Fermanagh, Sligo and Leitrim. Afterwards, we retired to the Ballroom of Romance in Glenfarne, near the border. Following the formalities, I mischievously ambushed Arlene and asked her to dance for the cameras. She hesitated and then uttered 'You are some rascal' cheerfully. We had the shortest waltz ever witnessed in that ballroom, but she took it all in good heart. Thank you, Arlene. It was a good day for cross-border relations.

Possibly the hardest task of all was the press adviser gig. Some said that no man or woman on earth had committed enough sins to deserve such punishment. Carol Hunt had proven courage when she stood for election to the Dáil without any political experience. She required much more when she accepted an invitation to organise my press affairs. My relationship with the media was distant at best. Carol wanted me to do more. I wanted to do less. Despite fighting ill-health, now thankfully recovered, she maintained a cheerful composure and ability throughout. She was the one who regularly delivered bad news. She did it with a smile. I hope I never shot such an upbeat messenger.

Chris Smith, my private secretary, was the most agreeable of civil servants. He ran the private office with the certainty of a practised veteran. He never made any mistakes. I must have challenged him on the information he provided a thousand times. He was always right and accurate. He never complained, even though he often would have had good cause. A keen football follower, I already miss our conversations about, of all teams, Blackburn and Scunthorpe.

John Bourke managed to fulfil a unique role. As a civil servant, he was allocated the task of dealing with non-political issues in the constituency office. He navigated his way around that minefield with skill, energy and good humour.

Two of the staff who had to endure the most were Ultan Sherlock and Pat Cullen. Both ex-Gardai, they had the unenviable task of driving me to the four corners of Ireland during the Dáil term. Both were in the vanguard of the 'Reopen Stepaside Garda Station' campaign. We ventured from Dublin to Donegal to West Cork to Wexford. They worked long hours and late nights, waiting for endless meetings to end. They performed way beyond the call of duty, while becoming experts in the skill of operating an electric car – within the speed limits of course!

Tony Williams and Catherine Halloran were Independent Alliance staff based in Government Buildings. Tony was our chief strategist, who spent much energy nudging the Judicial Appointments Bill so tantalisingly close to its conclusion, while Catherine was the person to turn to when the Alliance was at the height of media trouble. Both provided perfect bulwarks when the Blueshirts were becoming belligerent.

Publishers and agents never have an easy ride with opinionated authors. This book's adroit agent, Jonathan Williams, is obviously used to dealing with them. His relaxed outlook in all circumstances, his diligence in reading and rereading the transcript and in spotting possible inconsistencies has been stellar. He was never in a flap. His ability to operate in the modern world without a mobile phone may have something to do with his success.

Publishers Atlantic Books have been totally professional. Their confidence in deciding to publish the book, at a time when Covid-19 is a constant unknown, is an act of faith. To Clare Drysdale, Will Atkinson, Simon Hess, Clive Kintoff and Kate Ballard, thank you.

Research is essential. Many thanks to Tom Webb for his diligent research, in particular into the chapter on the FAI. Tom rescued me from committing a major gaffe by pointing out tactfully that the original draft suggested that I had attended the World Cup rather than the Euros in Poland in 2012! Ouch. Just imagine…

Finally, the jewel in the crown. When Michael Noonan met Aisling Dunne for the first time, he greeted her with the words, 'Ah, I hear you are the real minister.'

Aisling not only researched each chapter, she read every line. She edited the book. She saved me from indulging my unsubstantiated prejudices. She even refused to allow me to call Simon Coveney a Fine Gael 'toff'. Which he is, but she was right; he is a fine minister as well. She advised on the necessary inclusions and omissions. She provided many of the contemporaneous notes. She contacted many of the characters in the book to check on events and detail. As a qualified lawyer she read the transcript with a practised legal eye. I did what she left over.

Aisling was my special advisor. She was with me on every step of the journey. And she *was* Michael Noonan's 'real minister' in the sense that her diligence was beyond my comprehension. She read every line of legislation to come into the department, kept the peace between civil servants and the minister, foresaw the political pitfalls and benefits behind every measure. She was the source of many of the best initiatives to arise during the last term. She was landed with the results of many of my unforced errors and undoubtedly would have given me my P45 if the roles had been reversed. She bit her tongue on more occasions than she will ever admit. She was patient, scarily clever but managed to maintain a sense of humour in the worst of times.

Thank you to everyone.

Index